SEMANTIC MANAGEMENT OF MIDDLEWARE

SEMANTIC WEB AND BEYOND
Computing for Human Experience

Series Editors:

Ramesh Jain
University of California, Irvine
http://jain.faculty.gatech.edu/

Amit Sheth
University of Georgia
http://lsdis.cs.uga.edu/~amit

As computing becomes ubiquitous and pervasive, computing is increasingly becoming an extension of human, modifying or enhancing human experience. Today's car reacts to human perception of danger with a series of computers participating in how to handle the vehicle for human command and environmental conditions. Proliferating sensors help with observations, decision making as well as sensory modifications. The emergent semantic web will lead to machine understanding of data and help exploit heterogeneous, multi-source digital media. Emerging applications in situation monitoring and entertainment applications are resulting in development of experiential environments.

SEMANTIC WEB AND BEYOND
Computing for Human Experience
addresses the following goals:

> ➢ brings together forward looking research and technology that will shape our world more intimately than ever before as computing becomes an extension of human experience;

> ➢ covers all aspects of computing that is very closely tied to human perception, understanding and experience;

> ➢ brings together computing that deal with semantics, perception and experience;

> ➢ serves as the platform for exchange of both practical technologies and far reaching research.

Additional information about this series can be obtained from
http://www.springer.com

SEMANTIC MANAGEMENT OF MIDDLEWARE

by

Daniel Oberle
University of Karlsruhe, Germany

 Springer

Daniel Oberle
University of Karlsruhe
Institute of Applied Informatics and
Formal Descriptions Methods
D-76128 Karlsruhe
Germany

Library of Congress Control Number: 2005908104

Semantic Management of Middleware
by Daniel Oberle

ISBN-10: 0-387-0-387-27630-0   e-ISBN-10: 0-387-0-387-27631-9
ISBN-13: 978-0-387-27630-4   e-ISBN-13: 978-0-387-27631-1

Printed on acid-free paper.

Dissertation, genehmigt von der Fakultät für Wirtschaftswissenschaften der
Universität Fridericiana zu Karlsruhe, 2005. Referent: Prof. Dr. Rudi Studer,
Korreferenten: Prof. Dr. Bruno Neibecker, Prof. Dr. Steffen Staab

Cover art by Daniel Oberle, showing the architecture of the ontology-based
application server, from another perspective. The green object is a common
symbol for an ontology.

Printed in the United States of America.

9 8 7 6 5 4 3 2 1

springeronline.com

Dedicated to ...

... the Supervisors

Steffen Staab
Andreas Eberhart
Pascal Hitzler
Rudi Studer

... the Reviewers

Ed Curry
Robert Delaney
Aldo Gangemi
Peter Haase
Stefan Tai
Denny Vrandecic
Clare Waibel

... the Colleagues @ Semantic Karlsruhe

Andreas Abecker, Sudhir Agarwal, Stephan Bloehdorn, Saartje Brockmans, Philipp Cimiano, Christian Drumm, Marc Ehrig, Stephan Grimm, Siegfried Handschuh, Jens Hartmann, Andreas Hotho, Steffen Lamparter, Jens Lemcke, Alexander Mädche, Boris Motik, Kioumars Namiri, Gisela Schillinger, Lars Schmidt-Thieme, Christoph Schmitz, Ljiljana & Nenad Stojanovic, Gerd Stumme, York Sure, Julien Tane, Bernhard Tausch, Christoph Tempich, Max Völkel, Johanna Völker, Raphael Volz, Susanne Winter, Valentin Zacharias

... the Colleagues @ World

Sean Bechhofer, Bettina Berendt, Jorge Gonzalez, Nicola Guarino, Frank van Harmelen, Ian Horrocks, Hans-Arno Jacobsen, Holger Knublauch, Deborah McGuinness, Sheila McIlraith, Peter Mika, Christof Momm, Doug Lea, Jeff Pan, Helena Sofia Pinto, Debbie Richards, Marta Sabou, Jorge Santos, Rick Schantz, Luc Schneider, Swaminathan Sivasubramanian, Heiner Stuckenschmidt, Phil Tetlow, Peter Spyns, Mike Uschold, Werner Vogels, Frank Wolff

... and last but not least to my family & friends!

Contents

List of Figures

List of Tables

Preface

We have termed this series "Semantic Web and beyond: computing for human experience." Ramesh Jain (co-editor of this series) and I believe that semantics is going to be far more pervasive than portrayed by the current vision of the Semantic Web. Its role and values will certainly not be limited to the traditional Web. Semantics will also be one of the important components of a continuum leading to perception and experience, albeit one that will mature earlier in computational context. We also believe that computation, supported by techniques and technologies that deal with perception, semantics, and experiences, will improve and benefit human experience. Such a computation will have a far broader impact than the traditional drivers of information technology, such as improving efficiency, lowering cost, or productivity gains. In this context, we expect that this series intends to offer additional books covering topics in perception, semantics, and experiential computing as they relate to improving human experience involving interactions with computing devices and environments. Our series intends to offer research monographs, books for professional audiences, as well as text books for advance graduate courses.

This premier book in our series by Daniel Oberle is a good example of what we hope to cover in this series. It discusses the role of semantics in middleware — arguable the most important segment of the enterprise software market. This work demonstrates that semantics and the semantic (and Semantic Web) technologies have pervasive applications and uses. It is also an excellent training companion for active practitioners seeking to incorporate advanced and leading edge ontology-based approaches and technologies. It is a necessary preparation manual for researchers in distributed computing who see semantics as an important enabler for the next generation.

Middleware systems are complex. They need to integrate and manage multiple heterogeneous software systems. Just as semantics has been recognized as a key enabler of heterogeneous information integration, can semantics be a key enabler in integrating heterogeneous software systems? Daniel believes that is indeed the case, and he goes on to provide a detailed road map on how semantics and Semantic Web technologies can play a significant role in creating a middleware system and their use in managing heterogeneous software systems.

The first step in the road map is modelling which centers around using ontologies for specifying semantic models. This leads to the development of a semantic model for software components and Web services. We are introduced to the basics of middleware technology where technologies and design patterns from the past, such as message-oriented middleware or object monitors, help readers who are not familiar with the area to get the necessary background information. The discussion on ontologies achieves the same.

The subsequent part of this book offers a detailed discussion on the different ontology frameworks which can be used as a modelling basis. The requirements for the ontology are well laid out and each ontology framework is analyzed with respect to the requirements. DOLCE is chosen since it meets most of the requirements. The discussion on the semantic modelling of software systems is particularly interesting to read. The author addresses the different modelling issues at different phases of software component design. The modelling captures the intricate details and differences between fundamental concepts, such as data and software, and continues with component profiles, policies, and many more aspects. The modelling also captures the API of components and proposes a technique to discover dependent and conflicting libraries. Also presented is a model to capture workflows. A discussion on how such a modelling can meet the requirements and the advantages of using such an approach are presented in detail.

The next part provides a technical look at the different solutions. This includes discussing each aspect of the middleware system and the techniques to realize them as actual systems. The requirements of such a semantic middleware are presented and the system design is discussed with that central perspective. The system architecture along its different constituting components are discussed in detail. The application and reuse of the proposed ontology in the middleware system is also presented. The book ends with relating this approach to application management, Semantic Web Services and MDA.

Potentially, the most lasting engineering progress in this book, in my personal view, is that of taking semantics to the application server level. I foresee an emergence of Semantic Aware Networking, in which semantics not only facilitates network functions but significantly enhances its capability by pushing more functions. With the industry already taking initial steps in this direction, such as in CISCO's Application Oriented Networking products, the next step is quite likely the interplay between routers and application servers with semantics providing a bridge.

While there is plenty of work related to semantics of information and even Web services, this effort stands out in its attention to modelling the semantics of software components. In this context, it is a unique offering that goes beyond the mainstream Semantic Web research, while demonstrating a detailed and pervasive use of semantics in larger software systems context. This series will endeavor to offer more such books and for wider audiences.

Amit P. Sheth
Director, Large Scale Distributed Information Systems lab
Professor, Computer Science Department, University of Georgia
CTO and Cofounder, Semagix, Inc.
Athens, Georgia,
U.S.A.

Foreword

Which topic in computer science has been attracting researchers *and* developers from *artificial intelligence, business process modelling, conceptual modelling, databases, distributed systems, information systems, programming systems, security, software engineering, Web services* and *Web systems and engineering* (and probably many others whom I forgot to mention here)? It is the specification, development and management of component- and service-oriented architectures (SOAs).

The topic has become important to all of them. While the development of individual software systems is reasonably well understood and reasonably well-established practice (even when thousands of issues of such systems are and will have to be dealt with in more detail), the specification, development and maintenance of distributed software systems has in general not been understood to an extent that let their stakeholders gain the intended economic network benefits. On the upside, organizations that establish networking of their numerous distributed systems with the ones of other organizations may save costs, gain new customers or increase customer satisfaction. On the downside, if each minor change or minor disruption in one software system leads to a trickle down effect that results in expensive reprogramming of another system, all the potential positive network effects are overshadowed by the costs for joining and remaining in the network.

As the spectrum of interests indicates, the solution to this dilemma may require a multi-faceted approach. This book by Daniel Oberle significantly contributes towards this objective. Hence, the methods he proposes, revises and extends contribute to the plentiful, seminal research of several communities. I will name the ones that are most immediately affected, though I strongly believe that all of the above cited interest groups may benefit from building on his contribution:

Distributed Systems: Current middleware systems, such as application servers, are complex beasts that are very hard to tame because of the intricacies of distributed interactions. Hence, it has been a long-established practice to factorize configuration aspects of distributed interactions into corresponding declarative description files and — more recently — into XML files that follow the specification given by the various Web service standards.

Unfortunately, the semantics of these files is either given by the code of the concrete middleware system or — probably worse — by thousands of pages of specification documents consisting of raw textual explanations. We all know what went wrong with compilers in the 1960ies when programming language specifications were still at that stage.

Daniel here builds a rigorous approach towards giving the declarative descriptions of software components/Web services a well-defined meaning by defining ontological foundations *and* by showing how such foundations may be realized in practical, up-and-running systems.

Artificial Intelligence — Ontologies: Though all software developers use programming languages, only few specialists are actually able to formally define a programming language and develop a corresponding compiler: the formal foundation is not used to tutor the beginner, but to clarify the discussion and development by experts. The same is true for ontologies that underly a software management approach. They need to outlive many software development cycles, i.e., they need to have a formal foundation, yet one must also tutor the domain experts how to use them.

It is one of the successes of this work that it shows how to develop *and* use the ontological foundations of this work in a concrete software environment. This is done in a way that the usage of the resulting middleware infrastructure seems amenable to a sophisticated software developer even though the development of a complex foundational ontology may have to be left to some few specialists.

Web Services — Semantic Web Services: The analysis of the ontologies Daniel develops makes evident that *very few concepts* actually differ when "upgrading" from conventional middleware to Web services. It also makes clear that the use of declarative specifications, such as done in Web services, or formal declarative specifications, such as done for Semantic Web Services comes with economic modelling costs that need to be justified by savings in other places. This lets us presume that formal specifications with the objective of fully automatic Web service composition and orchestration remain a valid research topic — but one that will find its applications in niches rather than in wide-spread adoption by software developers.

Thus, the book covers an incredible depth and breadth of approaches. Its value lies in revising and extending existing methods thereby providing the cornerstones for specifying, developing and managing distributed applications in the coming decades — using semantics.

Prof. Dr. Steffen Staab
ISWeb — Information Systems and Semantic Web
Institute for Computer Science
University of Koblenz-Landau
Germany

Acknowledgments

This work was financed by WonderWeb — "Ontology Infrastructure for the Semantic Web," a European Union Information Society Technologies (IST) Future Emerging Technolgiges (FET) funded project under contract number IST-2001-33052 (2002-2004). I feel indebted to all the colleagues for the much valued cooperation and fruitful discussions we had throughout the project.

http://wonderweb.semanticweb.org

This work was financed by SmartWeb, a research project funded by the German Federal Ministry of Education and Research (BMBF). My appreciation to all the colleagues of another great project still running at the time of writing this book (2004-2007). It has been a joy working with you all!

http://smartweb.semanticweb.org

My appreciation to all the members of the Software Engineering Task Force (SETF). The task force is a part of the World Wide Web's Consortium (W3C) Semantic Web Best Practices and Deployment Working Group (SWBPD), where this work was also successfully exposed and revised [Tetlow et al., 2005].

http://www.w3.org/2001/sw/BestPractices/SE/

Finally, I would like to express my gratitude to Amit Sheth — the series editor — as well as the ladies at Springer: Susan Lagerstrom-Fife and Sharon Palleschi, who made the publication of this book possible.

PART I

FUNDAMENTALS

Chapter 1

INTRODUCTION

"There is already too much diversity of middleware for many customers and application developers to cope with ... the complexity of current middleware is untenable over the long term."
[Bernstein, 1996]

1. Motivation

Distributed information systems evolved in response to improvements in computer hardware and networks. Mainframes were the dominant computer architecture in the beginning of corporate IT. All three abstract layers of an information system (i.e., presentation logic, application logic and resource management) were blurred into a single tier running on a centralized computer. Once local area networks (LANs) appeared and PCs and workstations became powerful enough, it was possible to distribute the layers across at least two machines, with the LAN in between. The result was the well-known client/server architecture.

In order to implement such client/server systems, developers were in need of a powerful abstraction mechanism to hide the tedious communication details. Thus, a new breed of software was born, viz., *middleware*, whose essential role is to manage the complexity and heterogeneity of distributed information systems. Middleware offers programming abstractions that hide some of the complexities of the underlying network and operating system. Specific middleware solutions are almost always accompanied by a complex software infrastructure. These infrastructures tend to have a large footprint.

The magnitude of the challenge to develop and manage distributed, middleware-based applications became staggering. Companies are confronted with their legacy systems, hundreds to thousands of PCs in different configurations, several heterogeneous networks, operating systems, a myriad of server farms and links to business partners — all of which tied together by middleware infrastructures in a frequently changing and globalized environment. Although middleware is mandatory to realize such distributed applications, the sheer size and complexity of middleware-based applications makes their management very difficult.

Management of middleware can be considered as an endless loop of monitoring and controlling middleware elements (e.g., software components or Web services). We can think of monitoring as the passive activity of retrieving information about the middleware elements. Taking the gathered information as a basis, one might control, i.e., change, adapt or configure, specific aspects and elements of the middleware. Typical management efforts comprise: the assessing and controlling of middleware elements for their efficiency and productivity, their tailoring to make them operate properly, the definition and control of access rights and the provision of quantitative information about them.

It is the goal of this work to facilitate the development and management of middleware-based applications for developers and administrators. The novelty of our approach is to use, adapt, extend and apply *semantic technology* to automate some of the management tasks. The principal idea is to model semantic descriptions of specific middleware elements. Our approach uses a powerful semantic technology as a basis: *ontologies*. Ontologies are similar to conceptual modelling techniques, such as UML or Entity Relationship Models (ERM). However, ontologies typically feature logic-based representation languages with formal semantics and executable calculi. It is the executable calculi that allow developers and administrators to reason and query with semantic descriptions at development, deployment or run time. Therefore semantic descriptions of middleware elements may be queried, may foresight required actions, e.g., preloading of indirectly required components, or may be checked to avoid inconsistent system configurations — during development as well as during run time. Reasoning and querying make allowances to automate — or at least facilitate — management tasks, such as predicting or observing how middleware elements interact, get into conflict and behave — to name but a few tasks.

The earliest types of middleware were targeted at developing distributed applications from scratch and are referred to as *conventional middleware*. One of the oldest and probably best-known examples is the remote procedure call (RPC). RPC systems are still used as a foundation for almost all other forms of middleware today. The increase of computerization of business processes was — and still is — the main force driving the development of middleware. Transaction processing monitors, object brokers, object monitors and message-oriented middleware followed the RPC in the eighties and early nineties.

Conventional middleware was originally intended to integrate servers that reside in the resource management layer. Its increasing use led to the proliferation of distributed applications in companies. Each of the applications provided a higher level of abstraction and, thus, an added value. However, the functionality provided by these applications soon became the subject of further integration. Consequently, middleware for *enterprise application integration (EAI)* was created. Two prominent examples are message brokers and workflow management systems.

The need to integrate applications is not limited to the boundaries of a single company, however. Similar advantages can be obtained from inter-enterprise (or business-to-business, short B2B) application integration as much as from intra-enterprise application integration. The latest breed of middleware was thus developed to enable *B2B application integration*. It is obvious that the World-Wide Web plays the predominant role as a channel to access information systems here. In essence, we find two types of middleware in this category. First, *application servers* were the premier type of B2B application integration middleware to meet the new requirements. They comprise conventional middleware, but incorporate the Web as key access channel to the functionality implemented using the middleware. Second, we find *Web services*, which are expected to facilitate the development of infrastructures that support programmatic application integration, dynamic B2B marketplaces and the seamless integration of IT infrastructures from different cooperations.

While application servers and Web services offer many new possibilities for B2B application integration, they also bring about new challenges, which we want to address in this work. A significant aspect of application servers is the bundling of more and more functionality within the middleware platform. This is consistent with the current trend towards providing integrated support for many different middleware abstractions that we have witnessed in conventional middleware. Likewise, Web services middleware is almost universally being built as an additional tier over existing middleware platforms (mostly application servers), which are already too complex and cumbersome for developers and administrators. Introducing new tiers adds further complexity and complicates the management tasks even more.

2.   Research Questions

The usage of ontologies in application servers and Web services middleware brings about quite interesting research questions, such as the cardinal question below:

Cardinal Question *Can ontologies be used to facilitate the development and management of middleware-based applications for developers and administrators?*

Throughout this document we divide the Cardinal Question into three Main Questions, which are aligned with the parts of the book. We discuss middleware in general and have a closer look at application servers and Web services to learn about their complexity (Chapter 2). After introducing ontologies (Chapter 3), Chapter 4 considers these problems as a basis and proposes *semantic* management to automate *some* of the management tasks. The usage of semantic management does not come for free, however, as it relies on semantic descriptions of middleware elements. Modelling efforts, i.e., manual modelling or obtaining and integrating existing sources, have to be expended to arrive at semantic descriptions. As the modelling efforts should be kept as small as possible, we encounter the first Main Question:

Main Question I *How to find a good trade-off between modelling and management efforts?*

In Chapter 4 we approach the trade-off point. We follow the strategy that we first identify promising use cases for exploiting the semantic descriptions. Taking the use cases as a basis, we clarify who benefits from what kind of semantic descriptions, as well as when and for what purposes. The use cases are distinguished between application servers and Web services and embedded in respective scenarios. The scenarios pose additional requirements that have to be met by the system design later on. Chapter 4 answers the questions:

Question I.1 *Who uses semantic descriptions?*

Question I.2 *What are the semantic descriptions used for?*

Question I.3 *When are the semantic descriptions used?*

Question I.4 *Which aspects should be formalized by our ontology?*

The answers to the Question I.4 state a set of modelling requirements for deciding which aspects our ontology should formalize, that is, which aspects are relevant in order to realize semantic management of middleware. The modelling requirements serve as an input to Part II, which is concerned with answering the second Main Question:

Main Question II *How to build a suitable management ontology?*

Before modelling a management ontology from scratch, it is desirable to check if there are existing ontologies that we might reuse for our purpose. Thus, Chapter 5 analyzes existing ontologies for application servers and Web services, respectively. The conclusion is that their problematic aspects are typical for common ontologies. Their loose design and conceptual ambiguity prevents us from simply reusing them. Instead, we expect that a generic, high-quality ontology might serve us well as a modelling basis. The usage of such *foundational ontologies* fosters superior design and high quality of our management ontology. Based on specific ontological choices that are suitable in our case, Chapter 6 analyzes existing foundational ontologies and indicates an appropriate one.

Our goal is to save modelling efforts and to facilitate the reuse of our management ontology in any specific application server and Web service application. Hence, Chapter 7 discusses the design of a management ontology that captures a predefined set of semantic descriptions, which can be specialized to any specific platform. Consequently, the Main Question II can be subdivided into three questions:

Question II.1 *Can an existing ontology be reused for our purposes?*

Question II.2 *How to ensure high quality?*

Question II.3 *How to decrease modelling efforts and enable reuse?*

The formalization of an appropriate management ontology in Part II is the first step towards semantic management. The ontology provides a coherent formal model that allows the weaving together of separated aspects. The next step is to propose a way to realize semantic management, i.e., to automate some management tasks by reasoning and querying based on the ontology. Therefore, Part III is concerned with answering the third Main Question:

Main Question III *How to realize semantic management of middleware?*

In order to arrive at a suitable system design, Chapter 8 reflects on the following issues: First, we have to elaborate on a suitable target platform where the semantic technology can be integrated, e.g., enterprise application management tools, software IDE's, workflow engines or application servers. Second, we have to think about who or what will provide semantic descriptions. The number of semantic descriptions that are provided manually by the software developer must be as few as possible, because software developers will not be very willing to carry out additional work. Third, we have to consider the specific requirements of the scenarios introduced in Chapter 4.

In Chapter 9 we implement a prototype of the derived system design by applying an existing ontology tool suite in an existing application server. Finally, Chapter 10 discusses the steps necessary to reuse our management ontology in this concrete implementation. Thus, the Main Question III can be subdivided into:

Question III.1 *What is a suitable target platform?*

Question III.2 *Who provides semantic descriptions?*

Question III.3 *How to implement semantic management?*

Question III.4 *How to reuse the ontology?*

Part IV consolidates the related works of parts I to III into Chapter 11 followed by a conclusion and an outlook (Chapter 12). Each chapter starts with a short summary of the previous chapter and discusses the goals, as well as the what and the why of the current one. We give a list of publications if parts of the chapter have been published before.

3.   Contributions

The novelty of our approach is to use, adapt, extend and apply semantic technology to automate some of the management tasks of application server and Web services middleware. Such middleware solutions are very complex software products that are hard to tame because of the elaborately complex detail of building distributed systems. So far, their functionalities have mostly been developed and managed with the help of administration tools and corresponding configuration files, recently in XML. Though this constitutes a very flexible way of developing and administrating a distributed application, the disadvantage is that the conceptual model underlying the different configurations is *only implicit*. Hence, its bits and pieces are difficult to retrieve, survey, check for validity and maintain. To remedy such problems, we contribute an ontology-based approach to support the development and administration of middleware-based applications. The ontology captures properties of, relationships between and behaviors of the components and services that are required for development and administration purposes. The ontology is an *explicit* conceptual model with formal logic-based semantics. Therefore, its descriptions may be queried, may foresight required actions, or may be checked to avoid inconsistent system configurations. Thus, the ontology-based approach retains the original flexibility in configuring and running the middleware, but it adds new capabilities for the developer and user of the system. The proposed scheme is prototypically implemented in an open-source application server.

Our approach is one of the first that acknowledges and explicitly builds on the observation that there is a trade-off between expending efforts for management and expending efforts for semantic modelling. At the one end, the objective of full automation by semantic modelling will need very fine-grained, detailed modelling of all aspects of middleware elements — essentially everything that an intelligent human agent must know for managing the middleware. Thus, modelling efforts skyrocket at the end of fine-grained modelling. At the other end, where modelling is very coarse and little modelling facilitates management, management efforts of distributed systems soar. In this work, we approach the trade-off by identifying promising use cases. The use cases demonstrate that *some* management tasks can be facilitated by a justifiable amount of semantic modelling. In addition, the modelling requirements of the use cases give us clear indications of what concepts a suitable management ontology must contain. Although this seems quite a natural way of proceeding, it is rarely done in related research fields such as "Semantic Web Services," for instance. The approaches presented there usually aim at full automation and miss deriving modelling requirements for their respective ontologies.

Another contribution concerns the typical shortcomings of commonly and often naively built ontologies. Such ontologies suffer from conceptual ambiguity, poor axiomatization, loose design and narrow scope. They are often reduced to simple taxonomies and leave open many interpretations of their concepts and associations. We eliminate such shortcomings by adopting the advanced theory of Guarino and by introducing a new classification of ontologies in order to clarify their different usages. We carefully choose an appropriate foundational ontology on the basis of specific ontological choices. The foundational ontology is used as a modelling basis for the creation of a concisely axiomatized management ontology that may be reused in different middleware platforms. The extensive axiomatization of the management ontology and, thus, its reference characteristic, allows clarifying the meanings of overloaded terms such as "software component" or "Web service," allows the distinction among different kinds of entities, such as physical and information objects, and provides a superior design.

Chapter 2

MIDDLEWARE

This chapter introduces the reader to the notion of middleware. The essential role of *middleware* is to manage the complexity and heterogeneity of distributed infrastructures. On the one hand, middleware offers programming abstractions that hide some of the complexities of building a distributed application. On the other hand, there is a complex software infrastructure that implements these abstractions. With very few exceptions, this infrastructure tends to have a large footprint. The trend today is toward increasing complexity, as products try to provide more and more sophisticated programming abstractions and incorporate additional layers.

We advance chronologically and discuss briefly the earliest types of middleware targeted at *distributed application development* in Section 1. They are also referred to as *conventional middleware* and comprise the remote procedure call (RPC), transaction processing monitors, object brokers, object monitors and message-oriented middleware.

Conventional middleware is intended to facilitate the development of distributed applications from scratch. With the proliferation of distributed applications in companies, there arose the need for the integration of such applications as opposed the development from scratch. That triggered further the evolution of middleware leading to message brokers and workflow management systems to support *enterprise application integration*. Both types are discussed in Section 2.

The need to integrate applications is not limited to the boundaries of a single company, however. Similar advantages can be obtained from inter-enterprise (or business-to-business, short B2B) application integration as from intra-enterprise application integration. Therefore, the latest breed of middleware was developed to enable *B2B integration*. Application servers and Web services belong in this category. We have a closer look at both in Section

3. In order to limit the scope and hence the size of the problem we focus on application servers and Web services and neglect newer kinds of middleware. Examples for newer kinds are grid and peer-to-peer middleware [Junginger and Lee, 2004], which are also not yet mature enough.

A closer look at application servers and Web services reveals that both types are suffering from increasing complexity. Application servers bundle more and more functionality. Web services are almost universally being built as additional tiers over existing middleware platforms, e.g., application servers, which are already too complex and cumbersome. The complexity of developing and managing distributed applications with application servers is countered by the usage of deployment descriptors. Deployment descriptors are usually XML-files that reduce the amount of coding by specifying orthogonal issues in an declarative and application-independent way. In a similar vain, the Web service community is currently developing a set of standards, denoted WS*, to manage aspects, such as coordination or composition.

Although deployment descriptors and WS* descriptions constitute a very flexible way of developing and administrating a distributed application, we demonstrate by example that there are still many management efforts to be expended by developers and administrators. The reason is that the conceptual model underlying the different descriptions is *only implicit*. Hence, its bits and pieces are difficult to retrieve, survey, check for validity and maintain. This observation serves as input to Chapter 4 where we propose semantic management with the help of *explicit* conceptual models, i.e., ontologies (cf. Chapter 3).

Parts of this chapter provide an overview of middleware based on the significant book of [Alonso et al., 2004]. There are also parts based on [Mahmoud, 2004], as well as [Bernstein, 1996, Campbell et al., 1999]. The example of deployment descriptors is taken from [Oberle et al., 2005c], the one of WS* descriptors from [Oberle et al., 2005a].

1.   Middleware for Distributed Application Development

The essential role of *middleware* is to manage the complexity and heterogeneity of distributed infrastructures, thereby providing a simpler programming environment for distributed application developers. It is therefore useful to define middleware as any software layer that is placed above the infrastructure of a distributed system — the network and operating system — and below the application layer [Campbell et al., 1999].

Middleware platforms appear in many guises and it is sometimes difficult to identify their commonalities. Before addressing concrete types of middleware, it is worthwhile to spend some time clarifying the general aspects underlying all middleware platforms.

On the one hand, middleware offers programming abstractions that hide some of the complexities of building a distributed application. Instead of the programmer having to deal with every aspect of a distributed application, it is the middleware that takes care of some of them. Through these programming abstractions, the developer has access to functionality that otherwise would have to be implemented from scratch.

On the other hand, there is a complex software infrastructure that implements the abstractions mentioned above. With very few exceptions, this infrastructure tends to have a large footprint. The trend today is toward increasing complexity, as products try to provide more and more sophisticated programming abstractions and to incorporate additional layers. This makes middleware platforms very complex software systems [Alonso et al., 2004].

This section discusses the middleware used to construct distributed systems from scratch, i.e., middleware for *distributed application development* (also called *conventional middleware*). We further discuss middleware for enterprise application integration and business-to-business (B2B) integration in Sections 2 and 3, respectively. During our discussion we keep an eye on the paradigm shifts regarding the types and granularity of software building blocks because they influenced the evolution of middleware. As depicted in Figure 2.1, software building blocks evolved from *procedures* to *objects*, *workflows*, *components* and finally to *services*.

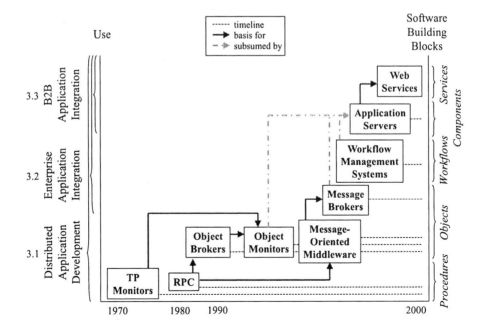

Figure 2.1. Types of middleware and historical overview.

TP Monitors In the early days of corporate IT, computer architectures were mainframe-based and interaction took place through terminals that only displayed the information as prepared by the mainframe.

Transaction processing monitors (TP Monitors), also called transaction processing middleware or simply transaction middleware, were initially designed to allow mainframes to support as many concurrent users as possible. As part of this task, TP monitors also needed to deal with multi-threading and data consistency, thereby extending core functionality with the concept of transactions. They are the oldest and best-known form of middleware. Today, distributed transaction monitors are prevailing to enable transactions spanning several isolated database management systems. [Gray and Reuter, 1993, Tai, 2004]

IBM CICS[1] was the first commercial product offering transaction protected distributed computing on an IBM mainframe. Nowadays, every major software vendor offers its own product, e.g., Microsoft Transaction Server (MTS)[2] or BEA Tuxedo.[3] Sun's Java Transaction API (JTA)[4] specifies standard Java interfaces between transaction monitors and involved parties.

RPC-based systems When the decentralization of corporate IT took place as a consequence of the introduction of the PC, functionality began to be distributed across a few servers. In order to realize distributed applications, developers were in need of a powerful abstraction mechanism to hide the tedious communication details.

The remote procedure call (RPC) responded to this need and was originally presented in [Birrell and Nelson, 1984] as a way to transparently call a procedure located on another machine. RPC established first the notion of a client (the program that calls a remote procedure) and a server (the program that implements the remote procedure being invoked). It also introduced many concepts still widely used today: the interface definition language (IDL), name and directory services, dynamic binding and service interfaces. Today, RPC systems are used as a foundation for almost all other forms of middleware, including Web services middleware (cf. Section 3.2).

Several RPC middleware infrastructures were developed that supported a wealth of functionality, e.g., the Distributed Computing Environment (DCE) provided by the Open Software Foundation (OSF) [Houston, 1996].

---

[1]Customer Information and Control System, cf. http://www.ibm.com/software/htp/cics/
[2]http://msdn.microsoft.com/library
[3]http://www.beasys.com/products/tuxedo
[4]http://java.sun.com/products/jta/

Object Brokers RPC was designed and developed at a time when the pre-dominant programming languages were procedural languages, i.e., software building blocks were *procedures*. With the advent of object-oriented (OO) languages, the *object* became the software building block, encapsulating data and behavior.

Platforms were developed to support the invocation of remote objects, thereby leading to object brokers. These platforms were more advanced in their specification than most RPC systems, but they did not significantly differ from them in terms of implementation. In practice, most of them used RPC as the underlying mechanism to implement remote object calls. [Alonso et al., 2004]

The most popular class of object brokers are those based on the Common Object Request Broker Architecture (CORBA),[5] defined and standardized by the Object Management Group (OMG).

Object Monitors When object brokers tried to specify and standardize the functionality of middleware platforms, it soon became apparent that much of this functionality was already available from TP Monitors. At the same time, TP monitors, initially developed for procedural languages, had to be extended to cope with object-oriented languages.

The result of these two trends was the convergence between TP monitors and object brokers that resulted in hybrid systems called object monitors. Object monitors are, for the most part, TP monitors extended with object-oriented interfaces. Vendors found it easier to make a TP monitor look like a standard-compliant object broker than to implement object brokers with all the features of a TP monitor and the required performance. [Alonso et al., 2004]

Examples of object monitors are Iona's OrbixOTM.[6] The aforementioned TP monitors, MTS from Microsoft and Tuxedo from BEA, can be classified as object monitors as well.

Message-oriented Middleware (MOM) The previous types of middleware are based on synchronous method invocation, where a client application invokes a method offered by a specific service provider. When the service provider has completed its job, it returns the response to the client. This rather "closely coupled" and "blocking" interoperability soon became too limiting for software developers.

---

[5]http://www.omg.org/corba/
[6]http://www.iona.com/products/orbix.htm

The answer to this limit was message-oriented middleware, enabling clients and servers[7] to communicate via messages, i.e., structured data sets typically characterized by a type and name-value-pairs. This kind of communication is made possible by message queues controlled by the MOM. Queues can be shared among multiple applications; recipients can decide when to process messages and do not have to listen continuously; priorities can be assigned, to name but a few advantages of this approach. [Curry, 2004b]

TIB/ETX from Tibco has been a popular product throughout the nineties.[8] Implementations of the Java Message Service (JMS)[9] can be regarded as message oriented middleware. Also, CORBA provides its own messaging service.

2.   Middleware for Enterprise Application Integration

The types of middleware discussed so far were originally intended to develop applications from scratch or to integrate database or file servers. The increasing use of such middleware led to the proliferation of distributed applications in companies. Each of the applications provided a higher level of abstraction, and, thus an added value. However, the functionality provided by these applications soon became the subject of further integration. The advantage of application integration is a higher level of abstraction that can be used to hide complex application and integration logic. The disadvantage is that now integration is not limited to database or file servers, but also to applications themselves. Unfortunately, while for databases there has been a significant effort to standardize the interfaces of specific types of databases, the same cannot be said of applications. As long as the integration of applications takes place within a single middleware platform, no significant problem should appear. Once the problem became the integration of applications provided by different middleware platforms, there was almost no infrastructure available that could help reduce the heterogeneity and standardize the interfaces, as well as the interactions between the systems.

The need for such *enterprise application integration (EAI)* further triggered the evolution of middleware, extending its capabilities to cope with application integration, as opposed to the development of new application logic. Such extensions involve significant changes in the way middleware is used. This section briefly discusses message brokers as the most versatile platform for integration and workflow management systems as the tools to make the integration logic explicit. Note that both types of middleware can also be used to develop distributed applications anew instead of integrating existing ones.

---

[7]Note that the distinction between clients and service providers becomes purely conceptual in the case of MOM. From the perspective of the middleware, all objects look alike.
[8]http://www.tibco.com
[9]http://java.sun.com/products/jms/

Message Brokers Message-oriented middleware (MOM) is rather static with regard to the selection of the queues to which the messages are delivered. For a generic EAI setting however, we need flexible and dynamic means for communication between arbitrary heterogeneous applications.

In response to those needs, message brokers extend MOM with the capability of routing, filtering and even processing the messages. In addition, most message brokers provide adapters that mask the heterogeneity and make it possible to access all kinds of applications with the same programming model and data exchange format. The combination of these two factors is seen as the key to supporting EAI. [Alonso et al., 2004]

Some of the best-known message brokers include IBM WebSphere MQ,[10] MSMQ by Microsoft[11] or BEA WebLogic Integration.[12]

Workflow Management Systems (WfMS) While message brokers are successful in providing flexible communication among heterogenous applications, the integration logic is still hard-coded and, thus, difficult to maintain.

Workflow management systems tackle the other side of the application integration problem: that of facilitating the definition and maintenance of the integration logic. Business processes are formally defined as a *workflow* and executed by a workflow engine. Workflows are seen as software building blocks for "programming in the large" because they compose coarse-grained activities and applications that can last hours. In addition, workflows compose large software modules, which are typically entire applications. [van der Aalst and van Hee, 2002, Georgakopoulos et al., 1995]

Examples of leading commercial workflow systems include WebSphere MQ Workflow[13] by IBM and Microsoft BizTalk Orchestration.[14]

3. Middleware for B2B Application Integration

So far we have studied middleware for creating and integrating distributed applications within the boundaries of a company. The need to integrate, however, is not limited to the systems within a single company. Similar advantages can be obtained from inter-enterprise (or business-to-business, short B2B) application integration as from intra-enterprise application integration.

With the Web being pervasively available, it goes without saying that some of the same technologies that enabled information sharing on the Web also form the basis for this kind of *B2B application integration*. In particular, HTTP is the

---

[10] http://www.ibm.com/software/integration/wmq/
[11] http://www.microsoft.com/msmq
[12] http://www.bea.com/products/weblogic/integration
[13] http://www.ibm.com/webspheremq/workflow
[14] http://msdn.microsoft.com/library/

basic protocol for applications to interact, and XML documents are the standard way to exchange information.

The need for B2B application integration triggered the evolution of middleware. Application servers and Web services provided the solution to the new requirements. Because this work focuses on application servers and Web services, we discuss them in more detail in the following sections. Note that both types of middleware can, of course, be used to develop distributed applications anew and to integrate applications within the boundaries of an enterprise. Most of the work on workflow management of the early nineties migrated to Web-based infrastructure in the late nineties to provide technical capabilities required for B2B applications.

3.1   Application Servers

The increasing use of the Web as a channel to access information systems forced conventional middleware platforms to provide support for Web access. This support is typically associated with application servers. Also, they foster component-based software engineering and introduce the use of deployment descriptors, all of which are discussed below.

The core functionality of an application server can be described by examining the major competing alternatives: application servers based on Sun's J2EE[15] and Microsoft's .NET.[16] Both are similar in terms of their functionality. However, we focus on J2EE in this section without loss of generality. Basically, J2EE is defined by a set of API specifications that is implemented by vendors. Examples are IBM WebSphere[17] or the open-source application server JBoss.[18]

Components and Frameworks

With the increasing complexity in system requirements and the tight development budget constraints, the process of programming applications from scratch is becoming less feasible. As we have seen throughout this chapter, the granularity of software building blocks ever increased and also influenced the evolution of middleware. Constructing applications from a collection of reusable components and frameworks is emerging as a popular approach to software development. This way of constructing applications can be seen as a new paradigm proposing that software should be built by gluing prefabricated components together as in the field of electronics or mechanics.

A (software) *component* is a functional discrete block of logic. Components can be full applications or encapsulated functionality that can be used as part of

---

[15]Java 2 Enterprise Edition, cf. `http://java.sun.com/j2ee/`

[16]`http://www.microsoft.com/net/`

[17]`http://www.ibm.com/software/websphere/`

[18]`http://www.jboss.org`

a larger application, enabling the construction of applications using components as software building blocks. Components have a number of benefits as they simplify application development and maintenance, allowing systems to be more adaptive and to respond rapidly to changing requirements. Reusable components are designed to encompass a reusable block of software, logic or functionality.

If components are analogous to building blocks, frameworks can be seen as the cement that holds them together. Frameworks are a collection of interfaces and interaction protocols that define how components interact with each other and the framework itself. In essence, frameworks allow components to be plugged into them. Examples of component frameworks include Enterprise JavaBeans (EJB)[19] in the case of J2EE and the Component Object Model (COM)[20] from Microsoft. Frameworks are most often integrated in application servers. [Curry, 2004a]

Application Servers as "Web-enabled" Middleware and Frameworks

Application servers incorporate the Web as a key access channel to the functionality implemented using conventional middleware, leading to "Web-enabled" middleware. Incorporating the Web as an access channel has several important implications. The most significant one is that the presentation logic of the application acquires a much more relevant role than in conventional middleware. This is a direct consequence of how HTTP and the Web work, where all forms of information exchange take place through documents. Preparing, dynamically generating, and managing these documents constitute main requirements to be met by an application server. An application server intends to support multiple types of clients including mobile phones, applications, such as those encountered in conventional middleware, Web services clients, i.e., applications that interact with the server through standard Web services protocols (cf. Section 3.2) and Web browsers. Web browsers are by far the most common type of clients. They interact with the application server via its Web server and receive statically or dynamically generated HTML pages.

Figure 2.2 depicts the API's of the presentation logic layer in the case of J2EE. Dynamic pages are generated by servlets,[21] viz., Java code that handles HTTP requests and generally responds with HTML to be rendered by a requesting browser. A closely related technology is the JavaServer Pages (JSP).[22] JSP is based on servlets, but is more convenient by including Java-code in an HTML page. Support for parsing and transforming XML documents independent of

---

[19]http://java.sun.com/products/ejb/
[20]http://www.microsoft.com/com/
[21]http://java.sun.com/products/servlet
[22]http://java.sun.com/products/jsp

a specific XML processing implementation is provided by Java API for XML Processing (JAXP).[23] JavaMail[24] provides platform-independent and protocol-independent means to build mail and messaging applications. Furthermore, the Java Authentication and Authorization Service (JAAS)[25] enables developers to authenticate users and enforce access controls upon those users in their applications. By abstracting from the complex underlying authentication and authorization mechanisms, JAAS minimizes the risk of creating security vulnerabilities in application code.

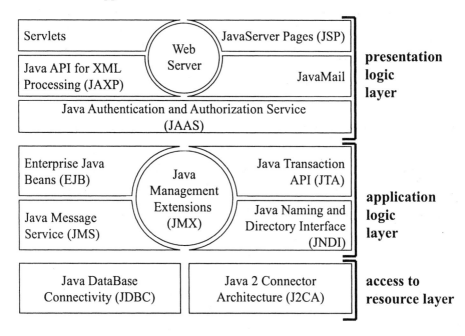

Figure 2.2.   J2EE API's divided into layers. [Alonso et al., 2004]

At the application layer, application servers conceptually resemble conventional middleware. The functionality provided is similar to that of TP monitors, CORBA and message brokers. However, component-based software engineering is typically fostered by application servers, which therefore provide a corresponding framework.

The middle section of Figure 2.2 depicts the API's of the application logic layer in the case of J2EE. We can find conventional middleware, such as JTA and JMS, together with directory services accessible via JNDI (cf. Section

---

[23]http://java.sun.com/xml/jaxp/
[24]http://java.sun.com/products/javamail/
[25]http://java.sun.com/products/jaas/

1). The framework for software components in the form of the Enterprise JavaBeans (EJB) container is a basic part of J2EE-based application servers. Specific EJB components are deployed in this container and contain the bulk of application logic. Some application servers use the recent Java Management Extensions (JMX)[26] technology to put EJB container, directory services and the like in coarser grained components, called managed beans (short MBeans). In contrast to EJB, JMX provides its own framework for such managed beans. The difference is that MBeans can be deployed, undeployed and monitored at run time. They also support interface evolution by a looser coupling.

Finally, J2EE addresses the problem of connecting to the resource layer. Two standards are leveraged in this case: (*i*) Java Database Connectivity (JDBC)[27] that enables developers to access almost any relational database, and (*ii*) the J2EE Connector Architecture (J2CA)[28] that is a generalization of JDBC in that it defines how to build arbitrary resource adapters.

As the complexity of J2EE shows, a significant aspect of application servers is the bundling of more and more functionality within the middleware platform. This is consistent with the trend toward providing integrated support for many different middleware abstractions that we have witnessed in conventional middleware. In fact, as software vendors continue to extend their middleware offerings and package them in many different ways, it becomes hard even to distinguish what is inside an application server and what is not. In many cases, the name originally given to the application server (e.g., IBM WebSphere) has been progressively used to label every middleware product offered by a company. For example, IBM messaging and workflow platforms are now marketed under the name WebSphere MQ.

Deployment Descriptors

Application servers try to tame the increasing complexity of their bundled functionality by managing orthogonal issues in an application independent way. They introduce vertical services, e.g., load balancing, pooling, caching, transactions, session management, user rights and persistence, that span all layers. Thus, the responsibility is shifted from the development to the deployment process, i.e., "the process whereby software is installed into an operational environment" according to the J2EE glossary.

XML files are used to describe how components and applications should be deployed and how vertical services should be configured. Such deployment descriptors[29] direct deployment tools to deploy a component, an application

---

[26]http://java.sun.com/products/JavaManagement/

[27]http://java.sun.com/products/jdbc

[28]http://java.sun.com/j2ee/connector/

[29]J2EE deployment descriptor, http://java.sun.com/j2ee/j2ee-1_4-fr-spec.pdf

or a vertical service with specific options and describe specific configuration requirements that a deployer must resolve.

While it is always a good idea to reduce the amount of source code that has to be written, the deployment process can be quite tricky in itself. Deployment tools merely act as an input mask, which generates the specific XML syntax for the user. This is definitely a nice feature; however, the developer must fully understand the quite complicated concepts that lie behind the options for the transactional behavior, for instance, and juggle all of them at the same time. The current deployment tools do not help to avoid or even actively repair configurations that may cause harmful system behavior. Even worse, this problem is duplicated, as there is a plethora of deployment descriptors for different kinds of components (servlets, EJBs, MBeans) and vertical services (security, transactions, etc.).

We here present a case of how tricky the deployment process can become. It is the interesting case of indirect permissions due to context switches (cf. Figure 2.3). As an example, consider the anonymous user who accesses a Web shop by the HTTP basic authentication. The script on this page, say a servlet, might connect to the CustomerEntityBean, an EJB, which in turn accesses the Customer table in the database. We assume that the database is only accessible by dbuser. Therefore, the EJB performs an explicit context switch (which is frequently described as the run-as paradigm). The call succeeds, because the user information will be propagated and the call will also be executed using the dbuser's credentials. This case is definitely not a bug; however, it remains a pure manual and tedious task for the administrator of the application server to keep track of such indirect permissions. [Oberle et al., 2005c]

Figure 2.3.   Example of indirect permission. [Oberle et al., 2005c]

In this example, the administrator needs to analyze two different deployment descriptors, as well as the source code to discover the situation outlined above. First, the deployment descriptor of the servlet container (web.xml) states that only authenticated users may access the WebShopServlet:

Example 2.1 (web.xml)

```
...
<security-constraint>
 <web-resource-collection>
  <web-resource-name>WebShopServlet</web-resource-name>
  <url-pattern>/servlet/WebShopServlet</url-pattern>
  <http-method>GET</http-method>
 </web-resource-collection>
</security-constraint>

<login-config>
 <auth-method>BASIC</auth-method>
</login-config>
...
```

Second, the WebShopServlet itself accesses the CustomerEntityBean. The servlet's doGet() method serves the incoming HTTP requests. In our case it queries user account information out of the Customer table by means of the bean in order to display it to the user. After retrieving a handle to the bean via the Home interface, the getCustomerName() method of the bean is invoked by the servlet.

Example 2.2 (WebShopServlet.java)

```
public class WebShopServlet extends HttpServlet {
 public void doGet(HttpServletRequest request,
  HttpServletResponse response)
 {
  ...
  //get customer info via CustomerEntityBean
  CustomerObject cObject = cHome.create()
  out.println(cObject.getCustomerName())
  ...
 }
 ...
}
```

Third, the deployment descriptor of the CustomerEntityBean, called ejb--jar.xml, states that the bean performs a context switch via the <run-as--specified-identity> tag. It thus accesses the database table with dbuser's credentials:

Example 2.3 (`ejb-jar.xml`)

```
...
<ejb-jar>
<enterprise-beans>
 <entity>
  <ejb-name>CustomerEntityBean</ejb-name>
  <ejb-class>edu.unika.aifb.CustomerEntityBean</ejb-class>
  ...
  <security-identity>
   <run-as-specified-identity>
    <role-name>dbuser</role-name>
   </run-as-specified-identity>
  </security-identity>
 </entity>
</enterprise-beans>
</ejb-jar>
...
```

Assessing such situations for any user, any EJB and any database table becomes an impossible task for developers and administrators. Rather, it is desirable to query a system from different perspectives, e.g., *"Are there any users with indirect permission to resources? And if yes, what are those resources?"* or *"Are there any indirect permissions on the* Customer *table? And if yes, who are the users?"* Such a system requires the explication of the conceptual model underlying the different descriptions. Each deployment descriptor introduces its own conceptual model implicitly in the corresponding XML-DTD. Therefore, it is difficult to arrive at conclusions that are a result of an integration of such descriptors. Consequently, Chapter 4 proposes the usage of ontologies to support developers and administrators in these tasks.

As we introduce in Chapter 3, ontologies are a means to formally specify a coherent conceptual model with logic-based semantics. The modelling of the computational domain has to be done rigorously, because we encounter fundamental ontological questions: *What is the difference between the users in the operating system, in the database system and within the application server's realm (where users are called principals)? Are there any conceptual differences except their placement in a different realm?* Also, we might be interested in the relationship between a user in an information system and the corresponding natural person. To infer the total of access rights granted for a natural person who might have several user accounts in and across information systems, might reveal further security holes.

3.2 Web Services

The types of middleware discussed so far are all based on tightly-coupled software building blocks (procedures, objects, workflows and components). That means interfaces between the different software building blocks of an application are closely interrelated in function and form, thus making them brittle when any form of change is required to parts or the whole application.

The need for B2B applications to adapt to changing environments is a key reason that made loosely-coupled systems attractive. In this section we explain how Web services came about and how they may meet the new requirements. First, one has to understand the paradigm of service-oriented architectures, which factorizes the functionality in loosely-coupled services. A second aspect is the way that Web services redesign the conventional middleware protocols. Finally, standardization plays a major role, which led to a set of specifications of different Web services aspects, labelled WS*.

Service-Oriented Architectures (SOA)

Today, businesses have to adopt quickly to changing environments, such as changing policies, business strengths, business focus, partnerships or industry standing. Businesses that are able to act flexibly in relation to their environment where change occurs as required, are called "on demand" businesses. They triggered the need for loosely-coupled systems in order to become more agile with respect to changing environments.

The SOA paradigm is the answer to this and other needs. The functionality of a distributed system is split into services instead of tightly-coupled objects or components. *Services* are loosely-coupled, autonomous and independent software building blocks. In order to work on a global scale, standards have to be defined for service invocation, description, discovery, coordination and composition.

SOA-based systems do not exclude the possibility that individual services can themselves be built with object-oriented design. It allows objects within the system and is as such object-based, but not as a whole object-oriented. The difference is that many aspects that were hard-coded before have to be specified dynamically and declaratively. One needs to specify how the overall application performs its workflow between services. The workflow may include services not just between departments, but even with other external partners. Policies have to be defined as to how relationships between services should transpire. All this has to work in an environment of trust and reliability, which is given implicitly when business partners know each other and agree on terms beforehand. [IBM developerWorks, 2004a]

Web Services as Middleware for SOA-based Systems

The Web-based middleware for SOA-based systems is called Web services. Web services subsume a set of protocols and XML-languages for interface description, invocation, discovery and composition of services. The minimalist Web services middleware is comprised of SOAP (Simple Object-based Access Protocol [Gudgin et al., 2003]), the standard for the invocation, and WSDL (Web Service Description Language [Christensen et al., 2001]), the standard for the interface description. Further standards for discovery, coordination and composition are being developed at the time of writing, as discussed below.[30]

The *evolutionary* nature of Web services presents them as extensions to conventional middleware that provides a set of simple interfaces for interactions across the Internet. These extensions make Web-based integration possible at least in simple scenarios (such as EAI or closed communities of business partners). SOAP and WSDL constitute yet another tier on the internal middleware of an organizational unit (cf. Figure 2.4).

External Middleware

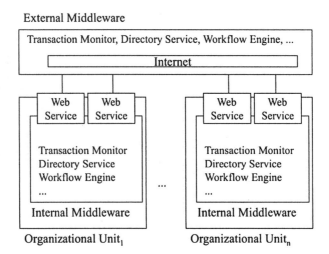

Figure 2.4.   Internal vs. external middleware. [Alonso et al., 2004]

Two organizational units are able to perform application integration if they both agree on using SOAP and WSDL, even if they use different internal middleware. For example, Web services might draw from components residing in application servers (internal middleware) distributed over different organizational units and heterogeneous platforms. Application servers are an obvious

---

[30]Message-oriented middleware is sometimes considered as middleware for SOA-based systems, too. In fact, it defines similar concepts, but lacks the standardization necessary to realize SOA-based systems on a global scale. We discuss these matters in the next section.

target to support such a "wrapping" by SOAP and WSDL, as they provide the basic infrastructure (Web server, XML parsers, etc.). In most cases, the developer is only required to mark a certain method with meta-tags in the source code. The application server cares for automatically generating the WSDL description and handling the SOAP messages.

The new tiers Web services add to the already overly complex internal middleware lead to significant performance overhead and increase the complexity of developing, tuning, maintaining, and evolving multi-tier systems. Translation to and from XML, tunnelling of invocations through SOAP, clients embedded in Web servers and many of the technologies typical of Web services do not come for free. Furthermore, Web services will introduce additional, external middleware, thus adding extra complexity.

The *revolutionary* view sees Web services as radically changing the way integration is achieved. The assumption seems to be that once SOAP and WSDL are used, then Web services will facilitate the development of infrastructures that support programmatic application integration, dynamic B2B marketplaces and the seamless integration of IT infrastructures from different cooperations.[31] However, the autonomous nature of such SOA-based systems demands the redesign of the middleware protocols to work in a loosely-coupled fashion and across organizational units.

Internal middleware protocols were designed based on assumptions that do not hold in cross-organizational interactions. For example, they assumed a central transaction coordinator and the possibility for this coordinator to lock resources indefinitely. Lack of trust and confidentiality issues often make a case against a central coordinator and, therefore, middleware protocols must now be redesigned to work in a fully distributed fashion and must be extended to allow more flexibility in terms of locking resources. Similar arguments can be made for all interaction and coordination protocols and, in general, for many of the other properties provided by conventional and internal middleware, such as reliability and guaranteed delivery. What was then achieved by a centralized platform must now be redesigned in terms of protocols that can work in a decentralized setting and across trust domains. One example of such "external" middleware is UDDI (Universal Description Discovery & Integration [UDDI Coalition, 2000]), allowing the discovery of Web services.

In order to facilitate application integration with Web services on a global scale, the external Web services middleware must rely on standards. These standards shape the current Web services landscape to a large extent. We have introduced SOAP, WSDL, as well as UDDI so far. We introduce additional ones in the next subsection.

---

[31]Today, Web services are not as revolutionary as one may think. They are mostly used in the evolutionary way for conventional EAI.

WS*

Having an SOA and redefining the middleware protocols is not sufficient to address loosely-coupled and dynamic application integration on a global scale, unless the language and protocols become standardized and widely adopted. Consortia, such as the Organization for the Advancement of Structured Information Standards (OASIS)[32] or the World Wide Web Consortium (W3C),[33] attempt to standardize all the different aspects beyond invocation (SOAP), description (WSDL) and discovery (UDDI). The commitment for standardization does not necessarily mean that there will be one specification for each aspect, however. Below, we give an incomplete overview of the aspects that are currently being specified. Altogether, they form an inscrutable set and are labelled *WS**. [Alonso et al., 2004]

WS-Coordination The primary goal of this specification is to create a framework for supporting coordination protocols. In this regard, it is intended as a meta-specification that will govern specifications that implement concrete forms of coordination protocols. [Cabrera et al., 2003]

WS-Transaction WS-Transaction is an example of a concrete coordination protocol specified by means of WS-Coordination. WS-Transaction is split into the WS-AtomicTransaction protocol for short duration transactions and WS-BusinessActivity to enable existing workflow systems to wrap their proprietary mechanisms and interoperate across trust boundaries. [Cabrera et al., 2004]

WS-BPEL The Business Process Execution Language for Web Services (WS-BPEL) is the de facto standard for specifying service composition. It also allows specifying coordination between Web services, thus acting as an alternative to WS-Coordination. [Andrews et al., 2005]

WS-Security WS-Security is an extension to SOAP for end-to-end application-level security that is otherwise ignored by underlying protocols, such as HTTPS. It adds to SOAP the mechanisms of signatures and encryption. [Atkinson et al., 2002]

WS-Policy is a proposal for a framework through which Web services can express their requirements, capabilities and preferences (commonly referred to as "policies") to each other in an interoperable manner. It defines a set of generic constructs for defining and grouping policy assertions. [Bajaj et al., 2004, Alonso et al., 2004]

---

[32]http://www.oasis-open.org
[33]http://www.w3.org

WS-Trust The Web Services Trust Language (WS-Trust) uses the secure messaging mechanisms of WS-Security to define additional primitives and extensions for security token exchange to enable the issuance and dissemination of credentials within different trust domains. [BEA Systems et al., 2004]

Other aspects and specifications include WS-Addressing, WS-Attachments, WS-Eventing, WS-Federation, WS-Inspection, WS-Manageability, WS-Meta-DataExchange, WS-Notification, WS-Routing, and many more. An overview is given in [IBM developerWorks, 2004b].

The advantages of WS* are multiple and have already benefited some industrial cases. Similar to deployment descriptors in application servers, WS* descriptions manage orthogonal aspects in an application independent way. XML-files declaratively describe how Web services should be deployed and configured. Thus, WS* descriptions are exchangeable and developers may use different implementations for the same Web service description. The disadvantages of WS*, however, are also visible; even though the different standards are complementary, they must overlap and one may produce models composed of different WS* descriptions, which are inconsistent, but do not easily reveal their inconsistencies. The reason is that there is no coherent formal model of WS* and, thus, it is impossible to ask for conclusions that come from integrating several WS* descriptions. Thus, discovering such Web Service management problems or asking for other kinds of conclusions that derive from the integration of WS* descriptions remains a purely manual task of the software developers accompanied by little or no formal machinery.

As an example for a trivial conclusion derived from both a WS-BPEL and WS-Policy description, consider the following case. Let's return to Example 2.1 on page 23 of a web shop and assume we have realized it with internal and external Web services composed and managed by a WS-BPEL engine. After the submission of an order, we have to check the customer's credit card for validity, depending on the credit card type (VISA, MasterCard, etc.). We assume that credit card providers offer this functionality via Web services. The corresponding WS-BPEL process `checkAccount` thus invokes one of the provider's Web services, depending on the customer's credit card. Example 2.4 shows a snippet of the WS-BPEL process definition.

Example 2.4 (WS-BPEL)

```
...
<process name="checkAccount">
 <switch ...>
  <case condition="getVariableData('card')='VISA'">
   <invoke partnerLink="toVISA"
    portType="visa:CCPortType"
```

```
    operation="checkCard"...>
   </invoke>
  </case>
  <case condition="getVariableData('card')='MasterCard'">
   <invoke partnerLink="toMastercard"
    portType="mastercard:CCPortType"
    operation="validateCardData"...>
   </invoke>
  </case>
 ...
 </switch>
</process>
 ...
```

Suppose now that the Web service of one credit card provider, say Master-Card, only accepts authenticated invocations conforming to Kerberos or X509. It states such policies in a corresponding WS-Policy document, such as the one sketched in Example 2.5. The invocation will fail unless the developer ensures that the policies are met. The developer has to check the policies manually at development time or has to implement this functionality to react to policies at run time, assuming that no policy matching engine is in place.

Example 2.5 (WS-Policy)
```
...
<wsp:Policy>
 <wsp:ExactlyOne>
  <wsse:SecurityToken>
   <wsse:TokenType>wsse:Kerberosv5TGT</wsse:TokenType>
  </wsse:SecurityToken>
  <wsse:SecurityToken>
   <wsse:TokenType>wsse:X509v3</wsse:TokenType>
  </wsse:SecurityToken>
 </wsp:ExactlyOne>
</wsp:Policy>
...
```

As we may recognize from this small example, it is desirable to support the developer with unambiguous specifications and formal machinery to arrive at such conclusions automatically. This is particularly helpful when we think of more sophisticated examples where we have large indirect process cascades or additional WS* descriptors to consider. However, it remains a manual task for the developer to discover and assess such situations. The reason is that there is no coherent conceptual model underlying the WS* descriptions — very similar to the case of deployment descriptors in application servers. As a consequence, Chapter 4 proposes the usage of ontologies in Web services middleware to support developers and administrators in performing such tasks.

Ontologies are a means to formally specify conceptual models with logic-based semantics. The domain of Web services demands a rigorous modelling because we are confronted with fundamental ontological questions. *What is the difference between a policy of a Web Service and an access right on a software component? Are they the same? Can workflows of Web services be modelled such as the invocation chain of software components?* Such questions call for a concise and fundamental introduction of ontologies, which is given in Chapter 3.

4. Summary

In this chapter we have discussed the evolution of middleware providing a brief overview for the reader. We have advanced from the earliest types of middleware targeted at distributed application development. With the proliferation of distributed applications in companies there arose the need for enterprise application integration. That triggered further the evolution of middleware resulting in middleware for enterprise application integration. Finally, we have had a closer look at the current state-of-the-art, viz., middleware for business-to-business (B2B) application integration. Application servers and Web services belong in this category. Both offer a wealth of functionalities for realizing business-to-business application integration via the Web. Application servers bundle more and more functionality and Web services are almost universally being built as additional layers over existing middleware platforms, which are already too complex and cumbersome. The complexity is countered by the usage of deployment descriptors that reduce the amount of coding by specifying orthogonal issues in an application independent way. In a similar vein, the Web service community is currently developing a set of standards, WS*, to manage aspects such as coordination or composition.

Though deployment descriptors and WS* descriptions constitute a very flexible way of developing and administrating a distributed application, we have demonstrated that developers and administrators still need to expend significant efforts. The reason is that the conceptual model underlying the different descriptions is *only implicit*. Hence, its bits and pieces are difficult to retrieve, survey and check for validity and maintain. It remains a manual task to arrive at conclusions that are the result of combining such descriptions. Hence, Chapter 3 introduces the reader to *ontologies* as a means to formally specify conceptual models with logic-based semantics. We have also demonstrated that the domain of software components and Web services demands a careful and rigorous ontological modelling.

Chapter 3

ONTOLOGIES

This chapter introduces the reader to ontologies as a means to *explicitly* specify conceptual models with logic-based semantics. Section 1 briefly discusses the original meaning of ontology as a philosophical discipline and continues by analyzing the definition of *an* ontology as used in the Artificial Intelligence and Database communities. In the latter case, we refer to an information object and engineering artifact defined by [Gruber, 1995] as an "explicit specification of a conceptualization." Subsequent sections explain how one can grasp the formal notion of a conceptualization and clarify the role of the explicit specification, i.e., the ontology itself. We also have a look at ontology quality criteria and a suitable representation formalism. The ontology quality criteria are later used to assess if existing ontologies can be reused for our purposes. Furthermore, the criteria allow us to motivate that a representation formalism with large expressiveness constitutes one possibility to increase ontology quality.

Section 2 elicits how one can classify ontologies according to the dimensions *purpose*, *expressiveness* and *specificity*. The classification acts as a guide throughout the document. It allows clarifying the different types of ontologies and the roles they play. In this chapter we take a closer look at foundational ontologies. They can be used as a starting point for building core and domain ontologies. In fact, Part II exploits a foundational ontology as a modelling basis for a management ontology. Its reference characteristics, extensive axiomatization and domain-independence are particularly suitable for this purpose. Using a foundational ontology as modelling basis means relating the concepts and associations of an ontology to the basic categories of human cognition investigated by philosophy, linguistics and psychology. This prompts the ontology engineer to sharpen his notions with respect to the distinctions made in the foundational ontology. Because the domain of software components and Web services demands a careful and rigorous modelling, foundational ontologies are a good basis to start from. We argue that the resulting core and domain ontologies have a better design by applying ontology design patterns captured by the foundational ontology.

A well-designed foundational ontology is very specific about the ontological choices to which it commits. Hence, by reusing a foundational ontology for modelling a universe of discourse, the ontology engineer is also prompted to decide whether the choices are suitable. This decision is often neglected or unconsciously made, leading to confusion later on. We discuss important ontological choices, which are also called ontology meta-criteria, in Section 4. In Part II we choose an appropriate foundational ontology on the basis of the ontological choices.

Although we acknowledge the original definition by [Gruber, 1995], we follow the work and theory of Guarino as depicted in his papers [Guarino et al., 1994, Guarino and Giaretta, 1995, Guarino, 1998, Guarino and Welty, 2002]. The notion of ontology quality and the ontological choices are taken from WonderWeb deliverables [Borgo et al., 2002, Masolo et al., 2002, Masolo et al., 2003], the formalism on quantified modal logic from [Schmitt, 2001]. The way to classify ontologies has not been published before (apart from [Oberle et al., 2004b] — an internal project report) and was created in cooperation with Aldo Gangemi. We also cite parts of [Varzi and Vieu, 2004].

1.   Definition

The word "ontology" is used with different meanings in different communities. We distinguish between Ontology (uncountable reading and capital initial) and *an* ontology (countable reading and lowercase initial) in the remainder of this book.

In the first case, we refer to a philosophical discipline, namely the branch of philosophy which deals with the nature and the organization of reality. Aristotle dealt with this subject in his Metaphysics[1] and defined Ontology[2] as the science of being. Unlike the special sciences, each of which investigates a class of beings and their determinations, Ontology regards all the species "... of being *qua* being and attributes which belong to it *qua* being ..." [Aristotle, 350 BC]. In this sense Ontology tries to answer the question: *What is being?* or, in

---

[1]The first books of Aristotle's treatises, known collectively as "Organon," deal with the nature of the world, i.e., physics. Metaphysics denotes the subjects dealt with in the rest of the books — among them Ontology. The Ancient Greek preposition μετά translates to the spatial "behind," i.e., what is meant by Metaphysics are the books next to the ones dealing with physics on the shelf. Hence, philosophers often equate Metaphysics and Ontology.

[2]Ontology is a Greek composite word put together by τὸ ὄν and ὁ λόγος. ὄν is the irregular active present participle of εἶναι, English "to be," whose complete stem is revealed in its genitive τοῦ ὄντος. ὁ λόγος is used by the Ancient Greek with at least five basic meanings, in this case it can be translated as "science."

a meaningful reformulation: *What are the features common to all beings?* [Guarino and Giaretta, 1995]

In the second case, we refer to an information object and engineering artifact as the most prevalent use in the Artificial Intelligence and Database communities. Ontologies are a means to formally model a specific universe of discourse. The ontology engineer analyzes relevant entities[3] and classifies them into concepts and instances.[4] The backbone of an ontology consists of a concept hierarchy, i.e., a taxonomy. Associations define relationships between concepts and can be instantiated accordingly. In our domain of middleware, "software component" and "enterprise bean" might be relevant concepts, where the first is the superconcept of the latter. "Depends on" can be considered a crucial association holding between software components. A concrete enterprise bean running on a computer would then be an instance of its corresponding concept.

In essence, ontologies are similar to existing conceptual modelling techniques, e.g., the Entity Relationship Model [Chen, 1976] or UML [Booch et al., 1998].[5] However, ontologies differ from existing methods and technologies in the following way: (*i*) the primary goal of ontologies is to enable agreement on the meaning of specific vocabulary terms and, thus, to facilitate information integration across individual applications; (*ii*) ontologies are formalized in logic-based representation languages. Their semantics are thus specified in an unambiguous way. (*iii*) The representation languages come with executable calculi enabling querying and reasoning at run time.

Gruber originally defined this notion of ontology as an "explicit specification of a conceptualization" [Gruber, 1995]. The following sections elaborate on the notion of conceptualization because it is hard to understand and is often confused with an ontology itself in common literature.

1.1   What is a Conceptualization?

[Gruber, 1995] refers to the notion of a conceptualization according to [Genesereth and Nilsson, 1987] who claim: "A body of formally represented knowledge is based on a conceptualization: the objects, concepts, and other entities that are assumed to exist in some area of interest and the relationships that hold among them. A conceptualization is an abstract, simplified view of the world that we wish to represent for some purpose. Every knowledge base,

---

[3]From Latin "ens; entis," the active present participle of "esse," derived from the Greek εἶναι, English "to be." Entity denotes the most general being, and, thus, subsumes subjects, objects, processes, ideas, etc.

[4]Smith made us aware that the notion of "concept" is quite ambiguous [Smith, 2004]. Therefore, we find another distinction in common literature. It is the distinction between universals and particulars that can be informally understood by taking the relation of instantiation as a primitive: particulars are entities which have no instances; universals are entities that can have instances. In this case, associations are usually considered as universals.

[5]In fact, we visualize ontologies by means of UML class diagrams throughout the document.

knowledge-based system, or knowledge-level agent is committed to some conceptualization, explicitly or implicitly." Formally, they define conceptualization as follows:

Definition 3.1 (Conceptualization according to Genesereth)
A conceptualization according to Genesereth is a tuple $(D, \mathbf{R})$ where

- *D is the universe*

- *$\mathbf{R}$ is a set of relations on D*

Genesereth and Nilsson's notion of conceptualization refers to ordinary mathematical relations on a set D (which we always denote by the letter D without further mention), i.e., extensional relations. These relations reflect a specific world such as the one depicted in Example 3.1.

Example 3.1
Let us consider an example of software components and their dependencies. A possible conceptualization of this universe of discourse might be $(D, \mathbf{R})$ with $D = \{sc_1, sc_2, sc_3, sc_4\}$ and $\mathbf{R} = \{SC, d\}$. The extensions of both relations might be $SC = \{sc_1, sc_2, sc_3, sc_4\}$ and $d = \{(sc_1, sc_2), (sc_1, sc_3), (sc_2, sc_3)\}$, i.e., SC comprises elements of the universe which are software components and d formalizes their dependency relations. The world is depicted in Figure 3.1.

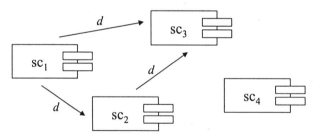

Figure 3.1. A specific world with software components and their dependencies.

Guarino made us aware that this notion of conceptualization is quite problematic, however. In [Guarino and Giaretta, 1995] he explains that another world has to be considered a different conceptualization according to this definition. In our universe of software components (Example 3.1), every specific dependency graph would be another conceptualization.

Example 3.2
Let us consider the following alteration of Example 3.1 with $D' = D$ and $\mathbf{R}' = \{SC, d'\}$ where $d' = d \cup \{(sc_1, sc_4)\}$. It is obvious that $(D, \mathbf{R}) \neq (D', \mathbf{R}')$ and, thus, we have two different conceptualizations according to Genesereth.

The problem is that the relations of **R** reflect a specific world. However, we need to focus on the meaning of those relations, independently of a world: for instance, the meaning of the d relation lies in the way it refers to certain pairs of software components according to their dependency. Therefore, we need to speak of intensional or conceptual relations. A standard way to represent intensions (and therefore conceptual relations) is to see them as functions from possible worlds into sets [Guarino, 1998].

Definition 3.2 (Conceptual Relation)
A conceptual relation ρ^n of arity n is a total function $\rho^n : W \rightarrow 2^{D^n}$ from the set W, which we call the set of possible worlds, into the set of all n-ary (extensional) relations on D.

We can consider our Examples 3.1 and 3.2 as two different worlds w_1 and w_2. Conceptual relations of SC and d look like follows: SC^1 maps every possible world to $\{sc_1, sc_2, sc_3, sc_4\}$ because software components cannot cease to be software components in any world we can think of (cf. the notion of rigidity in [Guarino and Welty, 2002]). d^2 maps to a specific dependency graph between the four software components. In Example 3.1 we have $d^2(w_1) = \{(sc_1, sc_2), (sc_1, sc_3), (sc_2, sc_3)\}$ and in Example 3.2 $d^2(w_2) = \{(sc_1, sc_2), (sc_1, sc_3), (sc_2, sc_3), (sc_1, sc_4)\}$. Having the notion of conceptual relations at hand, we are able to understand Guarino's notion of a conceptualization:

Definition 3.3 (Conceptualization according to Guarino)
A conceptualization according to Guarino is a triple $\mathbf{C} = (D, W, \Re)$ with

- *D the universe*

- *W a set of possible worlds*

- *$\Re$ a set of conceptual relations*

1.2 What is an Ontology?

Having clarified the notion of conceptualization, we can now draw our attention to the definition of an ontology as an "explicit specification of a conceptualization." The explicit specification is achieved by a logical theory, i.e., a set of logical axioms, expressed in a logical language **L**. Hence, an ontology can be regarded as a logical theory that accounts for the intended meaning of the vocabulary **V** of **L**. The vocabulary of a logical language usually consists of a set of constant, function and relation (predicate) symbols. We do not need function symbols for our purposes and limit our attention to constant and relation symbols.

This section explains how to grasp the intended meaning of a vocabulary following [Guarino, 1998]. We start with the logical language **L**, which is typically a variant of first-order logic. For the sake of brevity, we omit an extensive introduction of first-order logic and only give the usual definition of a first-order structure,[6] as well as the notion of satisfiability and model, which are required in the following definitions [Schöning, 2000].

Definition 3.4 (First-Order Structure, Model, Logical Theory)
A First-Order Structure M for a logical language **L** *with vocabulary* **V** *is a tuple* $M = (S, I)$ *with*

- $S = (D, \mathbf{R})$ *being a Conceptualization according to Genesereth*

- *I being an interpretation function* $I : \mathbf{V} \rightarrow D \cup \mathbf{R}$ *that maps vocabulary symbols of* **V** *to elements of the universe* D *or extensional relations of* **R***.*

A logical theory *F, consisting of a set of axioms, is* satisfiable *by a first-order structure M if all of its axioms are true. In this case, M is called a* model *of F, written* $M \models F$.

After introducing the language **L** we now clarify what is meant by the intended meaning of vocabulary of a language **L**. The key to this is the notion of ontological commitment. We say that a logical language **L** commits to a conceptualization **C** by means of an ontological commitment. Formally we write:

Definition 3.5 (Ontological Commitment)
An Ontological Commitment **K** *of a logical language* **L** *with vocabulary* **V** *is a tuple* $\mathbf{K} = (\mathbf{C}, \mathcal{I})$ *with*

- $\mathbf{C} = (D, W, \Re)$ *being a conceptualization according to Guarino and*

- $\mathcal{I}$ *being a total function* $\mathcal{I} : \mathbf{V} \rightarrow D \cup \Re$ *mapping vocabulary symbols of* **V** *to elements of the universe* D *or conceptual relations of* $\Re$.

The definition above is quite simple: We extend the usual mapping of vocabulary symbols to extensional relations in Definition 3.4 by a mapping to conceptual relations. We do so because we have learned that extensional relations are not suitable for expressing conceptualizations in the previous section. Coming back to our Example 3.1, we would commit the relation symbols SC and d to the conceptual relations SC^1 and d^2, respectively.

---

[6]We prefer to use the term "first-order structure" over "model" or "interpretation." The latter two are often used in common literature, but suffer from heavy overloading.

The notion of ontological commitment is the link between a conceptualization **C**, which is language independent in the first place, and an ontology, i.e., a logical theory expressed in **L** accounting for **K**. The next step is to formalize "accounting for" suitably, i.e., the logical theory should be designed so that its models approximate the conceptualization as tightly as possible. In other words, we need a notion of compatibility between the logical theory and the conceptualization:

Definition 3.6 (Compatibility: Logical Theory - Ontolog. Commitment)
A model $M = (S, I)$, *with* $S = (D, \mathbf{R})$ *a conceptualization according to Genesereth, of a logical theory expressed in* **L** *is compatible with an ontological commitment* $\mathbf{K} = (\mathbf{C}, \mathcal{I})$, *with* $\mathbf{C} = (D, W, \Re)$ *a conceptualization according to Guarino, iff*

1 there exists $w \in W$ *so that for all* $r \in \mathbf{R}$ *there exists at least one* $p \in \mathbf{V}$ *with* $r = \mathcal{I}(p)(w)$

2 for all constant symbols $c \in \mathbf{V}$ *we have* $I(c) = \mathcal{I}(c)$

3 for all relation symbols $p \in \mathbf{V}$ *there exists at least one* $\rho \in \Re$ *with* $\mathcal{I}(p) = \rho$

4 there exists $w \in W$ *so that for all relation symbols* $p \in \mathbf{V}$ *there exists at least one* $\rho \in \Re$ *with* $I(p) = \rho(w)$

The set $\mathbf{I_K(L)}$ *of all models of* **L** *that are compatible with* **K** *is called the set of* intended models *of* **L** *according to* **K**.

Condition 1 states that the extensional relations of **R** have to be equal to a conceptual relation in a specific world. In Example 3.1, we have $r = \{sc_1, sc_2, sc_3, sc_4\} = SC^1(w_1)$ and $r = \{(sc_1, sc_2), (sc_1, sc_3), (sc_2, sc_3)\} = d^2(w_1)$. Condition 2 is simple and just requires that the mapping of constant symbols to elements of the universe is identical. Example 3.1 does not introduce any constant symbols. In condition 3 we demand that the interpretation $\mathcal{I}$, defined in our ontological commitment, maps every relation symbol p to a conceptual relation ρ. In the example, the relation symbols SC and d have to be mapped to the conceptual relations SC^1 and d^2, respectively. Finally, condition 4 demands that the interpretations of relation symbols are elements of a corresponding conceptual relation in a specific world. In Example 3.1, $I(d)$ has to be equal to $d^2(w_1) = \{(sc_1, sc_2), (sc_1, sc_3), (sc_2, sc_3)\}$.

With the notion of compatibility at hand, we can now clarify the role of an ontology, considered as a logical theory designed to account for the intended meaning of a vocabulary **V** of **L**. With all of our clarifications, we arrive at the following definition:

Definition 3.7 (Ontology)

*Given a language **L** with ontological commitment **K**, an ontology **O** for **L** is a logical theory designed so that the set of its models approximates as best as possible the set of compatible, i.e., intended, models of **L** according to **K** (cf. Figure 3.2)*

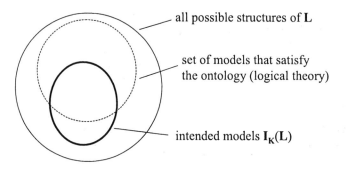

all possible structures of **L**

set of models that satisfy
the ontology (logical theory)

intended models $I_K(L)$

Figure 3.2.   Intended models vs. models of the ontology. [Guarino, 1998]

In general, it is not easy (nor always convenient) to find the right logical theory mainly because of cognitive reasons. Everybody conceives the world differently, applies individual meanings to concepts and changes his or her mind over time with respect to the meanings. Therefore, an ontology admits other models besides the intended ones. An ontology can "specify" a conceptualization only in a very indirect way, since (*i*) it can only approximate the intended models; (*ii*) such a set of intended models is only a weak characterization of a conceptualization. The reason for (*i*) and (*ii*) is that there is no way to reconstruct the ontological commitment of a language from a set of its intended models, since a model does not necessarily reflect a specific world. In fact, since the relevant relations considered may not be enough to completely characterize a world, a model may actually describe a situation common to many worlds. This means that it is impossible to reconstruct the correspondence between worlds and extensional relations established by the underlying conceptualization.

Therefore, we shall say that an ontology **O** for a language **L** approximates a conceptualization **C** if there exists an ontological commitment **K** so that the intended models of **L** according to **K** are included in the models of **O**. That leads us to the notion of ontology quality [Borgo et al., 2002]:[7]

---

[7]The notions of precision and completeness can be compared to the measures of precision and recall of intended models known from information retrieval. Accuracy can be understood as the product of precision and recall but calculated on worlds, i.e., specific situations, instead of intended models.

Definition 3.8 (Ontology Quality)

- *An ontology* O_1 *is* more precise than *an ontology* O_2 *if the models of* O_1 *cover fewer unintended models. This is the case when the axiomatization of* O_1 *is richer than that of* O_2. *In an ideal case, the models of the ontology and the intended models are identical.*

- *An ontology* O_1 *is* more complete than *an ontology* O_2 *if the models of* O_1 *cover more intended models. This is the case when* O_1 *adopts more relevant conceptual relations in its vocabulary than* O_2.

- *An ontology* O_1 *is* more accurate than *an ontology* O_2 *if the models of* O_1 *exclude more unintended situations. A precise and complete ontology might not be enough to fully characterize a world. The reason is that the intended models actually describe a situation common to many worlds.*

A typical case for an ontology not being precise enough is depicted in Figure 3.2, where the models of the ontology comprise also unintended models. In our running example, we do not specify our understanding of software component (SC) in the form of axioms. Software component is a very broad concept that leaves open a multitude of interpretations ranging from "part of an application" to very specific ones, such as enterprise bean. Hence, our ontology comprises also unindended models. The ontology depicted in Figure 3.2 is also not complete enough because it does not cover all intended models. In our running example, we are not complete enough if we understand software component as "part of an application" because "part" and "application" are missing in the vocabulary. Finally, a way to make an ontology more accurate is to enrich the universe of the underlying conceptualization. In our running example, we do not specify whether software components can also depend on Web services or vice versa simply because our universe does not contain enough relevant entities.

The criteria are used in Part II to assess if the quality of existing ontologies suffices for our purposes. A way to increase ontology quality is to adopt a modal logic, which allows one to express constraints across worlds. We discuss a suitable modal logic in the next section.

1.3   A Suitable Representation Formalism

When choosing a suitable representation formalism for ontologies, one always encounters the dilemma between *expressiveness* and *decidability*. On the one hand, the representation formalism should enable us to be as precise as possible. On the other hand, we need a decidable and efficient calculus for our language to allow reasoning at run time.

In this section, our intention is to approximate the intended models of a conceptualization as closely as possible, so we choose a rich representation formalism. Quantified modal logic has proven to be suitable because it introduces primitives that allow us to quantify over worlds. The reader may note that this choice does not exclude using a computable and efficient, yet less expressive, language later on at run time, e.g., a description logic. We elaborate on this issue in Section 2.

Quantified modal logic is based on first-order logic, but introduces a set W, which is called the set of possible worlds, and an accessibility relation A between worlds. Both are defined by means of a Kripke structure. The modal operators $\Box$ and $\Diamond$ allow us to quantify over these worlds. $\Box F$ is interpreted as "F is true in all worlds" and $\Diamond F$ as "there exists one world in which F is true."

Definition 3.9 (Quantified Modal Logic)

A Kripke structure $\mathcal{K}$ is a triple $\mathcal{K} = (W, A, M)$ with

- *a set W called the set of possible worlds*

- *$A \subseteq W \times W$ a binary relation on W (called the accessibility relation or alternativeness relation)*

- *a first-order structure $M_w = (S, I)$ that can be different in any $w \in W$*

If $\mathcal{K}$ is a Kripke Structure, $w \in W$ and F a modal formula, then we define $(\mathcal{K}, w) \models F$, i.e., F is true in world w of Kripke Structure $\mathcal{K}$, recursively as follows:

- *$(\mathcal{K}, w) \models r(c_1, ..., c_k)$ iff $M_w \models r(c_1, ..., c_k)$ for all relation symbols r and constant symbols c_i with $1 \leq i \leq k$*

- *$(\mathcal{K}, w) \models F \wedge G$ iff $(\mathcal{K}, w) \models F$ and $(\mathcal{K}, w) \models G$*

- *$(\mathcal{K}, w) \models F \vee G$ iff $(\mathcal{K}, w) \models F$ or $(\mathcal{K}, w) \models G$*

- *$(\mathcal{K}, w) \models F \rightarrow G$ iff $(\mathcal{K}, w) \not\models F$ or $(\mathcal{K}, w) \models G$*

- *$(\mathcal{K}, w) \models \neg F$ iff $(\mathcal{K}, w) \not\models F$*

- *$(\mathcal{K}, w) \models \Box F$ iff for all w_1 with $A(w, w_1)$ we have $(\mathcal{K}, w_1) \models F$*

- *$(\mathcal{K}, w) \models \Diamond F$ iff there exists w_1 with $A(w, w_1)$ so that $(\mathcal{K}, w_1) \models F$*

- *$(\mathcal{K}, w) \models \forall x F(x)$ iff for all $d \in D$ holds $(\mathcal{K}, w) \models F(d)$*

- *$(\mathcal{K}, w) \models \exists x F(x)$ iff there exists $d \in D$ with $(\mathcal{K}, w) \models F(d)$*

We want to give A the meaning of an ontological compatibility relation. Sets of worlds must be mutually inaccessible if they do not share the same assumptions. Coming back to our running example, a set of worlds in which d

is given another meaning, e.g., location in time, would not be compatible with the worlds in which we considered it as a dependency relation between software components.

To capture such intuitions, A must be an equivalence relation, i.e., reflexive, transitive and symmetric. If A is an equivalence relation it partitions worlds into equivalence classes, which are mutually inaccessible. In Figure 3.3, class $[W_1]$ denotes all worlds in which d is interpreted as dependency relation; $[W_2]$ denotes all worlds in which d is interpreted as location in time, for instance.

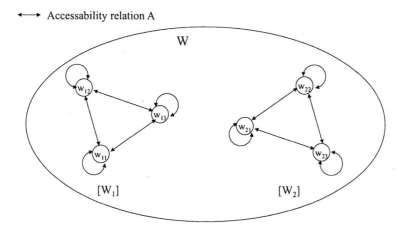

Figure 3.3. The equivalence relation A partitions the set of possible worlds W into equivalence classes $[W_1]$ and $[W_2]$. For the sake of brevity, we only consider three worlds per class. $[W_1] \cap [W_2] = \varnothing$ because both sets of worlds are ontologically incompatible.

We can force A to be the structure of an equivalence relation by adding specific axioms as tautologies to our modal logic. The relationship between A and the tautologies is well studied by correspondence theory [Schmitt, 2001]. In our case, the adopted modal logic is the system S5 [Guarino et al., 1994]. The system S5 introduces the axiom $\Box(A \to B) \to (\Box A \to \Box B)$, which leads to a reflexive A and the axiom $\neg\Box A \to \Box\neg\Box A$ which leads to a transitive and symmetric A.

2. Classification

In the previous section we have discussed the formal characterization of an ontology as a logical theory accounting for an ontological commitment. We have chosen a very rich representation formalism in order to approximate the intended models as closely as possible. In practice, however, less expressive languages are used in order to allow (efficient) reasoning at run time.

The difference with respect to *expressiveness* is only one dimension according to which we can classify ontologies. They also differ in *purpose* and *specificity*. In the first case, we distinguish between *reference* and *application* ontologies. In the latter case, we distinguish among *generic*, *core* and *domain* ontologies. All three dimensions are depicted in Figure 3.4 and are discussed below.

The classification acts as a guide throughout the document. It allows clarifying the different types of ontologies and the roles they play. For example, Section 3 introduces foundational ontologies which are *generic*, *heavyweight* and used for *reference* purposes. We exploit a foundational ontology as a starting point for the design of our management ontology in Part II. The management ontology acts as a *reference* for concepts and associations in our universe of discourse, is *heavyweight* and platform independent (*core* characteristic). Finally, Part III applies the management ontology in a concrete platform for reasoning and querying. Thus, its purpose shifts from *reference* to *application*. We have to reduce the axiomatization to fit a computable representation formalism resulting in a *lightweight* version. We also have to specialize concepts and associations to reflect the idiosyncracies of the platform resulting in a *domain* version.[8]

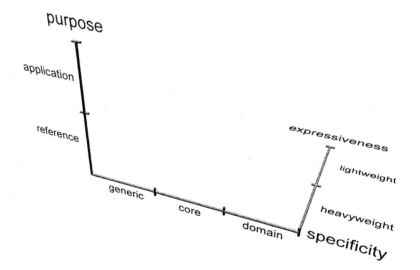

Figure 3.4.   Classification of ontologies.

---

[8]There exist other types of ontologies, e.g., *linguistic* or *terminological* ontologies [Gangemi et al., 2003a], and other classifications, e.g., [van Heijst, 1995, Sheth and Ramakrishnan, 2003, Guarino, 1998].

2.1 Classification according to Purpose

We can distinguish between detailed *reference* ontologies and *application* ontologies. The first are only accessed from time to time for reference purposes, while the latter support reasoning at run time [Borgo et al., 2002].

Application Ontology Used during run time of a specific application putting constraints on the axiomatization for the terminological service, i.e., the reasoner. The typical trade-off between expressiveness and decidability requires a limited representation formalism. As an example, consider the TBox of an ontology in description logics. Note that application ontologies may also describe specific worlds (called "semantic descriptions," "knowledge base," "metadata," "semantic metadata" or simply "instances.") In description logics, the specific worlds are captured by the ABox.

Reference Ontology Used during development time of applications for mutual understanding and explanation between (human or artificial) agents belonging to different communities, for establishing consensus in a community that needs to adopt a new term or simply for explaining the meaning of a term to somebody new to the community. Although parts of the reference ontology can be formalized in a TBox as well, description logics are usually not expressive enough for reference purposes.

2.2 Classification according to Expressiveness

There is a tradeoff between a *lightweight* and a *heavyweight* ontology committing to the same conceptualization: *heavyweight* ontologies try to specify the intended meaning of a vocabulary as precisely as possible. Their primary motivation is to enable mutual understanding in a heterogeneous environment. Their drawback is that they may be hard to develop and to reason with, both because of the number of axioms and the expressiveness of the language adopted.

Lightweight ontologies, on the other hand, may consist of a minimal set of axioms written in a language of limited expressiveness. Such an ontology may support only a limited set of specific services, intended to be shared among users who already agree on the underlying conceptualization.

The tradeoff coincides with the dilemma between *expressiveness* and *decidability* of representation languages. On the one end, we find higher-order logic, full first-order logic or modal logic as that used in Section 1. On the other end, we find less stringent subsets of first-order logic, which typically feature executable calculi. They can be split in two major paradigms. First, languages from the family of *description logics (DL)* [Baader et al., 2003] are strict subsets of first-order logic. The second major paradigm comes from the tradition of *logic programming (LP)* [Das, 1992]. Though logic programming often uses a syntax comparable to first-order logics, it assumes a different interpretation of axioms. Unlike a Tarski-style model theory, logic programming selects only a subset of models to judge semantic entailment of sentences. There are different ways to select subsets of models resulting in different semantics — all of them geared to deal more efficiently with larger sets of data than common approaches based on first-order logic. One of the most prominent differences resulting from this different style of logical models is that expressive logic programming axiomatizations become non-monotonic.

Heavyweight Ontology Heavyweight ontologies are extensively axiomatized and, thus, represent ontological commitment explicitly. The purpose of the axiomatization is to exclude terminological and conceptual ambiguities, which are due to unintended interpretations. Every heavyweight ontology can have a lightweight version. As with all dimensions, the borderline between lightweight and heavyweight is not clearly delimited.

Lightweight Ontology Ontologies are often reduced to a simple taxonomy of concepts and a small number of associations. We classify such ontologies as lightweight ontologies because they are hardly axiomatized, as opposed to heavyweight ontologies. Lightweight ontologies are used when the intended meaning of the concepts used by the community is more or less known in advance by all members, and the ontology can be limited to those structural relationships among concepts that are considered as relevant.

2.3   Classification according to Specificity

The classification according to specificity introduces three layers: generic, core and domain ontologies. The reader may note that "pure" layers are impossible, since domain ontologies are mixed up with excerpts of other domains, other cores, etc. Moreover, the domain layer can shift with detail, application, or even evolution of a domain. [Guarino, 1998]

Generic Ontology The concepts defined by this layer are considered to be generic across many fields. Typically, generic ontologies (synonyms are "upper level" or "top-level" ontology) define concepts such as state, event, process, action, component, etc.

Core Ontology Core ontologies define concepts which are generic across a set of domains. Therefore, they are situated in between the two extremes of generic and domain ontologies. The borderline between generic and core ontologies is not clearly defined because there is no exhaustive enumeration of fields and their conceptualizations. However, the distinction is intuitively meaningful and useful for building libraries.

Domain Ontology Domain ontologies express conceptualizations that are specific for a universe of discourse. The concepts in domain ontologies are often defined as specializations of concepts in the generic and core ontologies.

The borderline between core and domain ontologies is not clearly defined because core ontologies intend to be generic within a domain. Thus, it is usually hard to make a clear cut between generic and core as well as between core and domain ontologies. A concept, such as software component, would be placed in a core ontology for application servers for reuse in every possible domain ontology we can think of. However, a concept, such as enterprise bean, might only be relevant in a specific J2EE setting.

3. The Role of Foundational Ontologies

While the development of some kinds of applications may be easier if ambiguities in low quality ontologies are simply ignored, more sophisticated tasks necessitate the use of carefully designed ontological structures. This is the case when ontologies are used for meaning negotiation and explanation of terms, for establishing consensus in a community that needs to adopt a new term or simply for explaining the meaning of a term to somebody new to the community. Our first investigation of the domain of software components and Web services in Section 3 already revealed that a careful and rigorous ontological modelling is necessary. We encountered fundamental ontological questions, such as *What is the difference between the users in the operating system, in the database system and within the application server's realm?*, *How to model the relationship between a user in an information system and the corresponding natural person?* or *What is the difference between a policy of a Web Service and an access right on a software component? Are they the same?* Furthermore, it is crucial to concisely explain concepts, such as software component or Web service, when designing a management ontology in Part II. Such concepts typically suffer from ambiguity, i.e., users often differ in their understanding of such terms. An explicit representation of ontological commitment is required in order to exclude terminological and conceptual ambiguities bound to unintended interpretations. In this case, a rich axiomatization (in addition to an adequate informal documentation) seems to be unavoidable.

Even if two users or systems adopt the same vocabulary, there is no guarantee that they can agree on a certain definition unless they commit to the same conceptualization. Assuming that each system has its own conceptualization, a necessary condition in order to make an agreement possible is that the intended models of the original conceptualizations overlap. Supposing now that these two sets of intended models are approximated by two different ontologies, it may be the case that the two ontologies overlap while the intended models do not (right side of Figure 3.5). This means that a bottom-up approach to systems integration based on the integration of multiple local ontologies may not work, especially if the local ontologies are only focused on the conceptual relations relevant to a specific context. Therefore, they are only weak and ad hoc approximations of the intended models. Hence, it seems more convenient to agree on a generic ontology as a starting point for core and domain ontologies rather than relying on agreements based on the intersection of different ontologies (left side of Figure 3.5). [Guarino, 1998]

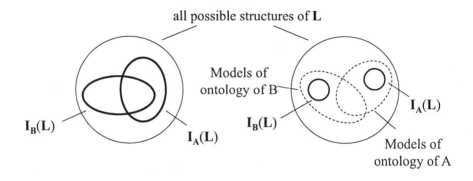

Figure 3.5.   Two agents A and B can only communicate if their intended models $I_A(L)$ and $I_B(L)$ overlap. [Borgo et al., 2002]

We shall use the term *foundational ontologies* for such ontologies, ultimately devoted to facilitate mutual understanding. Designing a foundational ontology is a tedious task and requires expert knowledge. Figure 3.6 depicts how foundational ontologies are categorized according to the three dimensions introduced. They are *heavyweight*, i.e., extensively axiomatized and *generic*, i.e., domain-independent. Their main purpose is to have a concise *reference* at development time. However, lightweight versions of a foundational ontology can also be used for reasoning at run time. In fact, Part II leverages a foundational ontology as a starting point for our management ontology to benefit from its advantages.

Because of their goals and nature, foundational ontologies need an expressive language in order to suitably characterize their intended models. Their computational requirements are less stringent, since their main purpose is for meaning negotiation (*reference* characteristic), rather than for terminological services, i.e., run time reasoning. However, in order to also leverage the foundational ontology in a running system, one usually adopts the following approach:

1 The foundational ontology is axiomatized in full first-order or modal logic.

2 The part of the axiomatization that can be expressed in an executable language is isolated and implemented in a specific application (together with core and domain ontologies).

3 The remaining part is added in the form of comments attached to concepts and associations.

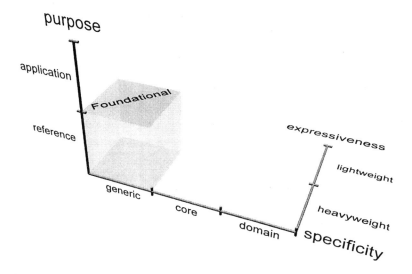

Figure 3.6. Classification of ontologies and the role of foundational ontologies.

Step 2 lets the ontology engineer choose a specific representation language that is executable, i.e., reasoning algorithms can be put into action during run time. This step requires the ontology engineer to manually adapt or remove the axioms of the foundational ontology. The result is a *lightweight* version of the foundational ontology.

Of course, building foundational ontologies is extremely hard, both conceptually and computationally. However, it only needs to be undertaken once, before a cooperation process starts. An ontology engineer should strive for reusing a proven foundational ontology before modelling a core or domain ontology. The ontology engineer can thus leverage a richly predefined set of generic concepts and associations. The assumption of such a top-down approach is that core and domain ontologies have a better design by applying ontology design patterns captured by the foundational ontology.[9] In addition, well-designed foundational ontology is very specific about the ontological choices to which it commits. This decision is often neglected or unconsciously made, leading to confusion later on. We discuss important ontological choices in the next section.

---

[9]Examples for ontology design patterns are locations in space and time, which can be applied and specialized. The World Wide Web Consortium has even introduced a task force for this subject, cf. http://www.w3.org/2001/sw/BestPractices/OEP/.

4.   Ontological Choices

Before addressing specific issues about the domain, its concepts and associations, it is important to clarify the general attitude towards ontological analysis, or — in other words —- the constraints and the motivations that influence the conceptualization of reality. This clarification is often unconsciously made and, thus, remains blurred, leading to confusion later on.

In an ideal case, a foundational ontology is used as a starting point for modelling a domain. A well-engineered foundational ontology is very specific about the ontological choices to which it commits. Hence, the ontology engineer is prompted to decide whether the ontological choices are suitable by reusing a foundational ontology. We discuss typical ontological choices, which are also called ontology meta-criteria, in the following sections. For the design of our management ontology, Part II chooses an appropriate foundational ontology on the basis of the ontological choices.

4.1   Descriptive vs. Revisionary

A *descriptive ontology* aims at describing the ontological assumptions behind language and cognition by taking the surface structure of natural language and common sense seriously. Under this approach, ontological categories are postulated in a rather unrestricted way, independently of evidence coming from other areas, such as physics or astronomy. In a descriptive ontology, the categories refer to cognitive artifacts, more or less depending on human perception, cultural imprints and social conventions. The distinction between things and events is typically considered as a human perception and is adopted by descriptive ontologies..

A *revisionary ontology*, on the other hand, gives less importance to linguistic and cognitive aspects, and does not hesitate to suggest paraphrases of linguistic expressions or re-interpretations of cognitive phenomena in order to avoid ontological assumptions considered debatable on scientific grounds. A revisionary ontology is committed to capture the intrinsic nature of the world. As a consequence, an ontology of this type may impose that only entities extended in space and time exist.

To give an example: common sense distinguishes between things (spatial or non-spatial objects), such as hardware or software components, and events (temporal objects), such as transactions or the lifecycle of a software component. In the wake of relativity theory, however, time is only another dimension for objects and some philosophers and computer scientists have come to believe that the commonsense distinction between things that are and things that happen should be abandoned for a view according to which everything extends in space and time. [Borgo et al., 2002]

4.2 Multiplicative vs. Reductionist

A *multiplicative ontology* aims at giving a reliable account of reality as it allows different entities to be co-localized in the same space-time. These co-localized entities are assumed to be different because they have incompatible essential properties. The drawback of this position is that it results in a larger number of basic concepts.

A *reductionist ontology* postulates that each space-time location contains at most one object: incompatible essential properties are regarded as being linked to different points of view from which one can look at the same spatio-temporal entity. Typically, a reductionist ontology describes a great number of ontological differences with a smaller number of concepts.

As an example, consider an application and the software components that make up the application. The multiplicativist states that these must be different entities, yet co-located: the application is constituted by a number of software components, but it is not a software component itself. When an application is formed, new properties are instantiated (e.g., the number of software components it uses), thus justifying the emergence of a new entity. The reductionist claims that the application and the software components are surely different, although not as entities, but as views of the same non-spatial object. [Borgo et al., 2002]

4.3 Possibilism vs. Actualism

The fundamental thesis of *actualism* is: "Everything that exists is actual." *Possibilism* is the denial of this thesis and there are various forms of possibilism that correspond to the various ways in which one can deny this thesis. Claims, such as, "it is possible that a software component sc_1 depends on sc_2" are known as modal claims, because the sentential prefix "it is possible that" indicates a mode in which the statements it precedes are true. Modal claims are ubiquitous in our thought and discourse. Many of our reflective and creative thoughts seem to be about possibilities and much of our logical reasoning involves drawing conclusions which, in some sense, necessarily follow from premises that we already believe.[10]

When committing to possibilism, we are able to represent possibilia, i.e., possible entities, in our domain. In this case, the representation language is required to express modalities, i.e., quantification over worlds. Basically, two approaches are possible: either one includes modal and temporal operators in the representation language from the very beginning or one reproduces modal reasoning into a first-order language, adding time and world parameters to the predicates. The first approach is called modal logic where we are able to literally

---

[10]http://plato.stanford.edu/entries/actualism/

translate the expression, "it is possible that a software component sc_1 depends on sc_2" into the formalism. The second approach only allows rephrasing the expression by, "there is a world in which sc_1 depends on sc_2."

4.4   Endurantism vs. Perdurantism

A fundamental ontological choice deals with the notion of change. What does it mean for an entity to change? This question raises the problem of variation in time and the related issue of the identity of the objects of experience. There are two main approaches, viz., *endurantism* (also called 3D paradigm) and *perdurantism* (also called 4D paradigm).

Perdurantism assumes that entities extend in time and in space. That means entities have both spatial and temporal parts (and, therefore, four dimensions). Therefore, a 4D entity (usually called perdurant, occurrence or simply process) is not wholly present at a point in time, but its whole is extended in space, as well as time. The entity at a point in time is a temporal part of the whole. For example, the lifecycle of a software component can be considered a 4D entity, where the phases of the initialization, the running state and the termination are its temporal parts.

Endurantism treats entities as 3D objects (sometimes called endurants or continuants) that pass through time and are wholly present at each point in time. Hence, 3D entities do not have temporal parts. A software component can be considered a 3D entity as opposed to its lifecycle (in which it participates). It is wholly present during all three phases of its life.[11] Generally speaking, the 3D approach corresponds well with the way that language works. Language has a focus around here, now, you and me as a context, and on the current state of affairs. This leads to efficient communication under the most common circumstances. [Stell and West, 2004]

4.5   Extrinsic Properties

Besides the ontological choices discussed above, several extrinsic properties of foundational ontologies play an important role. The ontology engineer might base his decision on the representation language, existing links to linguistic ontologies, as well as on modularization.

Representation Language We already discussed in Section 2 that representation languages typically encounter the trade-off between expressiveness and efficiency. We have undecidable languages, such as modal logic on the one hand and descriptions logics or logic programming on the other. Other criteria for the choice of the language include standardization. As an exam-

---

[11]Note that a software component is non-physical and, therefore, not extended in space. However, the distinction is meaningful also for non-physical objects.

ple, the World Wide Web Consortium recently published a recommendation for the Web Ontology Language (OWL) [McGuinness and van Harmelen, 2004], which is based on description logics.

Link to Linguistic Ontologies As mentioned in Section 2, linguistic or lexical ontologies express only classes corresponding to existing natural language terms. WordNet [Miller et al., 1990] is the most prominent representative. For some applications it might be of interest to have the foundational ontology linked to such linguistic information as well.

Modularization A well-designed foundational ontology should decrease the danger of over-commitment, i.e., the inclusion of theories that are not used or not shared by the engineer, by extensive modularization along the ontological choices and domains. It should be minimal and include only the most reusable and widely applicable generic categories. Typical theories that come in the form of ontology modules are: theories of time, plans, contextualization or information objects.

5. Summary

In this chapter we have introduced the reader to ontologies as a means to explicitly specify conceptual models with logic-based semantics. Such conceptual models are required to harmonize the implicit and incoherent models underlying the deployment and WS* descriptions of application servers and Web services middleware. We have discussed ontology quality criteria, which are used later on to assess whether the quality of existing ontologies is sufficient for our purposes.

We have also introduced a possible classification of ontologies, which acts as a guide throughout the document. It allows us to clarify the different types of ontologies and the roles they play. In this chapter we have had a closer look at foundational ontologies. Their role is that of a starting point for building core and domain ontologies. In Part II a foundational ontology is exploited as a modelling basis for our management ontology, i.e., we relate its concepts and associations to the basic categories of human cognition investigated by philosophy, linguistics and psychology. Thus, we are prompted to sharpen our notions with respect to the distinctions made in the foundational ontology. Having learned that the domain of software components and Web services demands a careful and rigorous modelling, foundational ontologies are a good basis from which to start modelling.

Each foundational ontology commits to specific ontological choices, such as endurantism, possibilism, etc. We have discussed the major ontological choices in this chapter because Part II decides chooses an appropriate foundational ontology based on these choices.

Chapter 4

TOWARDS SEMANTIC MANAGEMENT

In Chapter 2 we have discussed the evolution of middleware focussing on application servers and Web services. Their deployment descriptors and WS* descriptions make development and management very flexible. However, the conceptual model underlying the different descriptions is *only implicit*. Hence, its bits and pieces are difficult to retrieve, survey, check for validity and maintain.

To remedy such problems, we propose the semantic management of software components and Web services to support the developer and administrator. The underlying conceptual model of component and service descriptions has to be made *explicit* by formal logic-based semantics. As we have discussed in Chapter 3, this can be achieved by applying an ontology, which, in our case, has to capture properties of, relationships between and behaviors of the components and services that are required for management. Therefore, *semantic* descriptions of software components and Web services may be queried, may foresight required actions, or may be checked to avoid inconsistent system configurations (during development, as well as during run time). Thus, the ontology-based approach retains the original flexibility in configuring and running the middleware, but it adds new capabilities for the developer and administrator of the system.

However, semantic management does not come for free. Modelling efforts have to be expended by developers and administrators in order to arrive at semantic descriptions of components and services. We claim that the full breadth of management requires an understanding of the world that is too deep to be modelled explicitly. Instead, we foresee a more passive role for semantic management — one that is driven by the needs of the developers who must cope with the complexity and who could use valuable tools for integrating previously separated aspects.

This line of argumentation leads us to our working hypothesis: There is a *trade-off* between expending efforts for management and expending efforts for semantic modelling. The tradeoff is depicted qualitatively in Figure 4.1. On the one hand, typical *management efforts* comprise the assessing and controlling of components and services for their efficiency and productivity, their tailoring to make them operate properly, the definition and control of access rights and the provision of quantitative information about them. On the other hand, semantic descriptions require *modelling efforts* that comprise manual modelling or obtaining and integrating existing sources.

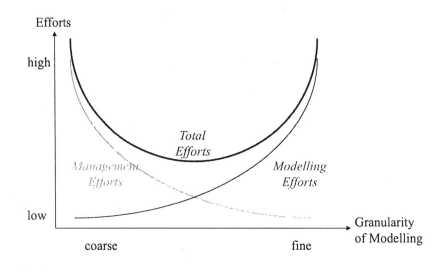

Figure 4.1.   Working Hypothesis.

The objective of automating all management tasks by semantic modelling needs very fine-grained, detailed modelling of all aspects — essentially everything that an intelligent human agent must know for managing the middleware. Thus, modelling efforts skyrocket at the end of fine-grained modelling. At the other end, where modelling is very coarse and little modelling facilitates management, efforts for managing distributed systems soar as experiences have shown in the past. No matter what the exact scale of granularity and efforts are, the qualitative indication of management and modelling efforts, such as depicted in Figure 4.1, leads to an overall total effort picture as indicated in the same figure.

In this chapter we elaborate on the Main Question I from the Introduction: *How to find a good trade-off between modelling and management efforts?* The answer is derived from an (inexhaustible) set of use cases (Section 2) that respond to the Questions I.1 *who uses the semantic descriptions?*, I.2 *what are they used for*, and I.3 *when do they occur?* The use cases also serve as an input to Part II for choosing which aspect our ontology should formalize (Question I.4). The use cases are embedded in scenarios for a specific type of application server and for a Web services application, respectively (Section 1).

Parts of this chapter have been published in conference proceedings and technical reports. The *Application Server for the Semantic Web* scenario was originally introduced in [Oberle et al., 2005d]. The *Web Services in SmartWeb* scenario stems from the German BMBF project of the same name. Application server use case are taken from [Oberle et al., 2004a], Web services use case from [Oberle et al., 2005a].

1.   Scenarios

In this section we discuss two scenarios in which we later embed our use cases. The first one stems from the concrete needs of the WonderWeb[1] project, whose objective was, among others, to provide a comprehensive infrastructure to link new and existing Semantic Web tools. We first introduce the reader to the Semantic Web, followed by the particular situation for application development it creates. The conclusion is that we need an *Application Server for the Semantic Web* extending common application servers for easier development of Semantic Web applications.

The second scenario, called *Web Services in SmartWeb*, stems from the project of the same name.[2] The goal of the SmartWeb project is to lay the foundations for multimodal user interfaces to distributed Web services on mobile devices. This results in the need to integrate a more or less confined set of several Web services into the system. Statical coding of the Web services invocations and compositions will lead to an inflexible system.

It is desirable to attach semantic descriptions to relevant components and services in both scenarios, such that some management tasks can be automated. We encounter the typical trade-off between management and modelling efforts that is addressed in Section 2 by discussing typical use cases.

1.1   An Application Server for the Semantic Web
The Semantic Web

The Internet and the WWW in particular were designed as an information space, with the goal that it should be useful not only for human-human communication, but also that machines would be able to participate and help. One of

---

[1]WonderWeb [Oberle et al., 2005e] has been a European Union IST (Information Society Technologies programme) project funded by the initiative on Future and Emerging Technologies (FET). `http://wonderweb.semanticweb.org`

[2]SmartWeb is funded by the German Federal Ministry of Education and Research (BMBF). `http://smartweb.semanticweb.org`

the major obstacles is the fact that most information on the WWW is designed for human consumption. Even if it was derived from a database with well defined meanings (in at least some terms), the meaning of the data is not evident to a web application system. [Berners-Lee, 1998]

The way out of this shortcoming is the Semantic Web, which augments the current WWW by giving information a well-defined meaning, thereby better enabling computers and people to work in cooperation. This is done by adding machine understandable content to Web resources. The results of this process are semantic descriptions that can be a simple statement, such as "site x's author is Daniel Oberle." Such descriptions are given their semantics by referring to an ontology (cf. Chapter 3). For example, in the statement above, we could express that "Daniel Oberle" is a PhD-Student and that PhD-Student is a specialization of Graduate-Student, where both concepts are introduced in an ontology.

In this section we want to introduce the reader to the architecture and languages of the Semantic Web. We start with the static part, which is depicted on the left hand side of Figure 4.2 [Berners-Lee, 2000], i.e., its language layers. Unicode, the URI and namespaces (NS) syntax and XML are used as a basis. XML's role is limited to that of a syntax carrier for data exchange. XML Schema [Biron and Malhotra, 2001] introduces simple data types, such as string, date or integer and allows us to define complex data types.

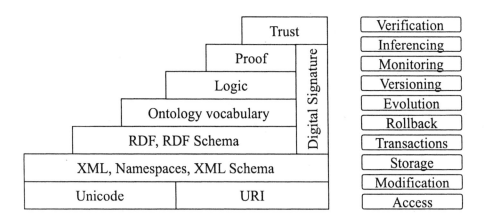

Figure 4.2.   Static and dynamic aspects of the Semantic Web layer cake.

The Resource Description Framework (RDF) may be used to make simple assertions about Web resources or any other entity that can be named. A simple assertion is a statement that an entity has a property with a specific value, for example, that the author of this work has a name property with value, "Daniel

Oberle." RDF Schema extends RDF by class and property hierarchies that enable the creation of simple ontologies.

RDF and RDFS are already standardized by the World Wide Web Consortium (W3C) [Manola and Miller, 2004]. Figure 4.3 depicts an example for semantic descriptions in the domain of research and academia. The ontology features a concept **Person**, along specializations, such as **Graduate-Student, PhD-Student**, as well as **AcademicStaff** and **Professor**. The modelling primitives of RDFS formalize the domain description as RDF statements, e.g., **PhD-Student rdfs:subClassOf Graduate-Student**. **CooperatesWith** is a symmetric property defined on **Person** by using the **rdfs:domain** and **rdfs:range** primitives.

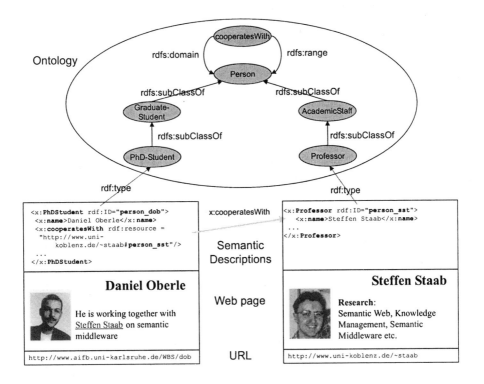

Figure 4.3. Semantic Web example in RDF(S) notation ([Manola and Miller, 2004]) where ovals represent concepts and edges represent associations.

XML serializations of RDF statements can be added to Web resources, such as the homepages of **PhD-Student** "Daniel Oberle" and **Professor** "Steffen Staab." The descriptions formally define both as instances of the ontology's concepts through the **rdf:type** primitive. Relationships are provided with formal semantics by referring to the ontology. A search engine could later infer that also "Steffen Staab" cooperates with "Daniel Oberle" because the property is defined to be symmetric.

The Ontology layer features the Web Ontology Language (OWL [McGuinness and van Harmelen, 2004]). OWL is a family of richer ontology languages consisting of OWL Lite, DL and Full. They augment RDF Schema and are based on the descriptions logics (DL) paradigm [Baader et al., 2003]. OWL Lite is the simplest of these. It is a limited version of OWL DL enabling a simple and efficient implementation. OWL DL is a richer subset of OWL Full for which reasoning is known to be decidable so complete reasoners may be constructed, though they will be less efficient than an OWL Lite reasoner. OWL Full is the full ontology language which is undecidable, however.

The Logic layer[3] will provide an interoperable language for describing the sets of deductions one can make from a collection of data. Given an ontology-based information base, one can derive new information from existing data via logical rules.

The Proof language will provide a way of describing the steps taken to reach a conclusion from the facts. These proofs can then be passed around and verified, providing short cuts to new facts in the system without having each node conduct the deductions themselves.

The Semantic Web's vision is that once all these layers are in place, we will have an environment in which we can place trust that the data we are seeing, the deductions we are making, and the claims we are receiving have some value. The goal is to make a user's life easier by the aggregation and creation of new, trusted information over the Web [Dumbill, 2001]. The standardization process has currently reached the Ontology layer, i.e., Logic, Proof and Trust layers are not specified yet.

The right hand side of Figure 4.2 depicts the Semantic Web's dynamic aspects that apply to data across all layers. Often, the dynamic aspects are neglected by the Semantic Web community; however, from our point of view, they are an inevitable part for putting the Semantic Web into practice. Transactions and rollbacks of Semantic Web data operations should be possible, following the well-known ACID properties (atomicity, consistency, independence, durability) of database management systems (DBMS). Evolution and versioning of ontologies are an important aspect; because ontologies usually are subject to change (cf. [Peters and Oezsu, 1997, Banerjee et al., 1987, Stojanovic et al., 2002a]). As in all distributed environments, monitoring of data operations

---

[3]A better description of this layer would be "Rule layer," as the Ontology layer already features a logic calculus with reasoning capabilities. We here use the naming given by Tim Berners-Lee in his roadmap.

becomes necessary for security reasons. Finally, reasoning engines are to be applied for the deduction of additional facts,[4] as well as for semantic validation

Application Development for the Semantic Web

Ontologies serve various needs in the Semantic Web, such as storage or exchange of data corresponding to an ontology, ontology-based reasoning or ontology-based navigation. Building a complex Semantic Web application, one may not rely on a single software module to deliver all these different services. The developer of such a system would rather want to easily combine different — preferably existing — software modules.

An example would be the domain ontology for an application supporting research and academia [Oberle and Spyns, 2004, Spyns et al., 2002, Hartmann and Sure, 2004]. Such an application manages information about a university's staff, their publications, students and courses. Its ontology can be easily expressed by Semantic Web languages and constructed by a corresponding editor (cf. Figure 4.4). There will be properties of concepts that require structured XML Schema data types [Biron and Malhotra, 2001] whose correctness can be checked by a validator. A description logic reasoner is usually applied for semantic validation of the ontology. An ontology store saves the ontology and can be reused by a research and academia portal. The latter may exploit a rule-based inference engine that is capable of handling large amounts of instances and deduction of additional information by rules.[5]

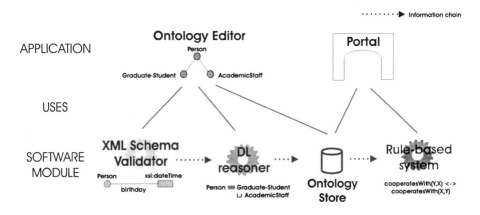

Figure 4.4. Information flow in the research and academia example.

---

[4]E.g., if cooperatesWith is defined as a symmetric property in OWL DL between persons. A reasoner should be able to deduce that B cooperatesWith A, given the fact that A cooperatesWith B.

[5]The reader may note that we neglect the details of translating between logic languages for the sake of a simple scenario.

So far, such integration of ontology-based modules had to be done in an ad hoc manner, generating a one-off endeavor, with little possibilities for re-use and future extensibility of individual modules or the overall system.

The new situation requires an infrastructure that facilitates plug'n'play engineering of ontology-based modules and, thus, the development and maintenance of comprehensive Semantic Web applications. The aim is to facilitate the re-use of existing modules, e.g., ontology stores, editors, and inference engines, to combine means to coordinate the information flow between such modules, to define dependencies, to broadcast events between different modules and to translate between ontology-based data formats. We shall adopt the concepts and technologies underlying common application servers in order to reach that goal. The result is an *Application Server for the Semantic Web (ASSW)* extending common application servers by means of easier development of Semantic Web applications. We build such an application server in Chapters 8 and 9.

1.2   Web Services in SmartWeb

SmartWeb — Mobile Broadband Access to the Semantic Web

Recent progress in mobile broadband communication and Semantic Web technology is enabling innovative internet functionality that provides advanced personalization and localization features. The goal of the SmartWeb project is to combine these functionalities and to lay the foundations for multimodal user interfaces to distributed Web services on mobile devices. The vision is to exploit the Web as a knowledge base to answer a broad range of user questions. The questions are asked by a human via a multimodal dialog system that combines speech, gesture, and facial expressions for input and output. Spontaneous speech understanding may be combined with the video-based recognition of natural gestures and facial expressions. Besides information-seeking dialogues, SmartWeb aims to support task-oriented dialogues, in which the user wants to perform a transaction (e.g., buy a ticket for a sports event or program his navigation system to find a souvenir shop).

SmartWeb is based on two parallel efforts in order to reach that goal. The first effort is the Semantic Web providing the explicit markup of the content of Web pages (cf. Section 1.1). Its contents may be exploited mainly for information-seeking dialogues. The size and dynamic nature of the Web and the fact that the content of most Web pages is encoded in natural language makes this an extremely difficult task. Therefore, SmartWeb exploits the machine-understandable content of Web pages for intelligent question-answering as a next step beyond today's search engines. Since semantically annotated Web pages are still very rare due to the time-consuming and costly semantic modelling, SmartWeb is using advanced language technology and information extraction methods for the automatic annotation of traditional Web pages encoded in HTML or XML.

The second effort is the integration of Web services in the system which allows task-oriented dialogs and user transactions. Multimodal user requests may lead to automatic Web service discovery and invocation, and also to the automatic composition, interoperation and execution monitoring of Web services — although with a more or less confined set of Web services as we learn below.

The context-aware user interface of SmartWeb supports the user in different roles, e.g., as a car driver, a motor biker, a pedestrian or a sports spectator. One of the demonstrators of the project is a personal guide for the 2006 FIFA world cup in Germany that provides mobile infotainment services to soccer fans, anywhere and anytime.

Another SmartWeb demonstrator is based on peer-to-peer communication between a car and a motor bike. When the car's sensors detect aqua-planing, for example, a succeeding motor biker may be warned by the system. The biker can interact with the system through speech and haptic feedback; the car driver can input speech and gestures.

The Role of Web Services

Figure 4.5 depicts a simplified view of the SmartWeb architecture. On the user's side, we find the SmartWeb Client incorporated by a UMTS cell phone. The client allows multimodal input, such as speech or browsing. The thus generated dialogue, i.e., user questions, is transmitted to the SmartWeb Server.

Within the server, dialogues are processed and analyzed by the Semantic Mediator. It exploits a knowledge base to answer information-seeking dialogues, which are structured according to an ontology. Semantically annotated Web pages and text mining results from common pages are the initial sources of the knowledge base. Basically, the Semantic Mediator has to deal with two cases: (*i*) the answer to the dialogue is already formalized in the knowledge base and (*ii*) the answer is missing or is incomplete. In the first case, a simple querying of the knowledge base might lead to several answers stemming from different sources with different timeliness and trustworthiness. Hence, the Semantic Mediator has to choose a suitable one according to corresponding algorithms. In the second case, the Semantic Mediator has to acquire additional information in order to answer the question. This can be achieved by applying reasoning on the knowledge base. By doing so, the answer might be deduced from existing facts. Otherwise, Web service access might help, e.g., by asking Google and processing its results in natural language. If this step is successful, the answer is asserted as an additional fact in the knowledge base.

The Web service Access module (cf. Figure 4.5) obtains answers to questions which are not derivable from the knowledge base. In this case the Google Web

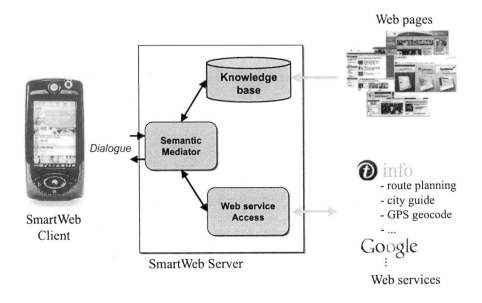

Figure 4.5. Simplified SmartWeb Architecture.

service might be exploited to complete the missing facts. Also, one of the project partners, viz., T-Info, provides several Web services for mobility and traffic information.[6] Examples comprise route planning functionality, a city guide, GPS geocode services, temperature, UV radiation, air quality and many more. They deliver very dynamic information, which is usually not asserted in a database.

Although further Web services enabling user transactions (e.g., buying a ticket) will be integrated in the system, this is a rather closed world. The obvious way to implement the Semantic Mediator and Web service Access module is to code which Web service has to be invoked given a specific query. For instance, when the user asks for weather information, the WeatherCondition service may deliver the answer. In addition, simple composition is necessary if the WeatherCondition service takes a GPS position as argument, but the question talks about zip codes.

Statically coding which of the several Web services has to be invoked is a very tedious task that leads to an inflexible application with high management efforts. The application would have to be recoded whenever a service changes or a new one should be integrated. Hence, it is be desirable to attach semantic descriptions to the relevant Web services in a way that invocation, simple com-

---

[6]http://services.t-info.de/soap

position and other management tasks can be automated. Here, we encounter the typical trade-off between management and modelling efforts. Automation does not come for free, but has to be bought by modelling all the Web services to a certain extent. We solve the trade-off in the next section by discussing typical use cases.

2. Use Cases

In order to approach the trade-off point mentioned at the beginning of this chapter, it is necessary to ask and to answer the following questions from the Introduction: *who uses the semantic descriptions?*, *what are they used for?* and *when do they occur?* The answers are derived from use cases which are embedded in the scenarios and split into application servers and Web services. Additionally, the use cases serve as an input to Part II by answering *which aspects* our ontology should formalize. The list below is neither exhaustive nor are the individual use cases mutually exclusive because there is a large number of use cases where semantic management may help the developer.

Question I.1 *Who uses semantic descriptions?*

We see two major groups of users constituted by (*i*) software developers and (*ii*) administrators. These two groups of users have the need to predict or observe how software components and Web services interact, get into conflict, behave, etc. It will be very useful for them to query a system for semantic management that integrates aspects from multiple deployment or WS* descriptions — which has not been possible so far. As a third "group of users," we foresee that applications may also exploit the querying and reasoning capabilities to allow autonomous control of interaction. Thus, running components or Web services constitute a third group. We consider the autonomous exploitation by programmes a rather desirable side effect of our approach.

Question I.2 *What are the semantic descriptions used for?*

We consider management tasks consisting of five basic categories, namely fault, performance, configuration, security and accounting. They are introduced in the definition of "network management" by the International Standards Organization (ISO), but general enough to be applied here, too. The bare essence of *fault management* is monitoring in order to detect anomalies (faults) as soon as they occur and taking the necessary corrective action. *Performance management* consists of assessing and controlling the efficiency and productivity of the managed elements. *Configuration management* is generally thought of as tailoring a managed element so that it will operate in the desired way. The aim of *security management* is to define who may perform which task and under what conditions. Finally, *accounting management* is the task of providing quantitative information of resource utilization. [Sturm and Bumpus, 1998]

Question I.3 *When are the semantic descriptions used?*

We consider three different stages, viz., development time, deployment time and run time.

Question I.4 *Which aspects should be formalized by our ontology?*

On the one hand, we want to be able to automate management tasks covering a broad range of aspects (such as security, policies, interface descriptions, etc.). On the other hand, the complexity of the ontology has to be kept small to avoid overburdening the developer. In addition, the answers to the Question I.4 serve as modelling requirements for building a suitable management ontology in Part II.

2.1 Application Servers

The use cases below propose the facilitation of *some* typical application server management tasks by a justifiable amount of semantic descriptions. That means, we do not strive at full automation of all management tasks but approach the trade-off between modelling and management efforts.

Library Dependencies and Versioning

Software libraries often depend on other libraries and a specific library can contain several libraries at once. Given this information, semantic descriptions can be exploited to locate all the required libraries.[7] Furthermore, the user might be notified when two libraries require different versions of a third one. For instance, the multitude of versions of XML parsers cause a lot of trouble. Semantic management could comprise reasoning with this kind of information in order to make an educated suggestion or to display inconsistencies.

Who:	Developer
What for:	Configuration management
When:	Development and deployment time
Which aspects:	Libraries

Licensing

Similar to the library dependencies, we can describe licensing, trustworthiness and quality. Including an external module in one's software has effects on the licensing options. For instance, using external GPL licensed code prohibits

---

[7]This idea is the basis of the RPM package manager: http://www.rpm.org/. Semantic management could generalize this approach and integrate it with other tools for the developer.

distributing the bundle under a LGPL license. Along the same lines, ISO software certification or a security guideline of a government agency might prohibit certain external components to be used in mission critical software. In all of these cases, it would be useful to model development constraints and reason with these and semantic descriptions to avoid problems.

Who: Developer
What for: Configuration and security management
When: Development time
Which aspects: Licenses

Capability Descriptions

Component capabilities adhering to standard interfaces can be made explicit to the developer by component profiles, i.e., semantic descriptions of component capabilities. For example, there is a lowest common denominator interface for description logics reasoners that can be used by applications, such as ontology editors. However, the behavior and capabilities of the specific reasoners used can vary dramatically. For example, some reasoners support inferences with instances (called ABox reasoning) others do not.

Who: Developer and Administrator
What for: Configuration management
When: Development and deployment time
Which aspects: Component profiles

Component Classification and Discovery

Given API's of a specific type, e.g., ontology stores, one will find different implementations with essentially the same functionality. We suggest aligning the corresponding component profiles in application-specific component taxonomies. This will allow the developer to discover implementations for a certain taxonomy entry and to classify them.

Who: Developer
What for: Configuration management
When: Development time
Which aspects: Component taxonomy, semantic API description

Semantics of Parameters

Parameters and return types of methods are often implicitly encoded in the respective names. Providing meaningful names is considered to be an important practice when developing software systems. However, it is also desirable to relate the names with concepts and associations of a common, agreed-upon domain ontology. Different ontology stores will provide different names for methods with comparable functionality (e.g., `storeConcept()` vs. `addConcept()`). Just as the point mentioned before, this will allow more powerful searches over a large unfamiliar API. These descriptions can even be used to generate a sequence of method invocations in order to achieve a goal specified [Eberhart, 2004].

Who:	Developer
What for:	Configuration management
When:	Development time
Which aspects:	Semantic API description

Automatic Generation of Web Service Descriptions

Development toolkits usually provide functionality for creating stubs and skeletons or for automatically generating interface metadata à la java2wsdl. With an entire set of new markup languages, such as WS-BPEL [Andrews et al., 2005] or OWL-S [Martin et al., 2004] emerging, tool support for these new languages is needed. Whereas WSDL [Christensen et al., 2001] tools can obtain almost all of the required input directly from the source code, richer descriptions in these languages require additional metadata. If the respective metadata are already available within the system, automatically generated WS-BPEL or OWL-S descriptions can be a side product of a unified framework.

Who:	Developer and administrator
What for:	Configuration management
When:	Development, deployment and run time
Which aspects:	Component profile, (semantic) API description

Access Rights

The access control mechanisms of application servers are based on users and roles to whom access can be granted for certain resources and services. In addition, components can be run using the credentials of the caller or those of another user that runs the component on behalf of the caller. This is often referred to as the authentication problem [Gray and Reuter, 1993]. It is quite evident, that access rights within a large application can be very complex (cf. Example 2.1 on page 23). Semantic management could comprise assistance of the administrator in suggesting suitable settings and in determining potential flaws in the security design. We believe that formal reasoning over group memberships or resources being accessed by processes running on behalf of other users will prove to be valuable here.

Who:	Administrator
What for:	Security management
When:	Development and deployment time
Which aspects:	Access rights

Error Handling

Modern programming languages make heavy use of exceptions. Exceptions are raised and propagated along the calling stack in order to be handled at the appropriate level. In order to avoid the embarrassing situation that an exception is not handled at all and simply passed to the user interface or business partner, a consistency check can be put in place. Similar to the argument made in the previous example, rules describing how exceptions are thrown, passed across the calling stack and being caught or not can be applied in this case.

Who:	Developer
What for:	Fault management
When:	Development time
Which aspects:	API description (exceptions)

Transactional Settings

Ontology or RDF stores typically offer transactional recovery. This notion is extended to general software components (e.g., EJB), which access transactional resources. Methods can be declared to not support transactions, to initiate a new transaction or to participate in the caller's transaction. Again, a chain of calls across many components can contain inconsistent settings, such as a component which requires a transaction calling one that does not support transactions. A formalization of invocations and the possible transactional settings can be applied here.

Who:	Developer
What for:	Fault management
When:	Run time
Which aspects:	Component profile, workflow information

Secure Communication

Confidential data might be made accessible to business partners only. Settings on the application server typically determine that a digital signature has to be checked before the request is passed along and that a component can only be bound to a secure communication line or protocol. Similar to the arguments made above, semantic management should be able to detect that a confidential resource is accidentally made accessible via a non-encrypted communication channel.

Who:	Developer
What for:	Security management
When:	Development, deployment and run time
Which aspects:	Component profile, workflow information

2.2   Web Services

The use cases below propose the facilitation of *some* typical Web service management tasks by a justifiable amount of semantic descriptions. The research field of "Semantic Web Services" (cf. related work in Chapter 11, Section 3) addresses very similar use cases. However, the approaches in this field usually aim at full automation of *all* management tasks. In contrast, we approach the trade-off point between modelling and management efforts.

Analyzing Message Contexts

Message passing plays the central role for Web services. A message sent to a service can in turn trigger several other messages being sent out on behalf of the initial message. Messages may carry a context with information about the sender, the sender's credentials, or the message's transactional context. During the deployment of a service, the administrator makes important choices as to how messages are propagated. These include whether the sender information is carried along or whether the new message is sent on behalf of a new user (also called the run-as paradigm). Similar choices are made with respect to the transactional settings. Services can choose to always open a new transaction, require a prior transactional context, or open a new transaction when needed. In a scenario such as SmartWeb, where networks of direct and indirect invocations are possible, it is crucial to be able to detect configuration errors. As an example, consider a situation where a service switching to user context X and calling Y does not have user X in its access control list.

Who:	Administrator
What for:	Security and configuration management
When:	Deployment time
Which aspects:	Service profile, workflow information, access rights

Selecting Service Functionality

There are several approaches to automatized runtime service matching in the area of Semantic Web Services, e.g., [Li and Horrocks, 2003, Paolucci et al., 2002a, Paolucci et al., 2002b]. However, it remains to be seen whether the problems related to semantic interpretations of documents can be solved in the full generality needed for real-life interactions between corporations.

Instead, we want to provide developers with some tool support in browsing and selecting an appropriate service at *development* time. The canonical approach to this task is a taxonomic categorization of services together with semantic descriptions of their capabilities. Naturally, searching for services of a certain capability class C should also yield all services classified as instances of subclasses of C. In the case of our SmartWeb scenario, the WeatherCondition service would belong to the category of "Environment" services, for instance.

Who:	Developer
What for:	Configuration management
When:	Development time
Which aspects:	Service taxonomy, semantic API description

Policy Handling

Policies play an increasing role, as demonstrated by the recent WS-Policy [Bajaj et al., 2004] proposal. The idea of a policy is to lay out general rules and principles for service selection. Thus, rather than deciding whether an invocation is allowed on a case by case basis at run time, one excludes services whose policy violates the local policy at development time. The major benefit is that policies can be specified declaratively. The administrator can specify policies much in the same way as writing an SQL query, i.e., writing down what should be done instead of how to implement it.

This use case does not aim at fully automated policy matching at run time, as we think that the full generality of policy matching imposes further problems that remain to be solved. Let alone the lack of WS-Policy engines so far. Instead we propose to apply semantic modelling in order to make policy handling more convenient for the developer. As an example, consider a large WS-BPEL workflow where checking for external task service invocations which are associated with a policy remains a tedious and manual task. Semantic descriptions can help to notify the developer if an external Web service in the BPEL workflow is associated with a policy, for instance. This situation is depicted in Example 2.5 on page 30, where the WS-Policy document states that a credit card validation service is only invocable with specific authentication methods.

Who:	Developer, System

What for: Security management
When: Development and run time
Which aspects: Policies

Detecting Loops in Interorganizational Workflows

Web services based applications may use asynchronous messaging, bringing upon quite complex interaction protocols between business partners. Current workflow design workbenches only visualize the local flow and leave the orchestration of messages with the business partners up to the developer. We believe that sufficient information is available in machine-readable format so that semantic management can assist the developer in this task. For instance, the structure of the local flow can be combined with publicly available abstract flows of the partners in order to detect loops in interorganizational workflows that might lead to non-termination of the system.

   As shown in the bioinformatics domain [Lord et al., 2004], automated composition of workflows is likely to be inappropriate in most cases. Hence, we propose to support the developers in their management tasks and not to replace them.

Who: Developer
What for: Fault management
When: Development time
Which aspects: Workflow information

Incompatible Inputs and Outputs

Type checking is not as straightforward anymore, using loosely coupled services operated by a large number of organizations. Furthermore, the interpretation of a B2B term such as 'price' might be different, even though syntactically it refers to an agreed-upon XML Schema type. For instance, different, possibly international Web services used in SmartWeb might have different assumptions about the currency and taxation details. Semantic management, which could automatically compare communication inputs and outputs according to a more detailed ontology, would help to prevent unexpected behavior here.

   Note that a developer who uses Web services wants to check at *development* time whether some incompatible configuration exists. While a 100% solution, such as required for full automation, will remain unfeasible in most cases, ticking of 80% of problematic situations by semantic support is a very desirable feature of semantic management.

Who: Developer

What for: Configuration management
When: Development time
Which aspects: Semantic API description

Relating Communication Parameters

This use case is again motivated by e-business policies. Let us assume that every Web service provider in SmartWeb must be ISO 9000 certified. Enforcing this policy requires correlating communication paths with information about the organizations operating the communication endpoints. Another example would be a policy stating that confidential information should only be sent across a secure communication channel. In this case, knowledge about message payload types, such as credit card information, must be connected with the properties of the underlying transport.

Who: Developer, Administrator
What for: Configuration management
When: Development and deployment time
Which aspects: Service profile

Monitoring of Changes

A system no longer being under the tight control of a single organizational unit will definitely be prone to service versioning issues. Updating a single part already requires close cooperation between the parties involved and this will, without a doubt, be much harder in Web services based applications. Consequently, semantic management should provide support for this issue by monitoring the providers' service interface definitions, security or transactional settings.

Who: Developer
What for: Configuration management
When: Development time
Which aspects: API description

Aggregating Service Information

Services will often be implemented based on other services. A service provider publishes information about its service. This might include service level agreements indicating a guaranteed worst-case response time, the cost of the service, or average availability numbers. The service requestor, in this case a composite service under development, can collect this information from the respective service providers. In turn, it offers a service and needs to publish similar numbers. We envision semantic management to support the developer and administrator with this task by providing a first cut of this data by aggregating the data gathered from external providers. For sequential invocations, cost and time must be added. If services are invoked in parallel, cost is added and the time will be the maximum time one has to wait for an external call. Consequently, the respective queries must consider the local program or flow structure when performing the aggregation. The computation results could be used as default values, which can be overridden manually by the administrator (cf. also [Cardoso et al., 2004]).

Similar to the statements given in [Lord et al., 2004], we argue that full automatic generation of such data will probably yield unwanted and inappropriate results. We see the computation results as an estimate which can be overridden manually by the administrator.

Who:	Administrator
What for:	Accounting management
When:	Deployment time
Which aspects:	Service profiles (quality of service information)

Quality of Service

While the previous use case was based on data gathered from service providers, one might want to obtain his or her own statistics on the reliability and availability of business partners' IT infrastructure. Assuming the system is aware of potential endpoints implementing a required service, these endpoints can be pinged regularly. If an actual request arrives, aggregated availability information can be used to direct subsequent requests to one or the other third party service.

Likewise, a provider needs to make sure it offers an adequate service level for its customers. In case of performance bottlenecks, it might have to make an educated decision on which jobs to grant higher priority and which job to drop or decline. Existing service level agreements and, of course, the respective penalties play an important role here.

The up and coming technology of virtualization - currently provided by VM Ware and Microsoft Virtual Server - makes this issue much more important. Virtual machines, prepared to provide a certain service, can be started, stopped, suspended or even cloned on the fly. Thus, one can make quick and flexible decisions on what service to provide on the available bare metal servers at one's disposal. With the base technology in form of virtualization being available, it is important to provide the necessary intelligence for controlling the technology.

Obviously, new developments in the area of Grid Computing further emphasize this point, since the grid will provide new mechanisms for scheduling tasks and for outsourcing IT services in general.

Who:	Administrator, System
What for:	Performance management
When:	Run time
Which aspects:	Service profiles (quality of service information)

3.   Summary

In this chapter we have proposed the semantic management of software components and Web services that trades off between modelling and management efforts (Main Question I: *How to find a good trade-off between modelling and management efforts?*). The trade-off point has been approached by identifying a set of use cases. Each of them responded to the Questions I.1 *who uses the semantic descriptions?*, I.2 *what are they used for?*, and I.3 *when do they occur?* The use cases propose the facilitation of some typical management tasks by a justifiable modelling efforts. The modelling requirements of the use cases also give us clear indications of what concepts a suitable management ontology must contain (Question I.4: *Which aspects should be formalized by our ontology?*). The organization of these concepts in an appropriate management ontology is the subject of Part II.

PART II

DESIGN OF A MANAGEMENT ONTOLOGY

Chapter 5

ANALYSIS OF EXISTING ONTOLOGIES

In the previous chapter we have approached the trade-off between modelling and management efforts. We have identified use cases where semantic descriptions of components and services can be exploited to automate some of the typical management tasks. The use cases in Chapter 4, Section 2 let us derive a set of modelling requirements for choosing the aspects our ontology should formalize. Regarding the application server use cases starting on page 66 we have derived the following modelling requirements: (*i*) *libraries*, *licenses*, *component profiles*, *component taxonomies*, *API descriptions*, *semantic API descriptions*, *access rights* and *workflow information* of software components. Regarding the Web services use cases starting on page 70, we have to model *service profiles*, *service taxonomies*, *access rights*, *policies*, *workflow information*, *API descriptions*, as well as *semantic API descriptions* of Web services.

The modelling requirements are the input to this part of the document which is concerned with the Main Question II from the Introduction: *How to build a suitable management ontology?* Our goal is to arrive at a high-quality management ontology with reference, heavyweight and core characteristics (cf. Figure 5.1). We opt for a *reference* ontology because our first investigation of the domain of software components and Web services in Chapter 2, Section 3 already revealed that a careful and rigorous ontological modelling is necessary. We encountered fundamental ontological questions that demand a concise explanation of concepts such as software component or Web service. In turn, such a concise explanation typically requires *heavyweight* expressiveness to approximate the intended models as closely as possible. Finally, the ontology should be as specific as possible, but should not reflect the idiosyncrasies of a concrete platform. In this way, we facilitate reuse in concrete platforms because it is expected that concepts and associations can be specialized to capture the platform details. This requirement coincides with *core* specificity.

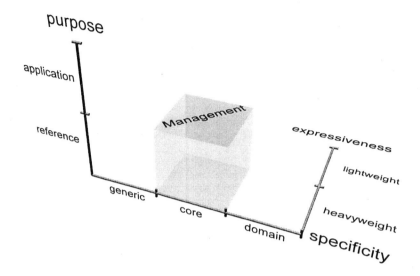

Figure 5.1.   The goal of Part II is to design a management ontology with *reference, heavyweight* and *core* characteristics (cf. classification in Chapter 3, Section 2).

Before modelling a management ontology from scratch, it is desirable to check if there are existing ontologies that we might reuse for our purpose (Question II.1: *Can an existing ontology be reused for our purposes?*). This chapter analyzes two commonly built ontologies. In Section 1 we review one of the earliest and most prominent Web service ontologies, viz., OWL-S. Section 2 talks about our own initial ontology of software components — one of the first efforts to semantically enhance application servers. It uses OWL-S as a basis, but extends and adopts it to model the idiosyncracies of software components. Finally, Section 3 inspects both ontologies and discusses their problematic aspects with respect to the ontology quality criteria we introduced in Definition 3.8 on page 41. A first conclusion is that both ontologies are a big step forward and that their reuse is possible in principle. However, both ontologies exhibit shortcomings that stand in conflict with our goals of having a high-quality, reference and heavyweight ontology. We claim that their shortcomings are typical for commonly built ontologies. A second conclusion is that most of the problems could have been avoided if a foundational ontology had been used as a modelling basis.

Parts of this chapter have been published in conference proceedings. The introduction to OWL-S is taken from the DAML Services initiative [Martin et al., 2004]. The initial ontology of software components is taken from [Oberle et al., 2003b, Oberle et al., 2003c, Sabou et al., 2004]. The analysis of their problematic aspects was done in [Mika, Oberle et al., 2004a].

1. OWL-S

OWL-S has been an initiative of the Semantic Web community to enable automatic discovery, invocation, composition, interoperation and monitoring of Web services through their semantic descriptions [Martin et al., 2004].[1] At the heart of this effort lies an ontology formalized in the OWL language [McGuinness and van Harmelen, 2004]. Its structuring is motivated by the need to provide three essential types of knowledge about a service, each characterized by the question it answers:

- *What does the service provide for prospective clients?* The answer to this question is given in the ServiceProfile.[2] It is used to advertise the service. The intention is to allow an agent to determine whether the service meets its needs. This form of representation includes a semantic description of inputs and outputs, preconditions and postconditions, as well as explanations in natural language. It allows associating the service with given classification and product schemes (e.g., the NAICS[3] and UNSPSC[4] categories). As an example, we might semantically describe a Web service for validating a credit card by stating that its input is a credit card number and its output is the result of the validation. Both would be concepts of an according domain ontology.

- *How is it used?* The answer to this question is given in the ServiceModel. It tells a client how to ask for the service and what happens when the service is carried out. For composed services (i.e., services invoking other services), this description may be used by an agent to coordinate the activities of the different participants during the course of the service enactment or to monitor the execution of the service. If our credit card validation service is composed of other services, the ServiceModel allows us to describe when and how the other services are invoked. This comes close to typical workflow descriptions made up of control constructs such as if-then-else, while, etc.

- *How does one interact with it?* The answer to this question is given in the ServiceGrounding. It specifies the details of how an agent can access a service. Typically a grounding specifies a communication protocol, message

---

[1]OWL-S was formerly called DAML-S as it is an outcome of the DAML program. After the standardization of the Web Ontology Language (OWL), it was renamed OWL-S (cf. http://www.daml.org/services/owl-s/).

[2]The reader may note that we use a sans serif font to denote names of ontologies, concepts and associations throughout Part II.

[3]North American Industry Classification System (NAICS), cf. http://www.census.gov/epcd/www/naics.html

[4]United Nations Standard Products and Services Code (UNSPSC), cf. http://www.unspsc.org/

formats and other service-specific details, such as port numbers. At the moment, there is only one grounding to align the semantic description with WSDL interface descriptions. In our example, we would map the credit card number as semantically described input to the respective WSDL parameters.

The ontology modules ServiceProfile, ServiceModel and Service-Grounding correspond to the three types of knowledge introduced above. Each module features a rich set of concepts and associations. Ontology modules are different from ontologies in that they depend on other ontologies or on other modules. An ontology module M_1 depends on M_2 if it specializes concepts of M_2, has associations with domains and ranges to M_2, or reuses its axioms. The three modules of OWL-S are linked to the Service module via presents, describes and supports associations. As depicted in Figure 5.2, the Service module acts as a container holding together profile, model and grounding information.[5] It basically consists of a concept of the same name which is to be instantiated for any service description.

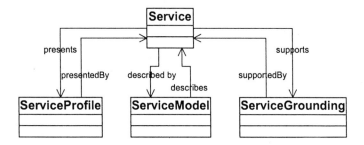

Figure 5.2. The OWL-S Service ontology module as UML class diagram. Classes represent concepts and arrows represent associations. Specializations of ServiceProfile, ServiceModel and ServiceGrounding are placed in their corresponding ontology modules.

The details of profiles, models and groundings may vary widely from one type of service to another. But each of these three service perspectives provides an essential type of information about the service. There are several interesting design principles underlying OWL-S [Sabou et al., 2004]:

Layering of Descriptions OWL-S is intended to provide a layer on top of existing WS* descriptions. The ServiceGrounding module provides a mapping between WSDL and OWL-S, thus facilitating flexible associations between them. For example, a certain semantic description can be mapped to several WSDL descriptions if the same semantic functionality is accessible in different ways. The other way around, a certain WSDL description can

---

[5]We visualize ontologies via UML class or object diagrams throughout the document.

be mapped to different semantic descriptions offering different views of the same service.

Core vs. Domain Knowledge The second principle which underlies the design of OWL-S is the separation between core and domain knowledge. OWL-S can be considered a core ontology offering a set of primitives to semantically describe any type of Web service. These descriptions can be enriched with domain knowledge specified in a separate domain ontology module (e.g., by specializing the concepts of the ServiceProfile in a domain profile). This modelling choice allows using the set of primitives across several domains just by varying the domain knowledge.

Modularity Another feature of OWL-S is the partitioning of the description over several ontology modules, as we have learned before. There are several advantages of this modular modelling. First, since the description is split up modules it is easy to reuse specific parts. Second, service description becomes flexible as it is possible to specify only the part that is relevant for the service (e.g., ServiceModel and ServiceGrounding can be omitted). Finally, OWL-S descriptions are easy to extend. If concepts are not detailed enough for a specific application domain one can specialize them in a separate ontology module.

In essence, we could reuse and extend OWL-S to capture at least the management aspects of Web services. OWL-S was a big step forward and features design principles that are suitable also for our use. Despite the advantages, however, OWL-S has several problematic aspects that endanger our goals of having a high-quality, reference and heavyweight ontology. Before discussing the problematic aspects in Section 3, we have a closer look at our own initial ontology of software components which has been based on OWL-S.

2. Initial Ontology of Software Components

In this section we briefly describe our initial ontology of software components for the semantic enhancement of an application server. In [Oberle et al., 2003b, Oberle et al., 2003c, Sabou et al., 2004] we derived the following ontology requirements based on scenarios:

R1 Interface Description and Code Details The ontology should contain means to model the interface description of software components, as well as relevant code details (version, required libraries, etc.).

R2 Component Profiles The ontology should contain means to model a software component's profile, i.e., the semantics of inputs and outputs in terms of the ontology, their classification according to a given taxonomy or information about the component provider.

R3 Consideration of Existing Efforts It was our intention to consider existing ontologies and reuse them whenever possible. If the ontology resembles
a well-known one, we might keep the learning curve low.

R4 Domain Independence The ontology should be reusable over a wider
range of domains; therefore we should separate core and domain specific
concepts.

In line with requirement R3, we have used OWL-S as a starting point for
our ontology. The design principles underlying OWL-S fit our purposes nicely,
e.g., its separation of core and domain knowledge corresponds to requirement
R4. Below we discuss the resulting ontology design. We have reused three of
the four ontology modules OWL-S introduced, adapted them for our purposes
and added further modules. Figure 5.3 compares both ontologies.

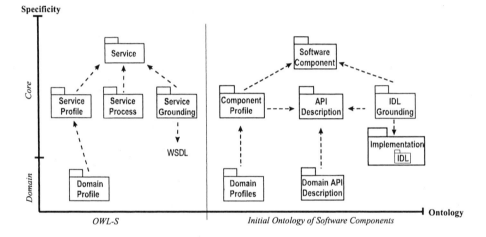

Figure 5.3.   The ontology modules of OWL-S in comparison with the modules of the initial ontology of software components as UML package diagram. Packages represent ontology modules
and dotted arrows represent dependencies between modules. An ontology module M_1 depends
on M_2 if it specializes concepts of M_2, has associations with domains and ranges to M_2 or
reuses its axioms. WSDL is not represented as package because it is not an ontology module.

SoftwareComponent This module is similar to OWL-S Service. However,
we performed some changes: (*i*) We have renamed the Service concept to
SoftwareComponent, as components are the software building blocks to
be described. (*ii*) We have excluded the link to the ServiceModel module,
since we are not interested in workflow information. (*iii*) We have replaced
the ServiceGrounding by the newly introduced IDLGrounding ontology
module which provides a mapping to components' interface descriptions.

ComponentProfile We have reused the OWL-S ServiceProfile module and renamed it ComponentProfile. It allows specifying the specific character-istics of a SoftwareComponent. In order to grasp the semantics of inputs and outputs we have added links to the APIDescription module that groups the information used to describe an API and is separated in a module of the same name. We separated it because we expect that components are able to reuse API descriptions (much more than the remaining profile information).

APIDescription As discussed above, the APIDescription module comple-ments the ComponentProfile by semantically describing the functionality offered by methods of API's and for classifying API types. In essence, the module introduces concepts such as API, Method, Input and Output and links them with associations. They can be specialized in terms of domain ontology concepts (see below).

IDLGrounding The IDLGrounding module provides a mapping between the APIDescription and the interface description captured by the IDL mod-ule. Thus, it resembles the OWL-S ServiceGrounding that maps between a semantic service description and existing WSDL interface descriptions. The mapping is straightforward: concepts InterfaceGrounding, Method-Grounding, InputGrounding and OutputGrounding map between respec-tive concepts from the APIDescription and IDL modules.

Implementation This module contains implementation level details of a component and, thus, responds to requirement R1. There are two aspects of the implementation: (*i*) CodeDetails that describe characteristics of the code, such as the class that implements the code, the required libraries or the version of the code. All these aspects are modelled as associations of the CodeDetails concept. (*ii*) The interface description. The name of the methods and their parameters are modelled using the module presented next (IDL).

IDL We have formalized a small subset of the IDL (Interface Description Lan-guage [Object Modelling Group, 2002]) specification into an ontology mod-ule that allows describing signatures of interfaces. The Interface concept corresponds to a described interface. It features an association called has-Operation which points to an Operation instance. Each Operation can have a set of (input) parameters of a certain type. Also, each Operation returns an OperationType.

Domain Ontologies We can build domain ontologies that specialize two of the modules presented above. By isolating domain knowledge in separate modules, we conform to requirement R4 (Domain Independence). On the one hand, DomainProfiles may distinguish several categories of software components and propose a set of characteristics for each category. These characteristics can be used as a framework for comparing components. On the other hand, **DomainAPIDescriptions** may introduce a set of common API's and methods. For example, one can declare a **DatabaseAdapterAPI** concept and define it as providing a **retrieveData** method and a **storeData** method. The intention is that such information allows performing a flexible search over the existing API's at development time.

Table 5.1 shows the relationship between requirements and ontology modules, confirming the major influence that these requirements had on our design. Much like OWL-S, we could reuse and extend this ontology to capture at least the management aspects of software components. However, OWL-S features several problematic aspects that endanger our goals of having a high-quality, reference and heavyweight ontology. It does not come as a surprise that our initial ontology of software components inherits similar problematic aspects as OWL-S because it is based on OWL-S. We elaborate on the problematic aspects in the following section.

Table 5.1.   Dependencies between requirements and ontology modules.

Requirement \ Ontology module	SoftwareComponent	ComponentProfile	APIDescription	Implementation	IDL	IDLGrounding	Domain Ontologies
R1 Interface description & code details				×	×	
R2 Component profiles		×	×			
R3 Consideration of existing efforts	×	×			×	×
R4 Domain Independence							×

3.   Problematic Aspects

This section identifies and illustrates some of the problematic aspects of OWL-S and our initial ontology of software components from the perspective of the ontology quality criteria introduced in Definition 3.8 on page 41. As the latter is derived from the first, the problems that the two exhibit are similar.

For each of the four problematic aspects, viz., *conceptual ambiguity, poor axiomatization, loose design, narrow scope*, we present examples and suggest improvements. The conclusion is that many problems could have been avoided by exploiting a high-quality foundational ontology as a modelling basis.

3.1   Conceptual Ambiguity

When it is difficult for users to understand the intended meaning of concepts, the associations between these concepts, as well as how they relate to the modelled entities, we speak of *conceptual ambiguity* of an ontology. The reason for conceptual ambiguity in our case is that the underlying logical theory is not complete enough. Furthermore, some concept definitions are too precise (despite the fact that the ontology is not precise enough in general, as we learn in 3.2 and 3.3).

Examples.   Conceptual ambiguity in OWL-S particularly affects the notion of a service which is introduced in [Martin et al., 2004] as follows: "By 'service' we mean Web sites that do not merely provide static information, but allow one to effect some action or change in the world, such as the sale of a product or the control of a physical device." Later, we read that "any Web-accessible program/sensor/device that is declared as a service will be regarded as a service."

However, neither of these definitions is formalized since neither the concept of a "Web site" nor the "Web" appears in the ontology. This is where OWL-S is not complete enough, i.e., its vocabulary lacks terms used in the natural language definition. Instead, the notion of a service is characterized solely by its relationship to a number of ServiceProfiles, at most one ServiceModel and any number of ServiceGroundings, which is not sufficient to understand the concept of Service considered by OWL-S. This prevents us from considering alternative ServiceModels, or from evaluating the relationship between a ServiceModel required by a customer's guideline, or by a legal regulation and the one underlying the provider's system, for instance. Thus, OWL-S actually excludes intended models in this case, making it too precise in terms of our ontology quality criteria (cf. Definition 3.8 on page 41).

The debates about the intended meaning of terms both within the OWL-S coalition and in public mailing lists[6] were plentiful. The reason is that terms such as Web service and closely related terms (e-Service, Service, etc.) typically suffer from overloading. In our search for possible formalizations, we found a variety of definitions emphasizing different aspects of a service [Gangemi et al., 2003b]: offering functionality (usefulness for a specific task) or interoperability using standards or providing an interface to an existing system. We also refer the reader to the work of [Baida et al., 2004], which compares and contrasts the definitions used in the business literature, in software engineering and in information sciences.

In our initial ontology of software components we find a similar dilemma regarding the plethora of meanings and definitions of terms such as component,

---

[6]cf. http://www.daml.org/services

software component or software module. The ontology fails to convey its intended meanings of such terms and leaves the interpretation to the ontology user.

Suggested Improvement. Even if there are several ways to formalize concepts such as service or component, using a foundational ontology as a modelling basis would allow comparison between alternative definitions and foster discussion about alternative conceptualizations. Using a foundational ontology as a modelling basis means relating the concepts and associations of an ontology to the basic categories of human cognition investigated by philosophy, linguistics or psychology. This prompts the ontology engineer to sharpen his notions with respect to the distinctions made in the foundational ontology. What is typically gained is an increased understanding of one's own ontology.

3.2   Poor Axiomatization

Both OWL-S and the initial ontology of software components are typical application ontologies, i.e., they are to be used at run time for reasoning purposes. Hence, it is important that each concept is characterized by an axiomatization in order to support meaningful inferences. Unlike the problem mentioned in the previous section, *poor axiomatization* reflects the lesser problem when the definition of concepts is clear, but axiomatization in the ontology itself needs improvement (in order to make it more precise). In particular, we believe that the level of axiomatization in OWL-S needs to be raised if it hopes to support the complex reasoning tasks put forward by its coalition.

Examples.   In both ontologies there is no firm concept or association hierarchy. That means that most concepts and associations are direct subconcepts of the top level concept (owl:Thing) or association (owl:Property), and that several associations declare owl:Thing as their domain or range. In essence, there is not much more than the concept hierarchy and domain and range restrictions. Therefore, reasoning is limited to subsumption checking and domain and range inferencing, although further reasoning could be usefully employed.

To give a concrete example: ControlConstructs in OWL-S are used to define how composite processes are combined together. Typical specializations are Sequence, Split, Choice or If-Then-Else. The components association relates ControlConstructs to lists or bags of further ControlConstructs or invocations of other processes. In OWL-S, the components association is described merely as a specialization of owl:Property with a domain of Control-Construct. It would be desirable to concisely axiomatize this association in order to support more meaningful consistency checks. We could axiomatize its mereological and temporal properties, e.g., being a functional and temporal proper part of a ControlConstruct. Both properties could be further characterized with formal restrictions on its application to other basic concepts, such as objects or events.

Suggested Improvement. The level of axiomatization can be increased by using a foundational ontology as a modelling basis. By specializing concepts of the foundational ontology, its extensive axiomatization is automatically inherited. It also promotes reuse by highlighting commonalities, which especially helps to reduce the proliferation of associations that is typical for application ontologies.

As an example, foundational ontologies typically incorporate precise theories for plans, formalizing constructs that are directly comparable to the Control-Constructs of OWL-S, but provide a higher level of axiomatization. Such a predefined theory could be leveraged in our case. Higher axiomatization can also be leveraged by the links to a theory of time — another theory often included in foundational ontologies — for describing constraints on temporal relations between process elements when they are executions of a plan. OWL-S would also need such an ontology of time. Then, it would be natural to adopt or reference an existing ontology instead of creating an ontology from scratch.

3.3 Loose Design

A further problematic aspect from an ontologist's point of view is the loose design of both ontologies. The reason for *loose design* is, amongst others, inherited by the limitations of the representation language's expressiveness, i.e., the ontologies are not precise enough.

At the heart of this problem lies the fact that both ontologies try to provide descriptions of components and services to support a number of different tasks (e.g., component or service discovery, composition, invocation). Besides the functional dimension, such descriptions should be contextualized to represent various points of view, possibly with different granularity.[7] Most of these views, however, are overlapping in that they concern some of the same attributes of a component or service.

A straightforward modularization in such cases results in an entangled ontology, where the placement of specific knowledge becomes arbitrary and intensive mapping is required between modules. This phenomenon is well described in object-oriented design, where the notion of *aspects* [Elrad et al., 2001] was recently proposed to encapsulate concerns that cross-cut the concept hierarchy of a software.

---

[7]The OWL-S specification mentions the ability to use the ServiceProfile for providing such views. However, no actual constructs are provided to map them to possible service executions or to each other.

Examples.   A case in point is the application of attribute binding in OWL-S. The construct of attribute binding is necessary in OWL-S to express, for example, that the output of a process is the input to another process or that the output of a composite process is the same as the output of one of its subprocesses. In programming, such equivalences are expressed by the use of *variables*. Variables are governed by the rules of *scoping*, which define the boundaries of commitment.

Since OWL lacks the notion of variables, attribute binding is expressed by the Binding concept which is attached to a Process (cf. Figure 5.4). The Binding contains instances of the valueOf concept. The valueOf concept points to a Process and to one of its inputs or outputs via the fromProcess and theVar associations, respectively. For example, in case of two processes A and B where B takes the output of A as an input, the Binding would point to the Input of B via toParam. In addition, a corresponding valueOf instance would point to the Process A and the Output of A.

The reader may note that the intended meaning of the entire construct, namely, the equivalence of B's input and A's output, is not encoded in the axiomatization. This is explained by the lack of expressiveness of the description logic used.

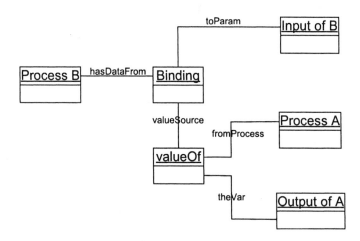

Figure 5.4.   The representation of attribute binding in OWL-S as UML object diagram. Concept instances are represented by objects and instantiated associations by object relations.

The representation of attribute binding is only one example where we find modelling artifacts in OWL-S. Modelling artifacts are concepts and associations that do not bear ontological meaning, but are introduced because of unfortunate ontology design or because of limitations of the representation language.

A closer look at our initial ontology of software components also reveals the existence of modelling artifacts. For example, we can find the concept

Parameter two times. One is introduced in the IDL module for modelling the interface description. Another is introduced in the APIDescription module for its semantic description. Both model the same information object, yet in a different context. The concepts Method in the APIDescription and Operation in IDL demonstrate that this problem is not limited to equally named concepts.

Suggested Improvement. The use of contextualization as an ontology design pattern would allow us to move from a monolithic description to the representation of different, possibly conflicting views with various granularity. Some foundational ontologies incorporate such design patterns or offer them as additional theories. They provide the basic primitives of context modelling such as the notion of roles, which allows us to talk about inputs and outputs on the abstract level, i.e., independent of the objects that play such roles, for instance.

Using the ontology design pattern of contextualization results in a much more intuitive representation of attribute binding, with clearly defined semantics and scoping. Inputs and outputs can be modelled as functional roles, which serve as variables in our ontology. A single object — for example, a physical book — can play multiple roles within the same or different descriptions, and, thus it is natural to express that the given book is output with respect to one process, but input to another. Moreover, it is easier to represent the requirement that the input of a process *has to be* played by the same instance as the output of another process by putting constraints on the *objects* (and not the process or task) which play these roles (however, the expressiveness required is the same and, therefore, goes beyond the expresiveness of OWL DL).

3.4   Narrow Scope

Web services may carry out operations to support a real-world service, e.g., the ordering of goods. Thus, Web services exist on the boundary of the world inside an information system and the external world. Functionality, which is an essential property of a service, then arises from the entire process that comprises computational, as well as real-world activities. Web service descriptions are thus necessarily descriptions of two parallel worlds. In an information system, the world consists of software manipulating (representations of) information objects. Activities are sequenced by computational processes. Meanwhile in the real world, goods are being delivered to their destinations. The connection between these worlds is that some of the information objects represent real-world objects. Also, computational activities comprise part of the service execution in the real world. For example, an order needs to be entered by the Web agent into an information system, so that a warehouse knows which goods to deliver to a given address.

The scope of OWL-S needs to be extended to represent real-world services that naturally cross the lines between information systems and the physical world. While OWL-S acknowledges this aspect of services, it is unclear how a distinction could be made between the objects and events within an information system (regarding data and the manipulation of data) and the real-world objects and events external to such a system.

Such a *narrow scope* is a result of the ontology not being complete and accurate enough. Although the case of real-world activity descriptions is of less relevance for software components, narrow scope is a problem in both ontologies.

Examples.   It is hard, if not impossible, to distinguish among a physical object (e.g., a credit card), an information object (e.g., a credit card number) and a representation of such information using a specific description system (e.g., a string encoding) in OWL-S. In one of its use cases,[8] we find a concept CreditCard-Type, directly inherited from owl:Thing and defined as an enumeration consisting of MasterCard, AmericanExpress, VISA and DiscoverCard. The interpretation is left to the ontology user, whether it is the physical or the information object that is modelled.

We can find a very similar example in our initial ontology of software components, where a concept User is specialized directly from the top-level concept. One can only guess whether it is the natural person, a role played by the natural person, or his or her informational counterpart. It would be worthwhile to explicate such differences, e.g., when we want to infer the total of access rights granted for a natural person who might have several user accounts in and across information systems.

We are able to explain this problem by means of our ontology quality criteria introduced in Definition 3.8 on page 41: the ontology is not complete enough (its vocabulary is not rich enough to capture the difference) and it is not accurate enough (its universe is exclusively limited either to physical users or to the corresponding information objects).

Suggested Improvement.   We believe that this distinction is important for disambiguating the nature of services and components. This especially holds for semantic descriptions of Web services in the context of the Semantic Web.[9] The separation would naturally follow from the use of a foundational ontology,

---

[8]A fictitious Web shop, called Congo.com, cf. http://www.daml.org/services/owl-s/1.1/examples.html.

[9]In fact, the lack of this distinction stands behind the emergence of the "Semantic Web identity crisis" that results from the ambiguous use of identifiers in Semantic Web ontology languages such as RDF [Pepper and Schwab, 2003]. In practice, a URI can be used to reference a document on the Web, either to reference (a fragment of) a document containing some definition of a concept or to represent a concept (without any intended reference to an actual location on the Web). Unfortunately, no standard scheme exists to distinguish among the three kinds of identifiers even though they need to be resolved in different ways.

where the distinction is an important part of the characterization of concepts. In particular, it makes it possible to be more specific about the kinds of relationships that can occur among objects or between objects and events. Using a foundational ontology, it is possible and even required for the creator of a description to make such distinctions because they fundamentally affect the ontological nature of the objects and events concerned.

4. Summary

In this chapter we have analyzed whether existing ontologies are suitable for our purposes, thus answering the Question II.1: *Can an existing ontology be reused for our purposes?* We have inspected one of the earliest and most prominent Web service ontologies, viz., OWL-S, as well as our own initial ontology of software components. We conclude that both are a big step forward with design principles suitable also for our purposes. Their reuse is possible in principle. However, both ontologies exhibit shortcomings that stand in conflict with our goals of having a high-quality, reference and heavyweight ontology. Their problems are very common also in more recent efforts (some of them are discussed in the related work chapter). We further conclude that most of the problems could have been avoided if a foundational ontology had been used as a modelling basis. Thus, the remainder of this part designs a new management ontology on the basis of a foundational ontology.

Chapter 6

THE APPROPRIATE
FOUNDATIONAL ONTOLOGY

In the previous chapter we have analyzed whether existing ontologies can be reused and adapted for our purposes. We have had a closer look at OWL-S and our own initial ontology of software components. Although their reuse is possible, we would inherit severe problems that stand in conflict with our goals of high quality, reference purpose and heavyweight axiomatization. Their shortcomings have called for the use of a foundational ontology.

Redesigning OWL-S and our initial ontology of software components with a foundational ontology as a basis is a dilemma between improving their problematic aspects and keeping as much of the original structure as possible. As discussed in [Mika, Oberle et al., 2004a], the result is an ontology of higher quality, but with many "leftover" concepts of the original ontologies that complicate its usage. Therefore, this chapter marks the starting point for building a management ontology anew as it opts for an appropriate foundational ontology. In lack of an established standard, we follow the strategy to first identify requirements in terms of suitable ontological choices the foundational ontology should reflect (cf. Section 1). Suitable ontological choices are implicitly given by the domain we want to model. Furthermore, the analysis of problematic aspects of OWL-S and our own initial ontology of software components yields additional requirements. Section 2 briefly discusses the alternatives, i.e., the most prominent foundational ontologies, with respect to the requirements. After comparing the foundational ontologies, we conclude that the DOLCE foundational ontology is the primary choice for our purposes (Section 3).

Most of the chapter resembles [Oberle et al., 2004b], an internal project report, where we advanced similarly in choosing an appropriate foundational ontology. Bits and pieces of the ontologies' introductions are taken from [Varzi and Vieu, 2004] and [Borgo et al., 2002, Masolo et al., 2002, Masolo et al., 2003].

1.   Requirements for Ontological Choices

Finding the appropriate foundational ontology is dependent on the universe of discourse we want to model, as well as the use cases and target users. In our case, several aspects of software components and Web services are to be modelled. This yields the requirements for ontological choices listed below. Some of them are mandatory, whereas others are optional.

Descriptive We should aim at a descriptive ontology that captures the ontological categories underlying natural language and human common sense. Reading, creating and understanding semantic descriptions must be as intuitive as possible for the developer. Being descriptive is a mandatory requirement because revisionary ontologies, which model the intrinsic nature of the world, would complicate those tasks.

Multiplicative The appropriate foundational ontology should provide a clear and detailed treatment of objects and properties assuming that different entities can be co-located in the same space-time. The multiplicative approach is optional because we assume it to be more intuitive. The human user usually tends towards a multiplicative recognition.

Possibilism The examples of software components and their dependencies on page 36 (Chapter 3, Section 1) already provide evidence that modalities come in handy as a modelling primitive. Using a modal logic means committing to possibilism and provides us with a powerful means with respect to expressiveness. Basically, possibilism is desirable, but not mandatorily required.

Perdurantism The ability to model 4D entities, i.e., perdurants, is of central importance for our ontology, and, thus, a mandatory requirement. For example, when we want to model workflow information by computational activities (which would be perdurants in this case).

The use cases of Chapter 4, Section 2, as well as the analysis of problematic aspects of OWL-S and our own initial ontology of software components (cf. Chapter 5, Section 3) yield additional requirements that particularly affect the extrinsic properties:

Executable Language Our goal is to arrive at a core ontology with heavyweight axiomatization and reference purpose. Its intended models should be approximated as concisely as possible to achieve high quality. However, we should already take into account that we want to reason at run time eventually. Hence, the foundational ontology is mandatorily required to be available in a lightweight version, formalized in an executable language.

Modular As we learn throughout the chapter, some foundational ontologies feature a great number of concepts and associations, as well as an extensive axiomatization. If monolithic, choosing such an ontology as a modelling basis leads to over-commitment, i.e., the import of theories that will not be used later on. Hence, it is desirable, but not mandatorily required, that the appropriate foundational ontology consists of a minimal core and additional modules reflecting theories such as the three listed below:

Theory of Contextualization The analysis of existing ontologies in Chapter 5, Section 3.3 reveals the need for a concise theory of contextualization. It would allow us to move from an entangled, monolithic design to the representation of different, possibly conflicting views with various granularity. The existence of a theory of contextualization is optional because it could be formalized anew in principle.

Theory of Plans One of the modelling requirements derived from the use cases in Chapter 4, Section 2 is to formalize *workflow information* of components and services. Foundational ontologies typically provide such modelling capabilities by theories of plans. We have learned in Chapter 5, Section 3 that a rich axiomatization thereof would allow for meaningful inferences. It is desirable to reuse an existing theory, but not mandatorily required.

Theory of Information Objects Another conclusion of the analysis in Chapter 5, Section 3.4 has been that a concise distinction between entities in an information system and the real world is required. Hence, an elaborated theory of information objects is another requirement. As with all the other theories, this one could also be formalized from scratch, making the requirement an optional one.

2. Alternatives

This section provides a brief description of the basic assumptions and methodologies considered in the most prominent foundational ontologies, namely BFO, DOLCE, OCHRE, OpenCyc and SUMO. In particular, we analyze whether they meet the requirements put forward in the previous section.

There are further ontologies that label themselves "upper-level" which we do not consider here for several reasons. In common literature we find particularly John Sowa's upper-level ontology [Sowa, 2000], as well as Russell and Norvig's upper-level ontology [Russell and Norvig, 1995]. However, both are integrated in SUMO — one of the alternatives we consider below.

Besides, there are several linguistic ontologies that are considered as upper-level sometimes. In that category we find the PROTON Upper module,[1] which

---

[1] http://proton.semanticweb.org/

stems from a company called Ontotext, featuring several core and domain level concepts. Others are Sensus,[2] a 70,000-node terminology taxonomy and extension of WordNet, as well as Mikrokosmos[3] and the Generalized Upper Model.[4] All of them are "linguistically motivated ontologies" expressing classes corresponding to existing natural language, and, thus, unsuitable for our purposes.

2.1   BFO

The BFO (Basic Formal Ontology) belongs to the WonderWeb library of foundational ontologies [Masolo et al., 2003]. The goals of the library are to have: (*i*) starting points for building core and domain ontologies, (*ii*) a reference point for comparisons among different ontological approaches and (*iii*) a common framework for analyzing existing ontologies.

BFO is mainly known for its application in the bio-medical domain. An essential feature is its separation into two ontology modules: SNAP and SPAN. Each module represents a specific view on reality, according to the level of granularity chosen by the modeler to catch certain aspects of the world.

SNAP provides a set of all the entities existing in time to model "snapshots of reality." Such enduring entities are called Continuants in the case of BFO. They are categorized into Substantial Entities, Spatial Regions and Tropes. Substantial Entities are the bearers of properties and change, e.g., material objects, organs or portions of the atmosphere, and are further classified in Substances, Boundaries, etc. Tropes can be considered as the qualities that inhere in Substantial Entities. Examples are the color of a tomato or the temperature of a body. Tropes are subdivided into Qualities, Functions, Conditions, etc. Finally, there are Spatial Regions which can be geographical, cosmological, anatomical or topographical, for instance.

The SPAN module is a "catalogue" of perduring entities, called Occurants here, divided into Temporal Regions, Processes and Spatio-temporal Regions. Temporal Regions are pure temporal regions as opposed to Spatio-temporal Regions which include dimensions to identify the spatial location of an entity. Processes are happenings, occurring entities, or changes of various kinds in substantial entities, e.g., the raising of temperature, the acquisition of a social status, movements, activities, etc. Processes are further classified in Settings, Events, Aggregates, etc. Finally, Spatio-temporal Regions are the four dimensional regions of space-time. SNAP and SPAN are sketched in Figure 6.1.[5]

---

[2]http://www.isi.edu/natural-language/resources/sensus.html
[3]http://www.csee.umbc.edu/~dingli1/student/cmsc691k/mikrokosmos.htm
[4]http://www.fb10.uni-bremen.de/anglistik/langpro/webspace/jb/gum
[5]We visualize pure taxonomies as trees, because they are better suited than UML class diagrams for this purpose.

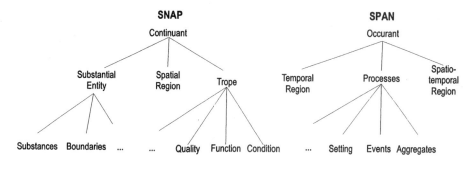

Figure 6.1. BFO Taxonomy.

BFO comes with a rich axiomatization in first-order logic without modalities, i.e., the ontology commits to *actualism*. Both 3D entities (Continuants) and 4D entities (Occurants) are considered, reflecting *endurantism* and *perdurantism* at the same time. Furthermore, BFO affirms that there are many views of reality which are equally veridical. These are views of entities in different domains, views of entities as seen from different perspectives or views of what exists on different levels of granularity (microscopic, mesoscopic, geographic). Thus, BFO commits to a *reductionist* stance with respect to co-localized entities. BFO assumes that reality and its constituents exist independently of our (linguistic, conceptual, theoretical, cultural) representations thereof. This position coincides with a *revisionary* ontological choice.

There is no publicly available version of BFO in an executable representation language. Although BFO is minimal and split into two modules, there are no additional theories for contextualization, plans or information objects.

2.2 DOLCE

DOLCE belongs to the WonderWeb library of foundational ontologies as well [Masolo et al., 2002]. It is intended to act as a starting point for comparing and elucidating the relationships with other ontologies of the library and also for clarifying the hidden assumptions underlying existing ontologies or linguistic resources such as WordNet [Miller et al., 1990]. It has been successfully applied in different domains, such as law [Gangemi et al., 2004c], biomedicine [Gangemi et al., 2004a] and agriculture [Gangemi et al., 2002].

DOLCE (Descriptive Ontology for Linguistic and Cognitive Engineering) is based on the fundamental distinction between enduring and perduring entities. The main relation between Endurants (i.e., objects or substances) and Perdurants (i.e., events or processes) is that of participation: an Endurant "lives" in time by participating in a Perdurant. For example, a software component, which is an Endurant, participates in its lifecycle, which is a Perdurant.

DOLCE introduces **Qualities** as another category that can be seen as the basic entities we can perceive or measure: shapes, colors, sizes, sounds, smells, as well as weights, lengths or electrical charges. Spatial locations (i.e., a special kind of physical quality) and temporal qualities encode the spatio-temporal attributes of objects or events. Finally, **Abstracts** do not have spatial or temporal qualities and they are not qualities themselves. An example are **Regions** used to encode the measurement of qualities as conventionalized in some metric or conceptual space. The basic concept hierarchy is sketched in Figure 6.2.

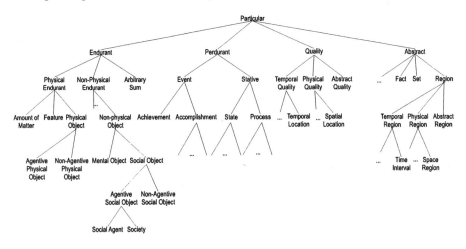

Figure 6.2. DOLCE Taxonomy.

As reflected by its name, DOLCE has a clear *descriptive* bias, in the sense that it aims at capturing the ontological categories underlying natural language and human common sense. DOLCE embraces the *multiplicative* approach: starting from the observation that one tends to associate objects to incompatible essential properties, DOLCE provides a clear and detailed treatment of objects and properties assuming that different entities can be co-located in the same space-time. DOLCE allows modelling 3D objects, i.e., **Endurants**, as well as 4D objects, i.e., **Perdurants**. Thus, it commits to both *endurantism* and *perdurantism*.

DOLCE features a rich reference axiomatization in modal logic S5, thereby committing to *possibilism*. The axiomatization captures ontology design patterns such as location in space and time, dependence or parthood. Its core is minimal in that it only includes the most general concepts and patterns. This makes it well-suited for modularization. In fact, there is a wealth of additional theories that can be included on demand. Examples are Descriptions & Situations for contextualization, the Ontology of Plans, the Ontology of Time or the Ontology of Information Objects [Gangemi et al., 2004b].

DOLCE is unique in that it provides a lightweight version (called DOLCE Lite). Thus, the application of DOLCE-based ontologies becomes possible in description logics such as DAML+OIL [Horrocks and Patel-Schneider, 2001] or OWL DL [McGuinness and van Harmelen, 2004]. The reference axiomatization has been adopted manually to fit the target language. Changes affect the DOLCE signature (associations may have the same name but different arities and domains), modal operators (which had to be omitted) and temporally-indexed associations (which are partly rearranged as compositions with temporal location associations).

2.3 OCHRE

OCHRE (Object-Centered High-level REference ontology) is the latest member of the WonderWeb library of foundational ontologies. In contrast to DOLCE and BFO, it puts strong emphasis on a clear and elegant mereological framework that gives a straightforward account of parthood relations between individuals. OCHRE does not offer the rich taxonomies of DOLCE. It has not been applied in real applications so far. [Schneider, 2003]

OCHRE is an ontology of perdurants (events and processes) and objects based on Tropes which are the mereological atoms out of which all denizens of reality are supposed to be built up. OCHRE gives a qualitative account of both objects and events as bundles of individual characteristics. Following the footsteps of Aristotle's metaphysics, OCHRE distinguishes between Thick and Thin Objects. Thick Objects are aggregations of Tropes that are extended in time and space. They are mereotopologically rigid, i.e., invariant in terms of composition and location. Change is reconstructed as the succession of such Thick Objects that share a same Thin Object. A Thin Object can be thought of as a core of essential properties that link a series of Thick Objects together.

For example, the Tropes of a ripening tomato are its color, its mass, its shape, etc. The change of a ripening tomato just pertains to different Thick Objects representing the tomato and its Tropes. That means, the Thick Objects are wholes centered around the bundle of core characteristics, e.g., the tomato's DNA, represented by a Thin Object. That one speaks of the same object through change is grounded in the existence of Thin Objects.

As depicted in Figure 6.3, OCHRE splits its entities in Tropes and Sums of Tropes. Tropes are the single characteristics of individuals which are temporally aggregated by Sums of Tropes. The latter are further specialized into Non Categorials and Categorials. As the name suggests, Non Categorials cannot be further categorized because they comprise arbitrary Sums of Tropes. In contrast, Categorials can be further categorized in Abstract and Concrete Categorials distinguished by spatio-temporal extension. Abstract Categorials comprise the Thin Objects, as well as Guises (sums of single

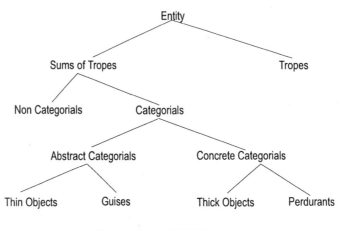

Figure 6.3.   OCHRE Taxonomy.

Thin Objects and the Tropes dependent on them). Concrete Categorials comprise the Thick Objects, as well as Perdurants.

OCHRE commits to ontological choices as follows: First, OCHRE adopts a *revisionary* approach because the distinction between Thick Objects and Thin Objects does not adhere to human common sense. Second, it is unclear if OCHRE adopts a *reductionist* stance. Though multiplying spatio-temporally co-located objects in OCHRE is avoided, it allows to distinguish between different Guises of the same Thick Object. Therefore, the same Thick Object may contain more than one Guise, and, thus, more than one Thin Object. E.g., a vase contains at least three Guises: its "material" (i.e., a bundle of material characteristics such as density or mass), its "form" (i.e., a bundle of formal characteristics such as shape) and its "function" (i.e., characteristics pertaining to its use). Despite its insistence on topological extensionality, OCHRE allows the multiplication of "abstract," i.e., non-spatial, parts of the same spatial entity. This is possible since OCHRE adopts a qualitative account of objects. Third, OCHRE commits to *endurantism*, because it considers events and processes being constituted by successions of Thick Objects. Indeed, an event as a basic perdurant corresponds to some elementary change, and, thus to the succession of two Thick Objects sharing a same Thin Object. Finally, the latest version of OCHRE commits to *possibilism* because it contains an account of possibilia (possible objects and possible worlds) in terms of Sums of tropes.

A version of OCHRE in an executable representation language is in the making at the time of writing this document. Compared to DOLCE, it lacks rich taxonomies which would allow a simple integration of domain-specific ontologies. However, it is not monolithic, since it has been designed to be extendable. Theories for contextualization, plans or information objects are missing but could possibly be implemented by introducing new subconcepts of Tropes, Thin and Thick objects and Perdurants.

2.4   OpenCyc

The Cyc project started in the mid eighties and was carried out by MCC (Microelectronics and Computer Consortium) which was later taken over by Cycorp. The project resulted in a complex knowledge-based system with a large corpus of commonsense knowledge. The knowledge is captured by an equally complex ontology, called UpperCyc, whose publicly available version, OpenCyc, is the focus of this section.[6]

OpenCyc captures millions of everyday terms, concepts and rules which try to formalize the human knowledge of reality. Due to problems of consistency within a huge knowledge base, the information in OpenCyc has been carved up according to hundreds of microtheories. A microtheory, in Cyc terms, usually concerns a specific domain of knowledge and bundles assertions that share common assumptions about the world thus representing a specific context. [Guha and Lenat, 1990]

The highest entity in the OpenCyc ontology is Thing which is further partitioned into MathematicalOrComputationalThing, PartiallyIntangible and Individual. All instances of MathematicalOrComputationalThing are abstract entities that do not have temporal or spatial properties. The collection of things that either are wholly intangible or have at least one intangible, i.e., immaterial, part are subsumed by PartiallyIntangible. Individual defines the set of individuals that are not a set or collection. The concept hierarchy is sketched in Figure 6.4.

OpenCyc appears to be deeply affected by cognitive assumptions, since its categories try to capture naive conceptions of the real world, that is, the human fund of commonsense knowledge. For this reason we can consider OpenCyc a *descriptive* ontology. Unfortunately, it must be said that the characterization of the commitments on underlying ontological choices seems to be a secondary task in the current state of the Cyc project. The documentation is still sketchy, and as a consequence, there is a lack of references to the established literature. That means there is no clear position which shows whether the ontology commits to *possibilism* or *actualism*, *endurantism* or *perdurantism* and whether it can be considered *multiplicative* or *reductionist*. [Borgo et al., 2002]

OpenCyc is primarily represented in CycL, which closely resembles KIF (Knowledge Interchange Format) [Genesereth and Fikes, 1992], basically equalling the expressiveness of first-order logic. It comes with a proprietary inference engine and application programmer's interface. The usage of mi-

---

[6]http://www.opencyc.org/

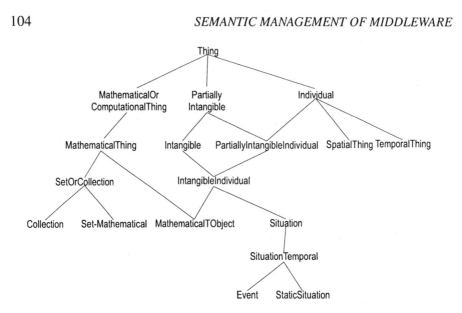

Figure 6.4.   OpenCyc Taxonomy.

crotheories partitions the ontology into modules. However, there is neither a microtheory for contextualization, nor for plans, or for information objects.

2.5   SUMO

The Suggested Upper Merged Ontology (SUMO)[7] is the most prominent proposal under consideration by the IEEE Standard Upper Ontology (SUO) working group[8] [Niles and Pease, 2001]. It is an attempt to link categories and relations coming from different top-level ontologies in order to improve interoperability, communication and search in the Semantic Web area. The development of SUMO was based on the merging of different ontology modules and theories: John Sowa's upper level ontology [Sowa, 2000], Russell and Norvig's upper level ontology [Russell and Norvig, 1995], James Allen's temporal axioms [Allen, 1984], Casati and Varzi's formal theory of holes [Casati and Varzi, 1995], Barry Smith's ontology of boundaries [Smith, 1996], Nicola Guarino's formal mereotopology [Borgo et al., 1996] and various formal representation of plans and processes, including the Core Plan Representation (CPR) [Pease, 1998] and the Process Specification Language (PSL) [Grüninger and Menzel, 2003].

A sketch of the taxonomy is depicted in Figure 6.5. The topmost concept in SUMO is Entity, which is further split into Physical and Abstract. Physical

---

[7]http://ontology.teknowledge.com/
[8]http://suo.ieee.org

entities are further divided into Objects and Processes. Other general topics, which are not shown in Figure 6.5, include: structural concepts (instance, subclass), general types of objects and processes, abstractions (including set theory, attributes, and relations, number, measures, temporal concepts, such as duration and parts and wholes). [Pease et al., 2002]

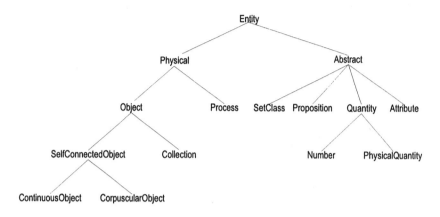

Figure 6.5. SUMO Taxonomy.

Because of its characteristic merging of different ontology modules and theories, SUMO is actually not influenced by any specific theoretical approach. Rather, it tends to adopt the general categories from various ontology proposals. In this context, we should say that SUMO does not clearly adopt either a *multiplicative* or a *reductionist* approach. We encounter the same dilemma regarding the choices *possibilism* vs. *actualism*, as well as *endurantism* vs. *perdurantism*. We classify SUMO as being *descriptive* because it adopts the commonsense distinction between objects and processes.

As we have learned above, SUMO is more or less modularized with respect to the different theories of which it consists. There is a theory of plans (the Core Plan Representation and the Process Specification Language), but no modules or theories for contextualization and information objects. SUMO provides quite a rich axiomatization formalized in the Standard Upper Ontology Knowledge Interchange Format (SUO-KIF), a variation and simplification of the Knowledge Interchange Format (KIF) [Genesereth and Fikes, 1992]. There also is an OWL Full version. Both require expressiveness equal to first-order logic.

3. Summary

In this chapter we have analyzed the most prominent foundational ontologies in light of the requirements put forward in Section 1. Tables 6.1 and 6.2 summarize the analysis and allow a clear comparison. The decision for the DOLCE foundational ontology as modelling basis is straightforward, since it meets all our requirements. Choosing DOLCE means opting for a conceptually clean approach with explicit commitment to ontological choices.

Table 6.1. The different alternatives compared to the requirements for ontological choices (mandatory requirements are written in italics; all the others are optional). Cells labelled with "unclear" express that there is no clear position to the corresponding ontological choice. This is a rather undesirable property of an ontology and is considered negatively.

Requirement \ Alternative	BFO	DOLCE	OCHRE	OpenCyc	SUMO
Descriptive	-	×	-	×	×
Multiplicative	-	×	unclear	unclear	unclear
Possibilism	-	×	×	unclear	unclear
Perdurantism	×	×	-	unclear	unclear

Another unique feature of DOLCE is the existence of a lightweight version. Its reference axiomatization has already been adapted to an executable description logic. This saves us a lot of work when we want to realize semantic management using our management ontology with DOLCE as a basis. In addition, DOLCE is unique in that it is well-modularized, providing all required theories for context modelling, plans and information objects. Thus, choosing DOLCE minimizes the risk of ontological over-commitment.

Table 6.2. The different alternatives compared to the requirements for extrinsic properties (mandatory requirements are written in italics; all the others are optional).

Requirement \ Alternative	BFO	DOLCE	OCHRE	OpenCyc	SUMO
Executable Language	-	×	×	×	×
Modularization	×	×	×	×	×
Theory of contextualization	-	×	-	-	-
Theory of plans	-	×	-	-	×
Theory of information objects	-	×	-	-	-

Chapter 7

AN ONTOLOGICAL FORMALIZATION OF SOFTWARE COMPONENTS AND WEB SERVICES

In the previous chapter we have analyzed the most prominent foundational ontologies in light of our requirements for ontological choices. We have decided to use the DOLCE foundational ontology as a starting point for modelling our management ontology.

This chapter is concerned with the design of an appropriate management ontology based on DOLCE. Appropriateness comprises: (*i*) to meet the modelling requirements derived from our use cases, (*ii*) to achieve high quality according to the ontology quality criteria and (*iii*) to enable reuse in specific platforms and to reduce modelling efforts to a minimum.

Regarding (*i*), the use cases of Section 2 in Chapter 4 on page 65 allowed deriving a set of modelling requirements to be met by the management ontology. In order to enable semantic management we have to model: (*a*) *libraries, licenses, component profiles, component taxonomies, API descriptions, semantic API descriptions, access rights* and *workflow information* of software components and (*b*) *service profiles, service taxonomies, policies, workflow information, API descriptions*, as well as *semantic API descriptions* of Web services.

Point (*ii*) coincides with the Question II.2: *How to ensure high quality?* Therefore, Definition 3.8 on page 41 introduced specific quality criteria. The general idea is to axiomatize the intended models of our universe of discourse as closely as possible. A high-quality ontology avoids the typical shortcomings of common ontologies as outlined in Chapter 5, viz., *conceptual ambiguity, poor axiomatization, loose design* and *narrow scope*. That means, e.g., to exclude unintended interpretations of overloaded terms, such as "software component" or "Web service." The management ontology should allow developers and administrators to disambiguate such overloaded terms. Hence, our management ontology has to have a *reference* characteristic. This is achieved by an extensive axiomatization, resulting in a *heavyweight* ontology.

Finally, (*iii*) requires the modelling to capture the idiosyncracies of software components and Web services *and* to be platform-independent at the same time. The answer to the corresponding research Question II.3 (*How to decrease modelling efforts and enable reuse?*) is to have a *core* ontology that can easily be reused and specialized in a concrete platform. In fact, Part III reuses and specializes the management ontology to realize semantic management in a concrete system. Modelling efforts can be decreased by leveraging the foundational ontology and its modules.

Figure 7.1 provides an overview of the reused ontology modules and the modules we contribute in this chapter. Besides DOLCE, we also need theories for contextualization, for plans and for information objects (as discussed in Chapter 6, Section 1, page 96). Descriptions & Situations, the Ontology of Plans, and the Ontology of Information Objects realize such theories and come in the form of ontology modules. All the modules are briefly explained in Section 1 in order to have a self-contained document. Our contributed ontology modules, viz., the Core Software Ontology, the Core Ontologies of Software Components and Web Services are introduced in Sections 2, 3 and 4. The reader may confer to the Appendix where we provide the taxonomies of all ontology modules. Finally, Section 5 shows how the management ontology responds to (*i*), (*ii*) and (*iii*) by examples.

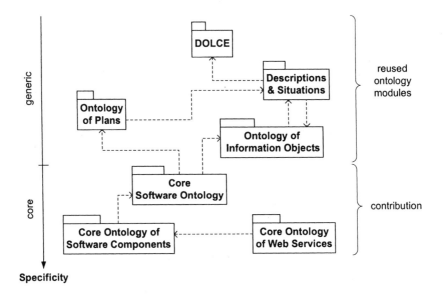

Figure 7.1. Overview of the management ontology as UML package diagram. Packages represent ontology modules; dotted lines represent dependencies between modules. An ontology module M_1 depends on M_2 if it specializes concepts of M_2, has associations with domains and ranges to M_2 or reuses its axioms.

Some of the ontology modules discussed in this chapter are reused as depicted in Figure 7.1. DOLCE is introduced in [Masolo et al., 2003], the Descriptions & Situations module, as well as the Ontology of Plans and the Ontology of Information Objects are discussed in [Gangemi et al., 2004b]. Parts of the Core Ontology of Web Services originate from [Mika, Oberle, et al., 2004a, Mika et al., 2004b, Gangemi et al., 2003b, Oberle et al., 2005b, Lamparter et al., 2005].

1.   Modelling Basis

When designing an ontology, it is desirable to start with an extensive and sound modelling basis. Hence, our methodology is geared towards reuse of generic ontology modules in order to reduce modelling efforts. Figure 7.1 already provided an overview of the reused ontology modules and the modules we contribute. We begin in this section by briefly discussing the reused ontology modules DOLCE, Descriptions & Situations, the Ontology of Plans, and the Ontology of Information Objects.

1.1   DOLCE

Foundational ontologies are *generic*, *heavyweight* and designed for *reference* purposes (cf. the classification of ontologies in Chapter 3, Section 2, on page 44). Using a foundational ontology as a modelling basis means relating core concepts and associations to some proposed invariant categories of human cognition (which are reflected in the foundational ontology itself). This prompts the ontology engineer to sharpen his notions with respect to the distinctions made in the foundational ontology. What is typically gained is an increased understanding of one's own ontology.

Chapter 6 has discussed our decision for the DOLCE foundational ontology. First, DOLCE provides the required theories for modelling contexts, plans and information objects. All of them are required for our ontologies and are explained below. Second, DOLCE commits to ontological choices (perdurantism, possibilism, being multiplicative, being descriptive) which are suitable for our domain. Third, DOLCE comes both in a reference and in an application version, axiomatized in quantified modal logic and implemented description logics (OWL DL), respectively. That allows us to formalize our own ontology with a maximum of expressiveness and to use it for run time reasoning later on.

We have already introduced DOLCE in Chapter 6, Section 2. However, we repeat it here in more detail and for the sake of readability. DOLCE (Descriptive Ontology for Linguistic and Cognitive Engineering) classifies entities into four categories. These are, as shown in Figure 7.2, Endurants, Perdurants, Qualities and Abstracts [Masolo et al., 2002]. The main relation between Endurants (i.e., objects or substances) and Perdurants (i.e., events or pro-

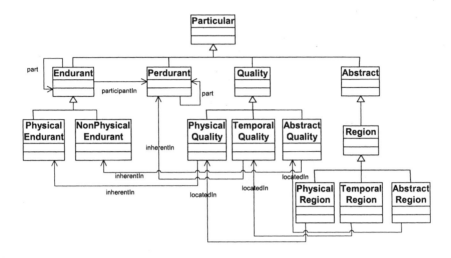

Figure 7.2.   Sketch of DOLCE as UML class diagram. [Gangemi et al., 2004b]

cesses) is that of participation: an Endurant "lives" in time by participating in a Perdurant. DOLCE introduces Qualities as another category that includes the properties of objects or events which we can perceive, measure or conventionally assert (e.g., color, density, legal validity). Finally, Abstracts do not have spatial or temporal qualities, nor are they qualities themselves. In particular, Regions are used to encode the representation of Qualities as conventionalized in some metric or conceptual space (e.g., a color space, a musical pitch space, a set of legal values). Every category features a whole taxonomy of specializations.

1.2   Descriptions & Situations (DnS)

The domain we want to model, namely that of software components and Web services, requires an ontological formalization of context. The most prominent examples for the need of context modelling are the different views that might exist on data. Data can play the role of both input and output, depending on the context considered. In Chapter 6, Section 1, page 96, we have already discussed that a theory for contextualization is required for that reason.

DOLCE provides an ontological theory of contexts that comes in the form of an ontology module. The module's name is Descriptions & Situations (DnS). DnS can be considered an *ontology design pattern* for structuring core and domain ontologies that require contextualization. The following paragraph provides a brief introduction. For a more detailed description please cf. [Gangemi et al., 2004b, Gangemi and Mika, 2003].

When Descriptions & Situations is used with DOLCE, the DOLCE entities are called *ground* entities and the newly introduced entities of Descriptions & Situations are called *descriptive* entities. We also visualize this distinction in Figure 7.3. Parameters, Roles and Courses are the descriptive entities which are special kinds of ConceptDescriptions (a DOLCE:NonAgentiveSocial-Object).[1] The descriptive entities "describe" the ground entities in the following way:[2] Parameters are valuedBy DOLCE:Regions, Roles are playedBy DOLCE:Endurants and Courses sequence DOLCE:Perdurants. The descriptive entities are aggregated by a SituationDescription via the defines association. The SituationDescription ontologically represents the context.

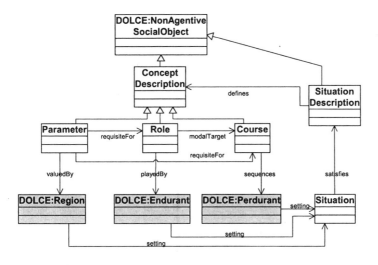

Figure 7.3.   The Descriptions & Situations (DnS) ontology module as UML class diagram. Grey classes represent the *ground* entities of DOLCE. *Descriptive Entities* are Parameters, Roles and Courses. [Gangemi et al., 2004b]

Furthermore, the module can be used to reify the satisfiability relation, viz., $\models$, of the underlying logic. As a result, we have a satisfies association between two sets of assertions. The first set is the Situation which groups ground entities via the setting association. The second set of assertions is the Situation-Description. A Situation satisfies a SituationDescription if its components describe the ground entities according to specified rules. The Descriptions & Situations module only defines the most generic satisfies association implying

---

[1]Throughout Chapter 7, concepts and associations are labelled in a namespace-like manner. Namespace-prefixes indicate the module where concepts and associations are defined. If no namespace is given, concepts and associations are assumed to be defined in the ontology module currently discussed.

[2]The reader may note, that we occasionally use concept and association names (written in sans serif and preceded by a namespace to clarify their origin) as subjects, objects and predicates of the sentences.

that at least some components of a SituationDescription must describe entities in the Situation. This constraint is minimal and for specialized Situation-Descriptions additional constraints should be given in order to reason with the satisfaction of candidate Situations. One example is the module discussed next: the Ontology of Plans.

1.3   Ontology of Plans (OoP)

One of the explicit requirements derived from the *Transactional Settings, Secure Communication, Analyzing Message Contexts* and *Detecting Loops in Interorganizational Workflows* use cases is the possibility to model workflow information between software components or between Web services. One of the DOLCE modules, the Ontology of Plans (OoP), formalizes a theory of plans in a generic way. It can be reused to model workflow information as well.

The Ontology of Plans applies the ontology design pattern of Descriptions & Situations to characterize planning concepts. The intended use of the module is to specify plans at an abstract level independent from existing calculi. It is expected that the concepts of the module are implemented as a framework to define detailed or approximate plans for any use (social, personal, computational) by appropriate tools. The resulting plans would then be grounded in some system that implements a set of functionalities and reasons according to the specifications given here. For a detailed description the reader is referred to [Gangemi et al., 2004b].

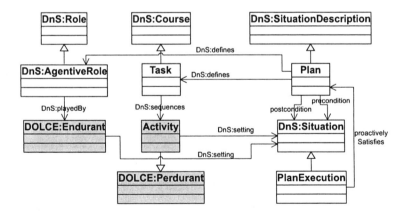

Figure 7.4.   The Ontology of Plans as UML class diagram. Grey classes represent *ground* entities. Concepts from Descriptions & Situations are labelled namespace-like with DnS. [Gangemi et al., 2004b]

Plans are special kinds of DnS:SituationDescriptions, which DnS:define Tasks (a special kind of DnS:Course). A typical hierarchy of Tasks (case, branching, synchronization, concurrency, cycling, etc.) is characterized with the help of succession relations. Furthermore, Tasks DnS:sequence Activities — a specialization of DOLCE:Perdurant. Activities are complex actions that are at least partly conventionally planned.

Specializations of the satisfies association of Descriptions & Situations are applied to express preconditions, postconditions, and several types of satisfaction between a Plan and specific DnS:Situations, e.g., proactively-Satisfies.

As an example we might consider the CustomerEntityBean which modifies the Customer table (cf. our motivating example in Chapter 2, Section 3.1, page 24). In order to formalize this setting, we introduce the *CustomerEntity-BeanPlan* which DnS:defines the *ModifyTable* task. An actual execution of this task is represented via the *23:58:00* instance to reflect its timestamp, i.e., DnS:sequences(*ModifyTable, 23:58:00*). We keep this as a running example, refine and extend it as we move along.

(Ex1) OoP:Plan(*CustomerEntityBeanPlan*)
(Ex2) DnS:defines(*CustomerEntityBeanPlan, ModifyTable*)
(Ex3) OoP:Task(*ModifyTable*)
(Ex4) DnS:sequences(*ModifyTable, 23:58:00*)
(Ex5) OoP:Activity(*23:58:00*)
(Ex6) OoP:PlanExecution(*ModifyTableExecution*)
(Ex7) DnS:setting(*23:58:00, ModifyTableExecution*)

1.4   Ontology of Information Objects (OIO)

In our motivating examples we have encountered fundamental ontological questions, e.g., how to model the relationship between a user in an information system and its corresponding natural person (cf. Section 3.1 in Chapter 2). Hence, another requirement for our ontology identified in Chapter 6, Section 1, is a concise distinction between entities in an information system and the real world.

The DOLCE library provides another module that allows us to formalize such relationships: the Ontology of Information Objects (OIO). Information objects are the core notion of a *semiotic ontology design pattern* which we briefly discuss here. For a more detailed discussion please cf. [Gangemi et al., 2004b].

A content (information) transferred in any modality is assumed to be equivalent to a kind of social object called InformationObject. InformationObjects are spatio-temporal entities of abstract information as described in Shannon's communication theory, hence they are assumed to be in time and realized by some entity.

Figure 7.5, which depicts the concepts and associations of the module, is best explained by a concrete example. The encoding of the CustomerEntity-Bean in Java could be considered an InformationObject. In this case, the

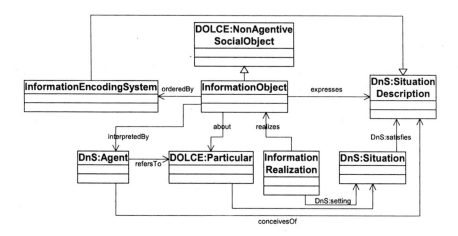

Figure 7.5.   The Ontology of Information Objects as UML class diagram. Concepts defined in DOLCE and Descriptions & Situations (DnS) are labelled with corresponding namespaces. [Gangemi et al., 2004b]

InformationObject would be orderedBy the Java language (the Information-EncodingSystem) and realizedBy a specific appearance of the algorithm in main memory (e.g., the contents between memory addresses *0x2112-0x5150*). The CustomerEntityBean expresses a specific OoP:Plan of computational tasks (such as *ModifyTable*) and is interpretedBy a CPU.[3]

(Ex8)   OIO:InformationObject(*CustomerEntityBean*)
(Ex9)   OIO:orderedBy(*CustomerEntityBean, Java*)
(Ex10) OIO:InformationEncodingSystem(*Java*)
(Ex11) OIO:realizedBy(*CustomerEntityBean, 0x2112-0x5150*)
(Ex12) OIO:InformationRealization(*0x2112-0x5150*)
(Ex13) OIO:expresses(*CustomerEntityBean, CustomerEntityBeanPlan*)
(Ex14) OIO:interpretedBy(*CustomerEntityBean,CPU*)
(Ex15) DOLCE:MaterialArtifact(*CPU*)

2.   Core Software Ontology (CSO)

   In order to model the required aspects of components and services, it is necessary to identify fundamental concepts, such as software or data, and to formalize them by reusing our modelling basis. In this section, we contribute the *Core Software Ontology*, which formalizes such fundamental concepts. The

---

[3]We assume without further mention that for any association there exists an inverse. The naming of associations and their inverses follows an intuitive scheme, e.g., the inverse of realizedBy is called realizes.

Core Software Ontology can be classified as *reference*, *core* and *heavyweight*, and is later reused to formalize the required aspects of components and services. Thus, the Core Software Ontology acts as a common basis for the Core Ontologies of Software Components and Web Services which are built in the subsequent sections.

Having a common basis is beneficial because it requires modelling the fundamental concepts only once. In essence, the Core Software Ontology meets all modelling requirements which are common to software components and Web services (as derived by our use cases starting on page 66). These are: *API descriptions, semantic API descriptions, workflow information, access rights* and *policies*. The modelling requirements constrain our modelling horizon and give us indications which concepts and associations we have to model. When formalizing concepts and associations, we usually specialize the ontology design patterns provided by DOLCE and its modules. If such design patterns are not applicable the modelling is left to our discretion. Note that we consider our contributed ontologies as being formalized in DOLCE's representation formalism, viz., modal logic S5. Although we do not explicitly use modal quantifiers, their usage is rooted in DOLCE's concepts and associations, cf. [Masolo et al., 2003], which we reuse for our modelling.

2.1   Software vs. Data

As mentioned above, the Core Software Ontology formalizes the most fundamental concepts required to model both components and services. We start in this section with a detailed discussion of software and data. In order to clarify both concepts, which are heavily inflicted by polysemy, it is necessary to identify and formalize the entities of the computational domain. The computational domain has a reality of its own, consisting of data manipulated by programs that implement algorithms. The programs that manipulate the data are usually referred to as software. Upon close inspection, it seems that the term software is overloaded and refers to at least three different concepts [Gangemi et al., 2003b]:

1 The encoding of an algorithm specification in some kind of representation (i.e., OIO:InformationEncodingSystem). Encoding can be either in mind, on paper or any other form. The CustomerEntityBean can be represented as Java or pseudo code, for instance. This is SoftwareAsCode and is a kind of OIO:InformationObject.

2 The realization of the code in a concrete hardware. These realizations are the DOLCE:PhysicalEndurants that are stored on hard disc or residing in memory. Henceforth, we will call them ComputationalObjects (a special kind of OIO:InformationRealization). This could be the appearance of the CustomerEntityBean in main memory that can be interpreted and

executed by the CPU. Hence, the difference between 1 and 2 is that 2 is physically present in some hardware.

3 The running system, which is the result of an execution of a Computational-Object. This is the form of software which manifests itself in a sequence of activities in the computational domain, e.g., the increment of a variable, the comparison of data, the storage of data on the hard disc, etc. This form of software is a DOLCE:Perdurant which we will call Computational-Activity.

ComputationalObjects (item 2) are a specialization of OIO:Information-Realization (any entity that realizes an OIO:InformationObject) as introduced in the Ontology of Information Objects. ComputationalActivities (item 3) are a specialization of OoP:Activity as introduced in the Ontology of Plans. ComputationalObjects and ComputationalActivities are the entities that live in the computational domain. The definitions below formalize the described properties.[4]

(D1) ComputationalObject(x) $=_{def}$ OIO:InformationRealization(x) $\wedge$
$\forall y$(DOLCE:participantIn(x, y) $\rightarrow$ ComputationalActivity(y)) $\wedge$
$\exists d$(DOLCE:specificallyConstantlyDependsOn(x, d) $\wedge$
Hardware(d))

(D2) ComputationalActivity(x) $=_{def}$ OoP:Activity(x) $\wedge$
$\forall y$(DOLCE:participantIn(y, x) $\rightarrow$ ComputationalObject(y)) $\wedge$
$\exists c$(DOLCE:specificallyConstantlyDependsOn(x, c) $\wedge$
ComputationalObject(c))

ComputationalObjects are characterized by the fact that they are necessarily dependent on Hardware which is a DOLCE:MaterialArtifact. The execution of a ComputationalObject may lead to ComputationalActivities. Hence, ComputationalActivities depend on the existence of a corresponding ComputationalObject. A suitable dependence association is axiomatized in DOLCE and is called specificallyConstantlyDependsOn:[5]

(D3) DOLCE:specificallyConstantlyDependsOn(x, y) $=_{def}$
$\Box(\exists t$(DOLCE:presentAt(x, t)) $\wedge$ $\forall t$(DOLCE:presentAt(x, t) $\rightarrow$
DOLCE:presentAt(y, t)))

---

[4]We consider unbound variables in definitions, axioms, and theorems as universally quantified.

[5]An entity that specificallyConstantlyDependsOn another entity is similar to weak entities in UML class diagrams. An entity x specificallyConstantlyDependsOn another entity y iff, at any time t, x cannot be present at t unless y is also present at t. DOLCE formalizes this association by using the DOLCE:presentAt(x, t) association that stands for "x is present (exists) during the time interval or instant t." Note that $ql_T(t', x)$ is the temporal location of x in t'. [Masolo et al., 2003]

(D4) DOLCE:presentAt$(x, t) =_{def}$
$\exists t'(\text{DOLCE:ql}_T(t', x) \land \text{DOLCE:part}(t, t'))$

As an example, we might consider the ComputationalObject residing in memory between addresses *0x2112* and *0x5150* whose (partial) execution leads to the ComputationalActivity carried out at and identified by the timestamp *23:58:00*. The ComputationalObject could be a concrete appearance of the `CustomerEntityBean` (cf. the motivating example on page 24) and the ComputationalActivity could be the execution of one of its methods.

(Ex16) ComputationalObject(*0x2112-0x5150*)
(Ex17) ComputationalActivity(*23:58:00*)
(Ex18) specificallyConstantlyDependsOn(*23:58:00, 0x2112-0x5150*)

Regarding item 1, we characterize SoftwareAsCode (which we abbreviate to Software) as an OIO:InformationObject. Accordingly, we specialize the design pattern represented by the Ontology of Information Objects (cf. Figure 7.5 on page 114). First, we constrain the OIO:realizedBy association to ComputationalObjects. Second, we say that Software OIO:expresses an OoP:Plan (cf. Figure 7.6 for an overview). The OoP:Plan consists of an arbitrary number of ComputationalTasks that DnS:sequence Computational-Activities (cf. Definition (D6) below). As explained in the Ontology of Plans (Section 1.3), Tasks are the descriptive counterparts of OoP:Activities which are actually carried out. Definition (D5) below captures this intuition of software.

(D5) Software$(x) =_{def}$
OIO:InformationObject$(x) \land \forall y(\text{OIO:realizedBy}(x, y) \rightarrow$
ComputationalObject$(y)) \land \exists p, t(\text{OoP:Plan}(p) \land$
OIO:expresses$(x, p) \land$ ComputationalTask$(t) \land$ DnS:defines$(p, t))$
(D6) ComputationalTask$(x) =_{def}$ OoP:Task$(x) \land$
$\forall y(\text{DnS:sequences}(x, y) \rightarrow$ ComputationalActivity$(y))$

The ComputationalObject introduced in (Ex16) can be regarded as a concrete realization of Software (in our case as the `CustomerEntityBean`). We have learned in our motivating example that the bean modifies the `Customer` table. Hence, its corresponding OoP:Plan DnS:defines a ComputationalTask that represents the modification.[6] The ComputationalActivity introduced in (Ex17) could be one specific execution of this task.

(Ex19) Software(*CustomerEntityBean*)

---

[6]Note that the detail of modelling ComputationalTasks is a matter of choice. In principle, *ModifyTable* can be considered a complex task and can be broken down to CPU operations.

(Ex20) OIO:realizes(*0x2112-0x5150*, *CustomerEntityBean*)
(Ex21) OIO:expresses(*CustomerEntityBean*, *CustomerEntityBeanPlan*)
(Ex22) OoP:Plan(*CustomerEntityBeanPlan*)
(Ex23) DnS:defines(*CustomerEntityBeanPlan*, *ModifyTable*)
(Ex24) ComputationalTask(*ModifyTable*)
(Ex25) DnS:sequences(*ModifyTable*, *23:58:00*)

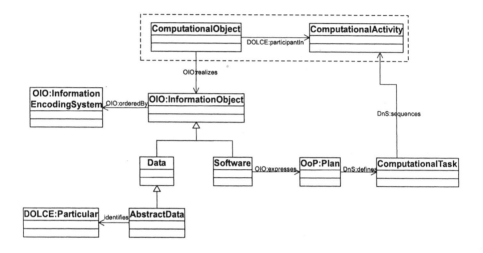

Figure 7.6. The classification of software and data. Concepts and associations taken from DOLCE, Descriptions & Situations (DnS), the Ontology of Plans (OoP), the Ontology of Information Objects (OIO) are labelled with a namespace.

We consider the data which are manipulated by the programs as ComputationalObjects as well. This reflects the fact that the appearances in the main memory or on the hard disc can be interpreted as instructions for the CPU (i.e., as software) or can be treated as data from the viewpoint of another program. For example, the operating system manipulates application software (loading and unloading it into memory, etc.) much like application software manipulates application data.

Hence, Data can also be considered as a special kind of OIO:Information-Object. The difference to Software is that Data does not OIO:express an OoP:Plan. Furthermore, we introduce AbstractData as a special kind of Data that identifies something different from itself. An example for Abstract-Data might be a user account in a Unix operating system which has a physical counterpart in the real world. Thus, we say that AbstractData identifies a DOLCE:Particular (a natural person, a company, a physical object) [Gangemi et al., 2004b]. The identifies association is a specialization of OIO:about. Definitions (D7), (D8), and (D9) capture these intuitions.

(D7) $\text{Data}(x) =_{def} \text{OIO:InformationObject}(x) \wedge$
$\forall y(\text{OIO:realizedBy}(x, y) \rightarrow \text{ComputationalObject}(y))$

(D8) $\text{AbstractData}(x) =_{def}$
$\text{Data}(x) \wedge \exists y(\text{DOLCE:Particular}(y) \wedge \text{identifies}(x, y))$

(D9) $\text{identifies}(x, y) =_{def}$
$\text{OIO:about}(x, y) \wedge \text{AbstractData}(x) \wedge \text{DOLCE:Particular}(y) \wedge x \neq y$

As an example, we might introduce another two ComputationalObjects that represent the dbuser and the Customer table in main memory. The dbuser is AbstractData because it identifies a DOLCE:NaturalPerson outside the computational domain, in this case the author.[7]

(Ex26) $\text{ComputationalObject}(\textit{0x22-0x23})$

(Ex27) $\text{ComputationalObject}(\textit{0x316-0x812})$

(Ex28) $\text{AbstractData}(\textit{dbuser})$

(Ex29) $\text{Data}(\textit{CustomerTable})$

(Ex30) $\text{OIO:realizedBy}(\textit{dbuser, 0x22-0x23})$

(Ex31) $\text{OIO:realizedBy}(\textit{CustomerTable, 0x316-0x812})$

(Ex32) $\text{identifies}(\textit{dbuser, DanielOberle})$

(Ex33) $\text{DOLCE:NaturalPerson}(\textit{DanielOberle})$

The theorem (T1) below is an entailment of our axiomatization. (T1) states that Software must also be considered as Data. As discussed before, this is intuitively clear because an algorithm can be considered as Data from the viewpoint of a compiler, for example. Comparing (D5) and (D7), we find that Software additionally OIO:expresses an OoP:Plan with at least one ComputationalTask. Thus, Software is more specific than Data.

(T1) $\text{Software}(x) \rightarrow \text{Data}(x)$

2.2 API Description

The formalization of fundamental concepts like Software and Data is a prerequisite for defining API descriptions which is explicitly required by the *Automatic Generation of Web Service Descriptions*, *Exception Handling* and *Monitoring of Changes* use cases. Assuming the object oriented paradigm (to which we limit ourselves in the remainder of this book), we need to model classes, methods, their inputs, outputs, and datatypes, as well as exceptions. Note that we do not strive to formalize all constructs of object orientation. We limit ourselves to the particular subset that is necessary to formalize simple

---

[7]Note that the Customer table as a whole is Data, but its specific rows, i.e., customer entries, are Abstract-Data.

API descriptions (e.g., we do not formalize specific objects, polymorphism or inheritance). Below, we give our understanding of those concepts.

(D10) $\text{Class}(x) =_{def} \text{Software}(x) \wedge \forall y(\text{DOLCE:properPart}(x, y) \rightarrow (\text{Data}(y) \vee \text{Method}(y)))$

(D11) $\text{Method}(x) =_{def} \text{Software}(x) \wedge \forall y(\text{DOLCE:properPart}(y, x) \rightarrow \text{Class}(y))$

(D12) $\text{Exception}(x) =_{def} \text{Class}(x) \wedge \forall y(\text{methodThrows}(y, x) \rightarrow \text{Method}(y))$

(D13) $\text{DOLCE:properPart}(x, y) =_{def}$
      $\text{DOLCE:part}(x, y) \wedge \neg \text{DOLCE:part}(y, x)$

(A1) $\text{methodRequires}(x, y) \rightarrow \text{Method}(x) \wedge \text{Data}(y)$

(A2) $\text{methodYields}(x, y) \rightarrow \text{Method}(x) \wedge \text{Data}(y)$

(A3) $\text{methodThrows}(x, y) \rightarrow \text{methodYields}(x, y) \wedge \text{Exception}(y)$

(A4) $\text{dataType}(x, y) \rightarrow \text{Data}(x) \wedge (\text{Region}(y) \vee \text{Data}(y))$

Definition (D10) considers a Class as a special kind of Software that encapsulates an arbitrary number of Data and an arbitrary number of Methods. Vice versa, a Method is defined as being a part of a Class, having input and output parameters and throwing exceptions. The associations between Methods and their parameters and exceptions are established via methodRequires, methodYields and methodThrows (cf. (D11), (A1), (A2), and (A3)). Exceptions are special kinds of Classes as defined in (D12). dataType relates Data with specific kinds of DOLCE:Regions in the case of simple datatypes, such as strings or integers, or with other Data in the case of complex datatypes, e.g., other classes (cf. Axiom (A4)).

As an example, both the CustomerEntityBean and the WebShopServlet would be Classes. For the bean, we just specialize the instance introduced in (Ex19) on page 117. The set of instances below also formalizes the servlet's doGet() method:

(Ex34) $\text{Class}(WebShopServlet)$

(Ex35) $\text{Class}(CustomerEntityBean)$

(Ex36) $\text{DOLCE:properPart}(WebShopServlet, doGet)$

(Ex37) $\text{Method}(doGet)$

(Ex38) $\text{methodRequires}(doGet, req)$

(Ex39) $\text{methodRequires}(doGet, resp)$

(Ex40) $\text{Data}(req)$

(Ex41) $\text{Data}(resp)$

(Ex42) $\text{dataType}(req, HttpServletRequest)$

(Ex43) $\text{dataType}(resp, HttpServletResponse)$

(Ex44) $\text{Class}(HttpServletRequest)$

(Ex45) $\text{Class}(HttpServletResponse)$

2.3   Semantic API Description

Another explicit requirement of the *Component Classification and Discovery*, *Semantics of Parameters*, *Selecting Service Functionality* and *Incompatible Inputs and Outputs* use cases is to model semantic API descriptions. The use cases propose to model the meaning of methods and parameters in order to allow for a more powerful search over a large unfamiliar API, for instance.

Our modelling so far already allows to achieve this goal. As depicted in Figure 7.7, the meaning or behavior of a Method can be modelled via OIO:expresses and a corresponding OoP:Plan. We already gave an example, namely the *CustomerEntityBeanPlan*, in (Ex22) on page 118. The semantics of parameters, as opposed to their datatypes, can be modelled via OIO:about which can point to any concept in the ontology. Thus, it is possible to model that the getPrice() method returns a specific Currency (a specialization of DOLCE:AbstractRegion), for example.

(Ex46) Method(*getPrice*)
(Ex47) methodYields(*getPrice, result*)
(Ex48) Data(*result*)
(Ex49) dataType(*result, xsd:float*)
(Ex50) OIO:about(*result, Euro*)
(Ex51) Currency(*Euro*)

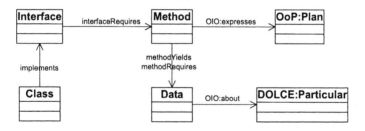

Figure 7.7.   Semantic API description.

We here introduce the notion of an Interface in order to group methods and parameters independently of the Classes they belong to (cf. (D14) and (A5) below). The Interface does not coincide with Java interfaces because it allows to grasp additional information as explained above. In our ontology, the Interface has to be classified as Data as it cannot be executed, i.e., it does not OIO:express an OoP:Plan. Different Classes may implement the same Interface as stated in (A6). In doing so, we are able to model that different classes provide different names for methods with comparable functionality (e.g., getPrice() vs. getCost()).

(D14)　Interface$(x) =_{def}$ Data$(x) \land \forall m$(inferfaceRequires$(x, m) \rightarrow$
　　　　　$(\exists p$(OIO:expresses$(m, p) \land$ OoP:Plan$(p)) \land$
　　　　　$\forall d$(methodRequires$(m, d) \rightarrow$
　　　　　$\exists e$(DOLCE:Particular$(e) \land$ OIO:about$(d, e)))))$

(A5)　interfaceRequires$(x, y) \rightarrow$
　　　　　DOLCE:properPart$(x, y) \land$ Interface$(x) \land$ Method(y)

(A6)　implements$(x, y) \rightarrow$ Class$(x) \land$ Interface$(y) \land$
　　　　　$\forall m_1 \exists m_2$(interfaceRequires$(y, m_1) \rightarrow$ DOLCE:properPart$(x, m_2))$

2.4　Workflow Information

The possibility of modelling workflow information, such as information about the WebShopServlet invoking the CustomerEntityBean, is explicitly required by the use cases *Transactional Settings*, *Secure Communication*, *Analyzing Message Contexts* and *Detecting Loops in Interorganizational Workflows*.

For modelling workflow information, we use and specialize the ontology design pattern of the Ontology of Plans (cf. Figure 7.4 on page 112) which in turn builds on Descriptions & Situations. We do so because the design pattern allows abstracting from concrete, i.e., actually executed, workflows. That means, we use ComputationalTasks, which are OoP:Tasks, to represent invocations, the addition of two integers, etc., rather than the actual executions of such tasks (which would be ComputationalActivities). ComputationalTasks are grouped and linked via the OoP:successor and OoP:predecessor associations in an OoP:Plan (a DnS:SituationDescription).

The workflow information we need to model is twofold. First, we have to model invocations between software. Second, we also need to model the inputs and outputs of tasks because the Ontology of Plans does not provide such capabilities.

Invocations Between Software

We start with two associations, viz., executes and accesses, to formalize invocations between Software. Below, (D15) introduces executes as "shortcut" between Software, such as Class or Method, and a ComputationalTask. For example, the doGet() method of our WebShopServlet executes an invocation task.

(D16) introduces accesses as "shortcut" between the ComputationalTask and the Software or Data that is being called or modified by the task. For example, the invocation task of the WebShopServlet accesses the Customer-EntityBean. The sequence of executes and accesses can be further abbreviated by invokes which is declared as being transitive (cf. (D17) and (A7)). Axioms (A8) and (A9) are introduced for convenience. Regarding (A8), we say that also a Class executes a ComputationalTask when one of its Methods executes this task. Regarding (A9), we state that invokes also holds when we have succeeding tasks.

(D15) executes$(x, y) =_{def}$ Software$(x) \wedge$ ComputationalTask$(y) \wedge$
$\exists co, ca, p($ComputationalObject$(co) \wedge$ ComputationalActivity$(ca) \wedge$
OoP:Plan$(p) \wedge$ OIO:realizedBy$(x, co) \wedge$ OIO:expresses$(x, p) \wedge$
DnS:defines$(p, y) \wedge$ DnS:sequences$(y, ca) \wedge$
DOLCE:participantIn$(co, ca))$

(D16) accesses$(x, y) =_{def}$
ComputationalTask$(x) \wedge$ Data$(y) \wedge \exists ca, co($DnS:sequences$(x, ca) \wedge$
ComputationalActivity$(ca) \wedge$ DOLCE:participantIn$(co, ca) \wedge$
ComputationalObject$(co) \wedge$ OIO:realizes$(co, y))$

(D17) invokes$(x, y) =_{def} \exists z($executes$(x, z) \wedge$ accesses$(z, y))$

(A7) invokes$(x, z) \leftarrow$ invokes$(x, y) \wedge$ invokes(y, z)

(A8) executes$(x, y) \leftarrow$
(executes$(z, y) \wedge$ Method$(z) \wedge$ DOLCE:properPart$(x, z) \wedge$ Class(x)

(A9) invokes$(x, z) \leftarrow$
executes$(x, y) \wedge$ OoP:successor$(y, t) \wedge$ accesses(t, z)

In some environments, calls are executed on behalf of a user whose identity can vary at run time or the authentication can be changed explicitly (called the run-as paradigm). Our running example requires us to express the context switch of the CustomerEntityBean, for instance. In order to model this kind of information we introduce the association contextUser as shown below.

(D18) contextUser$(x, y) =_{def}$
DnS:attitudeTowards$(x, y) \wedge$ User$(x) \wedge$ ComputationalTask(y)

Revisiting our example, we have a ComputationalTask that models the WebShopServlet's call of the CustomerEntityBean. We also have a task that models the modification of the Customer table on behalf of the bean. Note that this task is executed with dbuser's credentials. In the examples below, (Ex55) can be inferred from (Ex34), (Ex36), (Ex37), (Ex52), (Ex53), (Ex54), (A7) and (A8).

(Ex52) ComputationalTask(*CallBean*)
(Ex53) executes(*doGet, CallBean*)
(Ex54) accesses(*CallBean, CustomerEntityBean*)
(Ex55) (*Ex34*), ..., (*A8*) $\models$ invokes(*WebShopServlet, CustomerEntityBean*)
(Ex56) ComputationalTask(*ModifyTable*)
(Ex57) executes(*CustomerEntityBean, ModifyTable*)
(Ex58) contextUser(*dbuser, ModifyTable*)
(Ex59) accesses(*ModifyTable, CustomerTable*)

Inputs and Outputs

Besides invocations, we also need to model the Inputs and Outputs of tasks. The Ontology of Plans does not provide such capabilities. Inputs and Outputs are required when we want to represent the information of a WS-BPEL workflow, for instance. Inputs and Outputs are DnS:Roles which are both DnS:playedBy Data and DnS:definedBy an OoP:Plan (cf. (D19), (D20) and (A12)). The relationships between Inputs (Outputs) and Computational-Tasks are modelled by inputFor (outputFor) as specified in (A10) and (A11).[8] The difference between Inputs and Outputs is that the former must be present before the latter (cf. (A13)).

(D19) $\text{Input}(x) =_{def} \text{DnS:Role}(x) \wedge \forall y(\text{DnS:playedBy}(x,y) \rightarrow \text{Data}(y))$
(D20) $\text{Output}(x) =_{def} \text{DnS:Role}(x) \wedge \forall y(\text{DnS:playedBy}(x,y) \rightarrow \text{Data}(y))$

(A10) $\text{inputFor}(x,y) \rightarrow$
       $\text{DnS:modalTarget}(x,y) \wedge \text{Input}(x) \wedge \text{ComputationalTask}(y)$
(A11) $\text{outputFor}(x,y) \rightarrow$
       $\text{DnS:modalTarget}(x,y) \wedge \text{Output}(x) \wedge \text{ComputationalTask}(y)$
(A12) $\text{Input}(x) \vee \text{Output}(x) \rightarrow \exists p(\text{OoP:Plan}(p) \wedge \text{DnS:defines}(p,x))$
(A13) $\text{ComputationalTask}(ct) \rightarrow \forall d_1, d_2(\forall i, o(\text{inputFor}(i,ct) \wedge$
       $\text{DnS:playedBy}(i,d_1) \wedge \text{outputFor}(o,ct) \wedge \text{DnS:playedBy}(o,d_2)) \rightarrow$
       $\exists t_1, t_2(\text{presentAt}(d_1,t_1) \wedge \text{presentAt}(d_2,t_2) \wedge t_1 < t_2))$

As a concrete example, consider the Input for *ModifyTable* which would be the Customer table (cf. (Ex60), (Ex61) and (Ex62) below).

(Ex60) $\text{Input}(\textit{ModifyTableInput})$
(Ex61) $\text{DnS:playedBy}(\textit{ModifyTableInput}, \textit{CustomerTable})$
(Ex62) $\text{inputFor}(\textit{ModifyTableInput}, \textit{ModifyTable})$

2.5   Access Rights and Policies

The requirement to model access rights and policies stems from the *Access Rights, Analyzing Message Contexts* and *Policy Handling* use cases. In general, access rights are required to state that access is granted for a specific user on a specific resource. Policies can be regarded as a generalization of access rights. They define high-level guidelines that constrain the behavior of an information system.

We use and specialize Descriptions & Situations for modelling access rights and policies. The design pattern represented by Descriptions & Situations (cf. Figure 7.3 on page 111) provides us with the basic primitives of context

---

[8]Both are specializations of DnS:modalTarget, viz., the generic association holding between DnS:Roles and DnS:Courses.

modelling, such as the notion of roles, which allows us to talk about subjects and objects of a policy on the abstract level, i.e., independent of the entities that play such roles. As we have learned in Section 1.2, page 110, Descriptions & Situations therefore distinguishes between *descriptive* and *ground* entities.

In a first step, it is necessary to introduce further *ground* entities which are required later on. (D21) below specifies a User as a special kind of Abstract-Data which identifies a DnS:Agent. The intuition behind User is a user account in an operating system. Hence, Users identify DnS:Agents which are either DOLCE:AgentivePhysicalObjects or DOLCE:AgentiveSocial-Objects. Most frequently, but not always, a natural person is associated with such an account. We aggregate Users to a UserGroup by exploiting DOLCE:-Collection in (D22).

(D21) $\text{User}(x) =_{def} \text{AbstractData}(x) \land \forall y(\text{identifies}(x, y) \rightarrow \text{DnS:Agent}(y))$

(D22) $\text{UserGroup}(x) =_{def}$
$\text{DOLCE:Collection}(x) \land \forall y(\text{DOLCE:member}(x, y) \rightarrow \text{User}(y))$

In a second step, we specialize the *descriptive* entities of Descriptions & Situations, viz., DnS:Roles, DnS:Courses, DnS:Parameters, and DnS:SituationDescriptions as follows. First, we introduce two DnS:Roles to represent the subject and the object of a policy in (D23) and (D24). PolicySubjects are DnS:AgentiveRoles and can be DnS:playedBy Users or UserGroups. PolicyObjects are DnS:NonAgentiveRoles and can be DnS:playedBy Data. Second, we need to represent the predicate of a policy by a special kind of DnS:Course. (D6) on page 117 already introduced ComputationalTask which meets this requirement. We further aggregate such tasks to TaskCollections in (D25). The intuition behind Task-Collections are the security "roles" in operating or database systems. That means a TaskCollection groups ComputationalTasks, such as read, write or execute. Third, we introduce Constraints as special kinds of DnS:Parameter. The ComputationalTask or TaskCollections can be constrained in some way, e.g., a Web service policy might state that an invocation is only possible with Kerberos or X509 authentication (cf. (D26)). Finally, we construct a Policy-Description, viz., a special kind of DnS:SituationDescription, from the afore-mentioned concepts.[9] Figure 7.8 provides an overview.

(D23) $\text{PolicySubject}(x) =_{def}$
$\text{DnS:AgentiveRole}(x) \land \forall y(\text{DnS:playedBy}(x, y) \rightarrow$

---

[9]Note that DnS:unifies is the generic association between DnS:SituationDescriptions and DOLCE:Collections.

$(\mathsf{User}(y) \vee \mathsf{UserGroup}(y))) \wedge \forall z(\mathsf{DnS{:}attitudeTowards}(x,z) \rightarrow$
$(\mathsf{ComputationalTask}(y) \vee \mathsf{TaskCollection}(y)))$

(D24) $\mathsf{PolicyObject}(x) =_{def}$
$\mathsf{DnS{:}NonAgentiveRole}(x) \wedge \forall y(\mathsf{DnS{:}playedBy}(x,y) \rightarrow$
$\mathsf{Data}(y)) \wedge \forall z(\mathsf{DnS{:}attitudeTowards}(x,z) \rightarrow$
$(\mathsf{ComputationalTask}(y) \vee \mathsf{TaskCollection}(y)))$

(D25) $\mathsf{TaskCollection}(x) =_{def} \mathsf{DOLCE{:}Collection}(x) \wedge$
$\forall y(\mathsf{DOLCE{:}member}(x,y) \rightarrow \mathsf{ComputationalTask}(y))$

(D26) $\mathsf{Constraint}(x) =_{def}$
$\mathsf{DnS{:}Parameter}(x) \wedge \forall y(\mathsf{DnS{:}requisiteFor}(x,y) \rightarrow$
$(\mathsf{ComputationalTask}(y) \vee \mathsf{TaskCollection}(y))) \wedge$
$\forall z(\mathsf{DnS{:}defines}(z,x) \rightarrow \mathsf{PolicyDescription}(z))$

(D27) $\mathsf{PolicyDescription}(x) =_{def}$
$\mathsf{DnS{:}SituationDescription}(x) \wedge \forall y(\mathsf{DnS{:}unifies}(x,y) \rightarrow$
$\mathsf{TaskCollection}(y)) \wedge \forall z(\mathsf{DnS{:}defines}(x,z) \rightarrow \mathsf{Constraint}(z) \vee$
$\mathsf{ComputationalTask}(z) \vee \mathsf{PolicySubject}(z) \vee \mathsf{PolicyObject}(z))$

It is worthwhile to spend some words on the DnS:attitudeTowards association between DnS:Roles and DnS:Courses. The DnS:attitudeTowards
association is a special kind of DnS:modalTarget and can be considered the
descriptive counterpart of the DOLCE:participantIn association. It is used to
state attitudes, attention, or even subjection that an object can have with respect to an action or process. In our case, DnS:attitudeTowards it is used
to state the relationship between PolicySubjects, as well as PolicyObjects,
and the ComputationalTask or TaskCollection. Descriptions & Situations
provides us with three initial specializations of DnS:attitudeTowards, viz.,
DnS:rightTowards, DnS:empoweredTo, and DnS:obligedTo. We further
refine DnS:rightTowards in (A14) below.

(A14) $\mathsf{computationalRightTowards}(x,y) \rightarrow \mathsf{DnS{:}rightTowards}(x,y) \wedge$
$\mathsf{PolicySubject}(x) \wedge (\mathsf{ComputationalTask}(y) \vee \mathsf{TaskCollection}(y))$

(A15) $\mathsf{computationalRightTowards}(x,z) \leftarrow$
$\mathsf{computationalRightTowards}(x,y) \wedge \mathsf{TaskCollection}(y) \wedge$
$\mathsf{DOLCE{:}member}(y,z) \wedge \mathsf{ComputationalTask}(z)$

(A16) $\mathsf{DnS{:}playedBy}(x,y) \leftarrow \mathsf{DnS{:}playedBy}(x,z) \wedge \mathsf{PolicySubject}(x) \wedge$
$\mathsf{UserGroup}(z) \wedge \mathsf{DOLCE{:}member}(z,y) \wedge \mathsf{User}(y)$

(A15) and (A16) infer the closure of all resulting rights considering User-
Groups and TaskCollections. A PolicySubject is granted rights on all tasks
which are members of the TaskCollection. Similarly, a User is granted all
access rights which are granted for his UserGroup.

An analysis of the descriptor of our WebShopServlet (web.xml, cf. Example 2.1 on page 23) lets us derive the following PolicyDescription. The HTTP

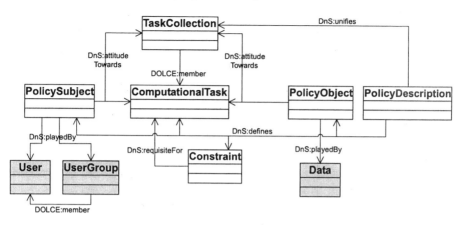

Figure 7.8. The Policy Description as UML class diagram. Grey classes represent *ground* entities, white classes the *descriptive* entities of Descriptions & Situations or specializations thereof.

basic authentication allows *anybody* to perform an HTTP GET on the servlet. We consider *anybody* as a UserGroup that has every User of the system as DOLCE:member.

(Ex63) PolicyDescription(*WebShopServletPolicy*)

(Ex64) DnS:defines(*WebShopServletPolicy*, *ServletCaller*)

(Ex65) PolicySubject(*ServletCaller*)

(Ex66) UserGroup(*anybody*)

(Ex67) DnS:playedBy(*ServletCaller*, *anybody*)

(Ex68) DnS:defines(*WebShopServletPolicy*, *GET*)

(Ex69) ComputationalTask(*GET*)

(Ex70) computationalRightTowards(*ServletCaller*, *GET*)

(Ex71) DnS:defines(*WebShopServletPolicy*, *ServletCallee*)

(Ex72) PolicyObject(*ServletCallee*)

(Ex73) Class(*WebShopServlet*)

(Ex74) DnS:playedBy(*ServletCallee*, *WebShopServlet*)

(Ex75) DnS:obligedTo(*ServletCallee*, *GET*)

3.   Core Ontology of Software Components (COSC)

In the last section we have presented a Core Software Ontology consisting of fundamental concepts and associations such as software, data, users, policies and so on. We separated the fundamental concepts in a core ontology to facilitate reuse.

Although some of the modelling requirements are already met by the Core Software Ontology, there remain further use cases that explicitly require the formalization of software component and Web service idiosyncracies. In this section, we present a possible *Core Ontology of Software Components* based on the Core Software Ontology that meets the remaining modelling requirements relevant for software components, viz., *Libraries and Licenses, Component Profiles*, and *Component Taxonomies* (cf. the application server use cases in Chapter 4, Section 2.1, page 66).

We start by formalizing our understanding of the term "software component." It requires special attention as there is a variety of interpretations that leads to ambiguity. We also put libraries and licenses in this core ontology because one of our use cases proposes to detect inconsistent configurations of components and their required libraries. Finally, we define a component profile that aggregates all relevant aspects of a component. We expect that this aggregation makes browsing and querying for developers more convenient. The component profile is envisioned to act as the central information source for software components rather than having bits and pieces all over the place. We finish by revisiting the Example 2.4 in Chapter 2, Section 3.2, and show how it can be formalized.

3.1   Formalization of the Term "Software Component"

Software componentry is a loosely defined term for a software technology proposing that software should be developed by glueing prefabricated components together as in the field of electronics or mechanics. Software componentry also proposes encapsulating software functionality for multiple use in a context-independent way, composable with other components and as a unit of independent deployment and versioning.[10]

Software components often assume the form of object-oriented classes conforming to a framework specification. However, software components differ from classes. The basic idea in object-oriented programming is that software should be written according to a mental model of the actual or imagined objects it represents. Software componentry, by contrast, makes no such assumptions.

The framework specifications prescribe (*i*) interfaces that must be implemented by components and (*ii*) protocols that define how components interact with each other. Examples of framework specifications are Enterprise JavaBeans (EJB) and the Component Object Model (COM) from Microsoft (cf. also Chapter 2, Section 3.1).

The definitions below formalize this intuition of software component as closely as possible. Assuming the object-oriented paradigm, (D30) below states that a SoftwareComponent is a special kind of CSO:Class that conforms to a FrameworkSpecification. According to the definition above, a

---

[10]Source: Wikipedia, http://en.wikipedia.org/wiki/Software_component, August 2005.

FrameworkSpecification is (*i*) a DOLCE:Collection of CSO:Interfaces and (*ii*) a special kind of OoP:Plan which specifies the interaction of components (cf. (D28)). Conformance means that at least one CSO:Interface prescribed by the FrameworkSpecification has to be implemented by the Software-Component (cf. (D29)).

(D28) FrameworkSpecification$(x) =_{def}$
OoP:Plan$(x) \wedge \exists y($DOLCE:Collection$(y) \wedge$ DnS:unifies$(x, y) \wedge$
$\forall z($DOLCE:member$(y, z) \rightarrow$ CSO:Interface$(z)))$
(D29) conforms$(x, y) =_{def}$ CSO:Class$(x) \wedge$ FrameworkSpecification$(y) \wedge$
$\exists i, c($CSO:Interface$(i) \wedge$ DOLCE:member$(c, i) \wedge$
DOLCE:Collection$(c) \wedge$ DnS:unifies$(y, c) \rightarrow$
CSO:implements$(x, i))$
(D30) SoftwareComponent$(x) =_{def}$
CSO:Class$(x) \wedge \exists y($conforms$(x, y) \wedge$ FrameworkSpecification$(y))$

Coming back to our running example, we would define the Customer-EntityBean as a SoftwareComponent that conforms to the *Enterprise-JavaBeans* FrameworkSpecification. In essence, the *EnterpriseJavaBeans* specification can be conceived as a set of Java interfaces (javax.ejb.*).

(Ex76) SoftwareComponent(*CustomerEntityBean*)
(Ex77) FrameworkSpecification(*EnterpriseJavaBeans*)
(Ex78) conforms(*CustomerEntityBean, EnterpriseJavaBeans*)

3.2 Libraries and Licenses

The *Library Dependencies and Versioning* and *Licensing* use cases require the modelling of libraries and licenses. Both use cases discuss the problem of conflicting libraries and incompatible licenses in the current configuration of an integrated software development environment (IDE). In the case of libraries, a lib1.jar might conflict with a lib2.jar in a specific version. For example, such information can be obtained from expert knowledge or from public sources, such as the RPM package manager.[11] However, the check for conflicts still remains a manual task. In the case of licenses, we find similar problems. Typically, software libraries are released under specific licenses such as GPL, LGPL, Apache, BSD, Public Domain, XFree86 or commercial closed source licenses.[12] The proliferation of different software licenses means increased work for software developers. They have to check whether used libraries have conflicting licenses.

---

[11]http://www.rpm.org
[12]http://www.gnu.org/philosophy/license-list.html

Therefore, the use cases propose an automatic check for conflicting libraries and incompatible licenses in an integrated software development environment (IDE) at development time. In order to realize either use case, we introduce the concepts of SoftwareLibrary and License in (D31) and (D32) below. A SoftwareLibrary consists of a number of CSO:Classes and is classified as CSO:Data because it cannot be executed as a whole. The concept License is a special kind of LegalContract as introduced in the Core Legal Ontology [Gangemi et al., 2004c].

(D31)   SoftwareLibrary$(x) =_{def}$
      CSO:Data$(x) \land \forall c($DOLCE:properPart$(x, c) \rightarrow$ CSO:Class$(c))$
(D32)   License$(x) =_{def}$
      LegalContract$(x) \land \exists y($CSO:Software$(y) \land$ DnS:involves$(x, y))$

Very often there are dependencies between libraries that are revealed only during run time by `ClassNotFoundExceptions`. For example, a library `lib1.jar` might depend on `lib2.jar` which in turn depends on `lib3.jar` and so forth. It is a very tedious task to keep track of such dependencies and, additionally, to check whether there are conflicts between libraries in this dependency graph. In order to reason with such information, we introduce the following associations and axioms: First, the transitive libraryDependsOn in (A17) and (A18) below. Second the symmetric libraryConflictsWith in (A19) and (A20). Finally, (A21) formalizes indirect conflicts.

The existence of incompatible licenses further complicates the situation. Even though libraries in the dependency graph do not conflict, they might have incompatible licenses. In order to reason with such information, we further introduce the association releasedUnder between SoftwareLibraries and Licenses in (A22), as well as the symmetric licenseIncompatibleWith in (A23) and (A24).

(A17)   libraryDependsOn$(x, y) \rightarrow$
      DOLCE:specificallyConstantlyDependsOn$(x, y) \land$
      SoftwareLibrary$(x) \land$ SoftwareLibrary(y)
(A18)   libraryDependsOn$(x, z) \leftarrow$
      libraryDependsOn$(x, y) \land$ libraryDependsOn(y, z)
(A19)   libraryConflictsWith$(x, y) \rightarrow$
      SoftwareLibrary$(x) \land$ SoftwareLibrary(y)
(A20)   libraryConflictsWith$(x, y) \leftrightarrow$ libraryConflictsWith(y, x)
(A21)   libraryConflictsWith$(x, z) \leftarrow$
      libraryDependsOn$(x, y) \land$ libraryConflictsWith(y, z)
(A22)   releasedUnder$(x, y) \rightarrow$
      OIO:expresses$(x, y) \land$ SoftwareLibrary$(x) \land$ License(y)
(A23)   licenseIncompatibleWith$(x, y) \rightarrow$ License$(x) \land$ License(y)

(A24) licenseIncompatibleWith$(x, y) \leftrightarrow$ licenseIncompatibleWith(y, x)

As an example, let us assume the `CustomerEntityBean` requires `lib1.jar`. Adding `lib1.jar` to the classpath in turn requires `lib2.jar` and `lib4.jar`. Adding `lib2.jar` to the classpath additionally requires `lib3.jar`. Furthermore, let us assume that `lib4.jar` conflicts with `lib3.jar`. Despite the small number of libraries, the situation becomes quite complex. Compiling and running the application will yield a run time exception. Given the modelling below we can infer libraryConflictsWith(*lib1.jar*, *lib4.jar*) because of (A18), (A20) and (A21).

(Ex79) SoftwareLibrary(*lib1.jar*)
(Ex80) SoftwareLibrary(*lib2.jar*)
(Ex81) SoftwareLibrary(*lib3.jar*)
(Ex82) SoftwareLibrary(*lib4.jar*)
(Ex83) libraryDependsOn(*lib1.jar*, *lib2.jar*)
(Ex84) libraryDependsOn(*lib1.jar*, *lib4.jar*)
(Ex85) libraryDependsOn(*lib2.jar*, *lib3.jar*)
(Ex86) libraryConflictsWith(*lib4.jar*, *lib3.jar*)
(Ex87) (Ex79), ..., (A21) $\models$ libraryConflictsWith(*lib1.jar*, *lib4.jar*)

3.3 Component Profiles and Taxonomies

So far, we have formalized several different aspects relevant for a software component such as interface and policy descriptions or plans. In this section we further aggregate the knowledge in component profiles. We expect that such an aggregation makes browsing and querying for developers more convenient. The component profile is envisioned to act as the central information source for a specific software component rather than having bits and pieces all over the place. Furthermore, the component profiles can be specialized and aligned in a taxonomy as required by the use cases *Capability Descriptions*, *Component Classification and Discovery*, *Automatic Generation of Web Service Descriptions*, *Transactional Settings* and *Secure Communication*.

(D33) and (A25) define a Profile as follows: First, it aggregates CSO:PolicyDescriptions, an OoP:Plan, the required SoftwareLibraries, the implemented Interfaces and additional Characteristics of a specific Software entity. Second, the link to the described Software is specified via the describes association. (D34) specializes this definition to ComponentProfile.

Often, we need to express certain capabilities or features of components, such as the version, transactional or security settings. For this purpose, we introduce Characteristics on a Profile in (D35). It is expected that Component-Profiles are specialized and put into a taxonomy. For example, we might define a DatabaseConnectorProfile as a ComponentProfile that provides for specific Characteristics describing whether the underlying database supports transactions or SQL-99. A taxonomic structure further accommodates the developer in browsing and querying for ComponentProfiles in his system.

Finally, (A26) specifies the profiles association as a "catch-all" for DnS:defines, DnS:unifies, OIO:about, as well as OIO:expressedBy. This is done for convenience in order to relieve the developer, who will certainly have to deal with such information, from such modelling details.

(D33) Profile(x) =$_{def}$ OIO:InformationObject$(x) \wedge \forall y$(profiles$(x, y) \rightarrow$
(CSO:PolicyDescription(y) ∨ SoftwareLibrary(y) ∨
CSO:Interface(y) ∨ OoP:Plan(y) ∨ Characteristic(y))) ∧
$\forall z$(describes$(x, z) \rightarrow$ Software(z))

(D34) ComponentProfile(x) =$_{def}$ Profile$(x) \wedge \forall y$(describes$(x, y) \rightarrow$
SoftwareComponent(y))

(D35) Characteristic(x) =$_{def}$
DnS:Parameter$(x) \wedge \forall y$(DnS:defines$(y, x) \rightarrow$
Profile(y)) ∧ $\forall z$(DnS:valuedBy$(x, z) \wedge$ DOLCE:AbstractRegion(z)))

(A25) describes$(x, y) \rightarrow$ OIO:about$(x, y) \wedge$ Profile$(x) \wedge$ CSO:Software(y)

(A26) profiles$(x, y) \rightarrow$ DnS:defines(x, y) ∨ DnS:unifies(x, y) ∨
OIO:about(x, y) ∨ OIO:expressedBy(x, y)

The information grouped by a ComponentProfile might have different origins. For example, a specific PolicyDescription might be automatically obtained from `ejb-jar.xml`, while manual modelling or source code analysis would result in an OoP:Plan. Hence, it is important to model also information-Timestamp and informationSource for parts of the ComponentProfile. We omit their definition because both are simple attributes with `xsd:string`.

As an example, we construct a profile for our `CustomerEntityBean` below. We assume the bean requires `lib1.jar`, implements the *javax.ejb.EntityBean* interface and has a policy description.

(Ex88) ComponentProfile(*CustomerBeanProfile*)

(Ex89) describes(*CustomerBeanProfile, CustomerEntityBean*)

(Ex90) profiles(*CustomerBeanProfile, lib1.jar*)

(Ex91) informationTimestamp(*lib1.jar, 050805-9:45:21*)

(Ex92) profiles(*CustomerBeanProfile, javax.ejb.EntityBean*)

(Ex93) CSO:Interface(*javax.ejb.EntityBean*)

(Ex94) profiles(*CustomerBeanProfile, CustomerEntityBeanPolicy*)

(Ex95) CSO:PolicyDescription(*CustomerEntityBeanPolicy*)

(Ex96) informationSource(*CustomerEntityBeanPolicy, file://ejb-jar.xml*)

3.4   Example

In this section, we revisit our running example (Example 2.1 on page 23) and show how it can be formalized with our ontology. We already introduced some of the instances in a piecemeal manner throughout the chapter. We collect the relevant instances to construct PolicyDescriptions and Plans so that a simple query can be used to detect if there are indirect permissions. An overview is given in Figure 7.9.

The descriptor files of the WebShopServlet (web.xml) and the Customer-EntityBean (ejb-jar.xml) result in two CSO:PolicyDescriptions. The third CSO:PolicyDescription below can be extracted from database metadata.

CSO:PolicyDescription(*WebShopServletPolicy*)
profiles(*WebShopServletPolicy*, *ServletCaller*)
CSO:PolicySubject(*ServletCaller*)
DnS:playedBy(*ServletCaller*, *anybody*)
CSO:UserGroup(*anybody*)
profiles(*WebShopServletPolicy*, *GET*)
CSO:ComputationalTask(*GET*)
CSO:computationalRightTowards(*ServletCaller*, *GET*)
profiles(*WebShopServletPolicy*, *ServletCallee*)
CSO:PolicyObject(*ServletCallee*)
DnS:playedBy(*ServletCallee*, *WebShopServlet*)
CSO:Class(*WebShopServlet*)
DnS:obligedTo(*ServletCallee*, *GET*)

CSO:PolicyDescription(*CustomerEntityBeanPolicy*)
profiles(*CustomerEntityBeanPolicy*, *BeanCaller*)
CSO:PolicySubject(*BeanCaller*)
DnS:playedBy(*BeanCaller*, *anybody*)
profiles(*CustomerEntityBeanPolicy*, *CallBean*)
CSO:ComputationalTask(*CallBean*)
CSO:computationalRightTowards(*BeanCaller*, *CallBean*)
profiles(*CustomerEntityBeanPolicy*, *BeanCallee*)
CSO:PolicyObject(*BeanCallee*)
DnS:playedBy(*BeanCallee*, *CustomerEntityBean*)
COSC:SoftwareComponent(*CustomerEntityBean*)
DnS:obligedTo(*BeanCallee*, *CallBean*)

CSO:PolicyDescription(*DatabasePolicy*)
profiles(*DatabasePolicy*, *DatabaseModifier*)
CSO:PolicySubject(*DatabaseModifier*)
DnS:playedBy(*DatabaseModifier*, *dbuser*)
CSO:User(*dbuser*)

profiles(*DatabasePolicy*, *ModifyTable*)
CSO:ComputationalTask(*ModifyTable*)
CSO:computationalRightTowards(*DatabaseModifier*, *ModifyTable*)
profiles(*DatabasePolicy*, *ModifiedTable*)
CSO:PolicyObject(*ModifiedTable*)
DnS:playedBy(*ModifiedTable*, *CustomerTable*)
CSO:Data(*CustomerTable*)
DnS:obligedTo(*ModifiedTable*, *ModifyTable*)

Source code analysis or manual modelling yields the *WebShopServlet-Plan* and the *CustomerEntityBeanPlan* below. A context switch is represented by the CSO:contextUser association between CSO:User and CSO:-ComputationalTask.

OoP:Plan(*WebShopServletPlan*)
profiles(*WebShopServletPlan*, *GET*)
profiles(*WebShopServletPlan*, *CallBean*)
CSO:accesses(*GET*, *WebShopServlet*)
CSO:executes(*WebShopServlet*, *CallBean*)
CSO:accesses(*CallBean*, *CustomerEntityBean*)
CSO:contextUser(*anybody*, *CallBean*)

OoP:Plan(*CustomerEntityBeanPlan*)
profiles(*CustomerEntityBeanPlan*, *CallBean*)
profiles(*CustomerEntityBeanPlan*, *ModifyTable*)
CSO:executes(*CustomerEntityBean*, *ModifyTable*)
CSO:accesses(*ModifyTable*, *CustomerTable*)
CSO:contextUser(*dbuser*, *ModifyTable*)

We can now define additional axioms to deduce all indirectly accessible resources for a user. First, Axiom (A27) infers the directly accessible resources r of a user u. The reader may note that axioms (A15) and (A16) on page 126 also infer the accessible resources which are a result of group memberships. Second, Axiom (A28) infers indirectly accessible resources, i.e., ones that are a result of a call with a context switch. With (A27) and (A28) we can infer indirectlyAccessibleResource(*CustomerTable*, *anybody*) — a result which otherwise would require tedious manual efforts.

(A27) directlyAccessibleResource(r, u) ←
        CSO:Data(r) ∧ CSO:User(u) ∧ DnS:playedBy(s, u) ∧
        CSO:PolicySubject(s) ∧ CSO:computationalRightTowards(s, ct) ∧
        CSO:ComputationalTask(ct) ∧ DnS:obligedTo(o, ct) ∧
        CSO:PolicyObject(o) ∧ DnS:playedBy(u, r)

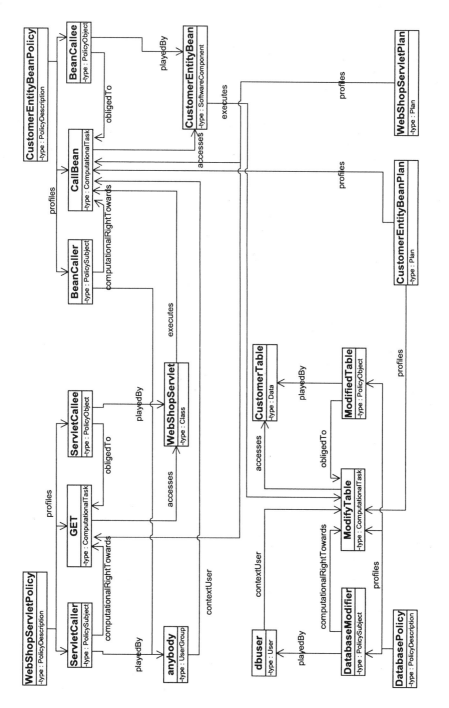

Figure 7.9. UML diagram of the software component example.

(A28)   indirectlyAccessibleResource(r_3, u) ←
        directlyAccessibleResource(r_1, u) ∧ CSO:invokes(r_1, r_2) ∧
        CSO:Software(r_2) ∧ CSO:executes(r_2, t) ∧
        CSO:ComputationalTask(t) ∧ CSO:accesses(t, r_3) ∧
        CSO:contextUser(u, t)

4.   Core Ontology of Web Services (COWS)

In this section we present a possible *Core Ontology of Web Services* to meet the remaining modelling requirements of *service profiles* and *service taxonomies*. The Core Ontology of Web Services is based on the Core Ontology of Software Components presented in Section 3. We start by formalizing our understanding of the term "Web service," introduce the notion of service profiles, revisit the motivating example (cf. Chapter 2, Section 3.2, page 30) and show how it can be formalized.

4.1   Formalization of the term "Web service"

On the one hand, Web services are often revelations of functionality residing in a class or component. Application servers typically provide support to automatically access the functionality via the standardized SOAP protocol and the automatic generation of standardized WSDL interface descriptions. However, the same can be done with the Java Remote Method Invocation (RMI) or CORBA although with different protocols and interface descriptions. On the other hand, a Web service can be defined as a composition of other Web services, e.g., by the Business Process Execution Language (WS-BPEL).[13] Again, this can be done with software components in common workflow engines as well.

So what is the difference between a software component and a Web service? We argue that standardization in terms of Web protocols and descriptions seems to be the major distinction. In any case, Web services are mandatorily accessible via the SOAP protocol and expose an interface description according to WSDL. This is in line with one of the many existing definitions:

"*A Web service is a software system identified by a URI, whose public interfaces and bindings are defined and described using XML. Its definition can be discovered by other software systems. These systems may then interact with the Web service in a manner prescribed by its definition, using XML based messages conveyed by internet protocols*" [Booth et al., 2004]

However, there are dozens of other, partly contrary, definitions of the term Web service. In [Gangemi et al., 2003b] we list several definitions and conclude

---

[13]http://www-128.ibm.com/developerworks/library/specification/ws-bpel/

that a concise axiomatization of such an overloaded term is necessary to avoid confusion among developers and ontology users.

(D36) follows the definition above and specifies WebService as a special kind of CSO:Software which is OIO:orderedBy a *WSDLEncoding*. The *WSDLEncoding* is an OIO:InformationEncodingSystem as defined in the Ontology of Information Objects. For our middleware domain, (A29) further constrains the intended meaning of WebService by axiomatizing that it is either a revelation of functionality residing in a COSC:SoftwareComponent or a combined service specified by an OoP:Plan.[14]

(D36) WebService$(x) =_{def}$
CSO:Software$(x) \land \forall y($OIO:orderedBy$(x, y) \land y = $*WSDLEncoding*$)$

(A29) WebService$(x) \rightarrow$
$(\exists sc($CSO:invokes$(x, sc) \land $COSC:SoftwareComponent$(sc)) \oplus$
$\exists p, t($CSO:executes$(x, t) \land $CSO:ComputationalTask$(t) \land$
DnS:defines$(p, t) \land $OoP:Plan$(p) \land $OIO:expresses$(x, p)))$

4.2 Service Profiles and Taxonomies

The *Analyzing Message Contexts*, *Selecting Service Functionality*, *Relating Communication Parameters*, *Aggregating Service Information* and *Quality of Service* use cases require the modelling of service profiles and taxonomies. Similar to COSC:ComponentProfiles, we group the different descriptions relevant for a Web service in a ServiceProfile in (D37) below. We expect that such a grouping makes browsing and querying for developers more convenient. The information grouped by a ServiceProfile might have different origins. Hence, we also add informationTimestamp and informationSource as simple attributes to parts of the profile. We omit their definition because both are simple attributes with xsd:string. Furthermore, ServiceProfiles can be specialized and put into a taxonomy.

ServiceProfiles differ from COSC:ComponentProfiles in two ways: First, they can have QualityOfService parameters. QualityOfService parameters are specializations of COSC:Characteristics and defined on ServiceProfiles as shown in (D38). Second, the ServiceProfile necessarily OIO:describes a WebService as opposed to COSC:ComponentProfiles which COSC:describe COSC:SoftwareComponents (cf. (A29)).

(D37) ServiceProfile$(x) =_{def}$
COSC:Profile$(x) \land \forall y($COSC:describes$(x, y) \rightarrow $WebService$(y))$
(D38) QualityOfService$(x) =_{def}$ COSC:Characteristic$(x) \land$
$\forall y($COSC:profiles$(y, x) \rightarrow $ServiceProfile$(y))$

---

[14]Note that the symbol $\oplus$ represents the logical xor (exclusive or) connective.

4.3   Example

In this section we revisit the Example 2.4 in Chapter 2, Section 3.2, page 30, and show how it can be formalized with our ontology. The WS-BPEL process description can be parsed and relevant information can be extracted leading to an OoP:Plan consisting of several ComputationalTasks. Figure 7.10 provides an overview.

ServiceProfile(*WebShopProfile*)
COSC:describes(*WebShopProfile, WebShopWS*)
WebService(*WebShopWS*)
COSC:profiles(*WebShopProfile, WebShopPlan*)
OoP:Plan(*WebShopPlan*)
COSC:profiles(*WebShopPlan, checkAccount*)
CSO:executes(*WebShopWS, checkAccount*)
OoP:ComplexTask(*checkAccount*)
COSC:profiles(*WebShopPlan, CallVisaWS*)
OoP:ComputationalTask(*CallVisaWS*)
COSC:profiles(*WebShopPlan, CallMastercardWS*)
OoP:ComputationalTask(*CallMastercardWS*)
WebService(*VisaWS*)
WebService(*MastercardWS*)
OoP:successor(*checkAccount, CallVisaWS*)
OoP:successor(*checkAccount, CallMastercardWS*)
CSO:accesses(*CallVisaWS, VisaWS*)
CSO:accesses(*CallMastercardWS, MastercardWS*)

Furthermore, the WS-Policy document of the external Mastercard service (cf. Example 2.5 on page 30) can be parsed and a corresponding CSO:Policy-Description created. Chapter 9, Section 3, discusses the procedure of how to obtain the instances below from WS-Policy documents.

ServiceProfile(*MastercardProfile*)
COSC:describes(*MastercardProfile, MastercardWS*)
COSC:profiles(*MastercardProfile, MastercardPolicy*)
CSO:PolicyDescription(*MastercardPolicy*)
COSC:profiles(*MastercardPolicy, MastercardCaller*)
CSO:PolicySubject(*MastercardCaller*)
DnS:playedBy(*MastercardCaller, anybody*)
CSO:UserGroup(*anybody*)
COSC:profiles(*MastercardPolicy, CallMastercardWS*)
CSO:computationalRightTowards(*MastercardCaller, CallMastercardWS*)
COSC:profiles(*MastercardPolicy, MastercardCallee*)
CSO:PolicyObject(*MastercardCallee*)

DnS:playedBy(*MastercardCallee*, *MastercardWS*)
COSC:profiles(*MastercardPolicy*, *AuthenticationProtocol*)
CSO:Constraint(*AuthenticationProtocol*)
DnS:requisiteFor(*AuthenticationProtocol*, *CallMastercardWS*)
DnS:valuedBy(*AuthenticationProtocol*, *AuthenticationProtocolValue*)
AuthenticationProtocolValue(x) → DOLCE:AbstractRegion(x)
AuthenticationProtocolValue(*Kerberos*)
AuthenticationProtocolValue(*X509*)

We can now introduce axiom (A30) below to infer all WebServices which CSO:invoke other WebServices with attached CSO:PolicyDescription. With (A9) on page 123 and executes(*WebShopWS*, *checkAccount*), OoP:successor(*checkAccount*, *CallMastercardWS*) and CSO:accesses (*CallMastercardWS*, *MastercardWS*) we can entail invokesWebServiceWithPolicy(*WebShopWS*, *MasterCardWS*). Without semantic management, obtaining this result would require tedious manual analyses of the WS-BPEL and WS-Policy descriptors.

(A30) invokesWebServiceWithPolicy(x, y) ←
    CSO:invokes(x, y) ∧ WebService(x) ∧ WebService(y) ∧
    COSC:describes(sp, y) ∧ ServiceProfile(sp) ∧
    COSC:profiles(sp, pd) ∧ CSO:PolicyDescription(pd)

5.   Proof of Concept

The chapter proposed the design of an appropriate management ontology. We have defined appropriateness at the beginning of the chapter as follows: (*i*) the management ontology should meet all the modelling requirements derived from our use cases, (*ii*) it should achieve high quality according to the ontology quality criteria and (*iii*) it should enable reuse in specific platforms and reduce modelling efforts to a minimum. In this section, we detail where and how our management ontology responds to (*i*), (*ii*) and (*iii*).

5.1   Meeting the Modelling Requirements

Tables 7.1 and 7.2 summarize which parts of the management ontology meet the requirements. The requirements comprise modelling (*i*) *libraries, licenses, component profiles, component taxonomies, API descriptions, semantic API descriptions, access rights* and *workflow information* of software components and (*ii*) *service profiles, service taxonomies, policies, workflow information, API descriptions*, as well as *semantic API descriptions* of Web services.

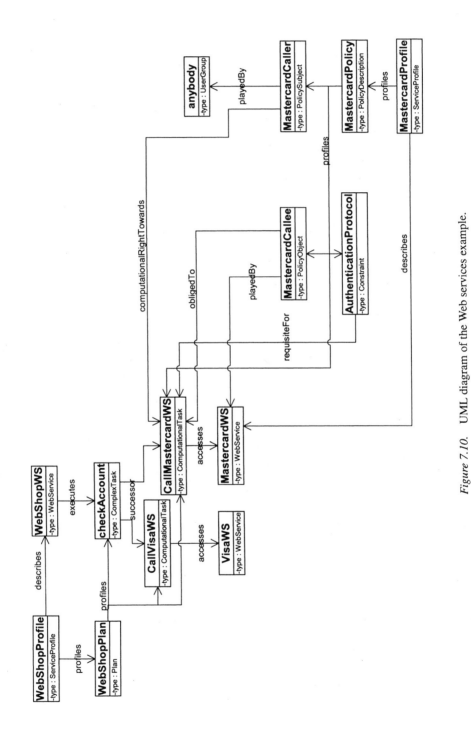

Figure 7.10.   UML diagram of the Web services example.

Table 7.1.   Modelling requirements for software components and the parts of the management ontology that meet the requirements.

Part of ontology \ Requirement	Libraries	Licenses	Component profiles	Component taxonomies	API descriptions	Semantic API descriptions	Access rights	Workflow information
OoP:Plan						×		×
CSO:Class,CSO:Method					×			
CSO:Interface						×		
CSO:PolicyDescription							×	
COSC:SoftwareLibrary	×							
COSC:License		×						
COSC:ComponentProfile			×	×				

Table 7.2.   Modelling requirements for Web services and the parts of the management ontology that meet the requirements.

Part of ontology \ Requirement	Service profiles	Service taxonomies	Policies	Workflow information	API descriptions	Semantic API descriptions
OoP:Plan				×		×
CSO:Class,CSO:Method					×	
CSO:Interface						×
CSO:PolicyDescription			×			
COWS:ServiceProfile	×	×				

5.2   Higher Quality

Besides meeting the requirements, a remaining question has been II.2: *How to ensure high quality?* Throughout the axiomatization, we have approximated the intended models of our universe of discourse as closely as possible. In particular, we have strived to avoid the typical shortcomings of common ontologies as outlined in Chapter 5, Section 3, viz., *conceptual ambiguity*, *poor axiomatization*, *loose design* and *narrow scope*. In the following we give some examples how the shortcomings are eliminated.

Conceptual Disambiguation

We have learned in Chapter 5, Section 3.1, that common ontologies such as OWL-S [Martin et al., 2004] and our initial ontology of software components [Sabou et al., 2004] suffer from conceptual ambiguity. An example is the notion of OWL-S:Service which is defined twice and differently in the specification. In turn, both definitions stand in conflict with the axiomatization of the concept in the ontology. In our initial ontology of software components, we have found a similar dilemma regarding the plethora of meanings and definitions of terms, such as component, software component or software module. Both ontologies fail to convey their intended meanings of such terms and leave the interpretation to the ontology user.

In contrast to such commonly built ontologies we have captured the intended meanings of concepts and associations as precisely as possible. Our definition of terms such as Web service (Definition (D36) on page 137) or software component (Definition (D30) on page 129) are in line with the natural language definitions prevailing in the middleware community. Comparing both definitions makes evident that very few concepts actually differ when "upgrading" from software components to Web services. Only minor extensions to the Core Software Ontology are required to capture the differences between software components and Web services.

While our definitions of the terms Web service and software component may not be the only ones, the fact that they are highly axiomatized allows comparing them to alternative definitions and allows fostering discussions on alternative conceptualizations. We argue that this will enable mutual understanding which is crucial for information integration of any kind.

Increased Axiomatization

Common ontologies are often reduced to a simple taxonomy with domain and range restrictions on associations. OWL-S and our initial ontology of software components are no exceptions as demonstrated in Section 3.2 of Chapter 5. An example are the OWL-S:ControlConstructs which define how composite processes are combined.

In our management ontology we have made use of the Ontology of Plans which provides extensive axiomatization of OoP:Tasks and subconcepts thereof. OoP:Tasks are directly comparable to the OWL-S:ControlConstructs, but provide a heavyweight axiomatization. An example is *SynchroTask* (an instance of OoP:ControlTask) which matches the concept of OWL-S:Join in the OWL-S:SplitJoin control construct. A *SynchroTask* joins a set of tasks after a branching and waits for the execution of all (except the optional ones) tasks that are direct successors to a *ConcurrencyTask* or *AnyOrderTask*. Below we give the axiomatization of the *SynchroTask* as introduced in [Gangemi et al., 2004b].

ControlTask$(SynchroTask) \rightarrow \exists t_1, t_2, t_3(t_1 = ConcurrencyTask \vee t_1 = AnyOrderTask) \wedge$ successor$(t_1, x) \wedge (ComplexTask(t_2) \vee ActionTask(t_2)) \wedge (ComplexTask(t_3) \vee ActionTask(t_3)) \wedge$ directSuccessor$(t_2, SynchroTask) \wedge$ directSuccessor$(t_3, SynchroTask)$

Another example is the OWL-S:components association, which is used to relate OWL-S:ControlConstructs to their components. In OWL-S this association is described merely as a subrelation of owl:Property with a domain of OWL-S:ControlConstruct. The Ontology of Plans exploits the DOLCE:-temporaryComponent association which has a firm foundation as a special kind of the more basic DOLCE:component mereological association and DOLCE:partlyCompresent temporally indexing association. Both are characterized by formal restrictions on their application to other basic concepts.

Improved Design

In our management ontology we propose to use contextualization as a design pattern. Contextualization allows us to move from monolithic component or service descriptions to the representation of different, possibly conflicting views with various granularity. The Descriptions & Situations ontology module provides us with the basic primitives of context modelling such as the notion of roles, which allows us to talk about inputs and outputs on the abstract level, i.e., independent of the objects that play such roles.

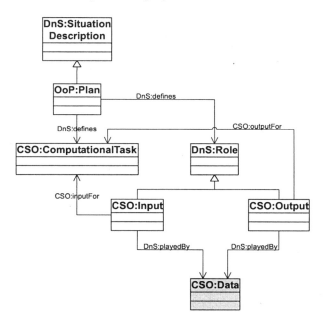

Figure 7.11.   Solution to the attribute binding problem. Data can play both the role of an Input and an Output at the same time. Inputs and Outputs can be linked to ComputationalTasks in a Plan. White classes represent descriptive entities, grey classes represent ground entities.

Using this pattern results in a much more intuitive representation of attribute binding than in OWL-S with clearly defined semantics and scoping provided by Descriptions & Situations. Attribute binding in OWL-S is necessary to express, e.g., that the output of a process is the input to another process as presented in Figure 5.4 on page 90. In our ontology, inputs and outputs can be modelled as DnS:Roles which serve as variables. Thus, CSO:Data can play multiple roles within the same or different descriptions. It is natural to express that the given CSO:Data is output with respect to one process, but input to another (cf. Figure 7.11).

Wider Scope

As we have seen in Chapter 5, Section 3.4, components and services exist on the boundary of the world inside an information system and the external world. Web services, in particular, may carry out operations to support a real-world service. Functionality, which is an essential property of a service, then arises from the entire process that comprises computational, as well as real-world activities.

The distinction between information objects, events and physical objects is not explicitly made in most ontologies. In our management ontology this separation naturally follows from the use of DOLCE and the Ontology of Information Objects, where the distinction is an important part of the characterization of concepts. In particular, it becomes possible to be more precise about the kinds of relationships that can occur among objects or between objects and events.

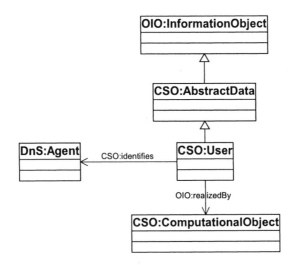

Figure 7.12.   Using the Ontology of Information Objects allows us to model the relationship between a user in an information system and its corresponding agent (e.g., a natural person).

For example, we can distinguish among a physical object (such as a natural person), an information object (such as user in an information system) and represent the link between them. The capabilities provided by our ontology are shown in Figure 7.12. It is worthwhile to explicate such differences, e.g., when we want to infer the total of access rights granted for a natural person who might have several users in and across information systems.

5.3   Enabling Reuse

Finally, we have designed the management ontology in a way to be platform-independent *and* as specific as possible at the same time. The answer to the corresponding research Question II.3 *How to decrease modelling efforts and enable reuse?* is to have a *core* ontology that can easily be reused and specialized in a concrete platform.

The following three steps have to be taken in order to allow for reuse in a specific platform: (*i*) specialization of the core concepts and associations to reflect the idiosyncracies of the platform. For example, we have to introduce EnterpriseBean as a special kind of COSC:SoftwareComponent in a J2EE-based platform. The result of this step is a *domain*, *reference* and *heavyweight* version of our management ontology. Step (*ii*) removes concepts and associations that have been introduced merely for reference purposes. As an example, it is unlikely and not required to model particular ComputationalObjects or ComputationalActivities for the reasoning at run time. Both were introduced to better explain concepts such as Software or Data. The result is a *domain*, *application* and *heavyweight* version. Finally, step (*iii*) requires a decision for an executable ontology language that can be reasoned with at run time. Accordingly, the axiomatization has to be adapted to this language. This might be a description logic, such as OWL DL, which is less expressive than the modal logic S5. The result of this step is a *domain*, *application* and *lightweight* version of the management ontology.

In fact, Part III reuses and specializes the management ontology according to the three steps. After designing and implementing an ontology-based application server in Chapters 8 and 9, Chapter 10 discusses the three steps in more detail.

6.   Summary

In this chapter we have been concerned with the design of an appropriate management ontology founded on a modelling basis. The modelling basis consists of DOLCE and three of its modules, viz., Descriptions & Situations, the Ontology of Plans and the Ontology of Information Objects. All of them have been introduced in Section 1. Subsequently, we have contributed a *Core Software Ontology* Section 2, which formalizes fundamental concepts of the computational domain. The Core Software Ontology acts as a common basis for the *Core Ontologies of Software Components and Services* which have been built in Sections 3 and 4, respectively. Finally, Section 5 showed (*i*) where we have met the modelling requirements derived from our use cases, (*ii*) how we have achieved high quality according to our ontology quality criteria and (*iii*) how we have enabled reuse in specific platforms.

In contrast to commonly built ontologies we have avoided their typical shortcomings of *conceptual ambiguity, poor axiomatization, loose design* and *narrow scope.* We have captured the intended meanings of concepts and association as precisely as possible. Our definition of terms such as "software component" or "Web service" are in line with the natural language definitions prevailing in the middleware community. Comparing both definitions makes evident that very few concepts actually differ when "upgrading" from software components to Web services. We argue that our concise axiomatization will enable mutual understanding which is crucial for information integration of any kind.

PART III

REALIZATION OF SEMANTIC MANAGEMENT

Chapter 8

DESIGN OF AN
ONTOLOGY-BASED APPLICATION SERVER

In Part II we have been concerned with answering the Main Question II: *How to build a suitable management ontology?* As a result, we have obtained a high-quality management ontology with reference, heavyweight and core characteristics, that meets all the modelling requirements derived from the use cases in Chapter 4, Section 2, page 65.

The ontology is a contribution in its own right. We have disambiguated overloaded terms such as "software component" or "Web service" by a concise axiomatization, making the ontology ideal for reference purposes. However, the ontology is merely a passive object. An inference engine is required to enable querying and reasoning with the semantic descriptions of components and services. In most cases, inference engines are based on logic calculi, which basically consist of a set of syntactic derivation rules. Furthermore, a whole infrastructure is required to embed the inference engine in and to obtain, model and use the semantic descriptions. We have to choose a specific platform and, ideally speaking, an existing ontology tool suite. Additional steps are required to reuse our management ontology in this specific platform and to adapt it to the idiosyncracies of the tool suite. It is the purpose of this part to elaborate on all these issues as a response to the Main Question III from the Introduction: *How to realize semantic management of middleware?*

We begin this chapter by discussing general design issues. In Section 1, we elicit where to apply the inference engine, thus answering the Question III.1: *What is a suitable target platform?* Besides the obvious platform of an application server, the inference engine can also be applied in workflow management systems, software IDE's, Web service composition engines and a lot more. Eventually, we choose an application server because many use cases can be realized. Section 1 also answers the Question III.2: *Who provides semantic descriptions?* The number of manually provided descriptions has to be kept as small as possible because developers and administrators do not want to adopt additional tasks. Hence, we elicit further options on how to arrive at semantic descriptions of components and services. We continue in Section 2 by designing an ontology-based application server in a piecewise manner. This comprises a careful elicitation of requirements and, subsequently, meeting the requirements by a suitable architecture. Section 2 concentrates on the semantic management of software components, whereas Section 3 focuses on the semantic management of Web services. Basically, the realization of semantic management of Web services boils down to an extension of the server.

Parts of this chapter have been published in conference proceedings and journals. The requirements for the application server, as well as its architecture, are taken from [Oberle et al., 2005d] and [Oberle et al., 2004a, Oberle, 2004], respectively. Possible platforms and the elicitation on how to apply the inference engine originate from [Oberle et al., 2005a].

1.   General Design Issues

Our management ontology meets the modelling requirements put forward in our use cases (cf. Chapter 4, Section 2). We have concisely defined its concepts and associations by a rich axiomatization. For every ontology-based application, however, an inference engine is required to enable the querying and reasoning with semantic descriptions. An *inference engine* (also known as *reasoner*) implements a calculus for the underlying logic which is defined by a set of syntactic derivation rules. The general purpose of the inference engine is to derive answers from semantic descriptions and to check an ontology for consistency. [Horrocks and Patel-Schneider, 2004]

In this section, we discuss *where* to apply the inference engine in 1.1, followed by an elicitation of potential sources of semantic descriptions in 1.2. Finally, we discuss *how* to integrate the inference engine in the middleware control in Section 1.3.

1.1   Possible Platforms

The first set of use cases presented in Chapter 4, Section 2, mainly focus on the semantic management of software components. It is the primary choice to integrate the inference engine in an application server to realize this set of use cases because application servers typically foster component-based software development. However, this section discusses additional platforms for two reasons: (*i*) the platform for the second set of use cases, i.e., the ones dealing with Web services, is not obvious at all and (*ii*) other platforms may benefit as well from semantic management, making it worthwhile to elaborate on them.

Application Servers We have already discussed application servers in Chapter 2, Section 3.1. Application servers are ideal as a platform to integrate the semantic management of software components. In addition, they typically provide Web service support and, thus, can also be considered for some of the Web service use cases. The inference engine cannot only become an integral part of J2EE-based application servers, such as IBM WebSphere or JBoss, but also of Microsoft .NET.

Software IDE's An integrated development environment (IDE) is an application or a set of tools that allows a programmer to write, compile, edit and, in some cases, test and debug within an integrated, interactive graphical user interface. The most prominent examples are Eclipse, JBuilder or Microsoft Visual Studio.

IDE's are possible platforms because some of the use cases require information about the source code. The internal datamodels of the IDE can be leveraged to obtain such information. Information about calls or exceptions can be easily obtained and integrated into the ontology as semantic descriptions.

Application Management Systems The infrastructure that manages the whole bandwidth from network monitoring to software distribution to the desktop is called an enterprise application management system. Examples of commonly used application management systems are HP OpenView, Computer Associates Unicenter and IBM Tivoli.

Such systems are a possible target platform because management of middleware-based applications is a part of application management (cf. related work in Chapter 11, Section 1 for a detailed discussion). Some of our use cases of semantic management of middleware are shared by the application management use cases.

Web Service Management Systems Application management is currently extended to Web services. Web services management defines the manageability model for managing Web services as a resource and explains how to describe and access that manageability (cf. also related work in Chapter 11, Section 1).

Such management systems share some of our use cases. Integrating semantic technology makes them even more powerful by reasoning capabilities. It is thus worthwhile to regard them as a possible platform. Existing application management systems, such as HP OpenView, already support Web services management.

Workflow Management Systems Workflow management systems (WfMS) facilitate the definition and maintenance of the integration logic of distributed applications (cf. Chapter 2, Section 3.1). Business processes are formally defined as a workflow and executed by a workflow engine. Workflows are seen as software building blocks for "programming in the large" because they compose large software modules which are typically entire applications. Examples of leading commercial workflow systems include IBM WebSphere MQ Workflow and Microsoft BizTalk Orchestration.

Reasoning with workflow information is proposed by some of the use cases in Chapter 4, Section 2. Therefore, workflow management systems can also benefit from semantic technology to facilitate the management of some tasks.

Web Service Composition Engines Web service composition engines are similar to workflow management systems and mainly use WS-BPEL (cf. Chapter 2, Section 3.2) as a process specification language. Corresponding BPEL-engines care for executing the composite services. Examples are activeBPEL,[1] Bexee,[2] or the BPEL engines that ship with application servers.

We believe that Web service composition engines are the primary choice as a platform for the semantic management of Web services. The reason is that they allow for the realization of all of the Web services use cases introduced in Chapter 4, Section 2.

For the remainder of this part we limit ourselves to the integration of an inference engine in an application server. We do so because of the following reasons: (*i*) although a Web service composition engine allows realizing all the Web services use cases, it is not suited for the semantic management of software components. Regarding both the semantic management of software components and of Web services, application servers allow the realization of most of our use cases. (*ii*) the scenario discussed in Chapter 4, Section 1.1, on page 57, proposes an *Application Server for the Semantic Web* which we build in the remainder of this chapter.

1.2 Obtaining Semantic Descriptions

After having decided *where* to use the inference engine, namely, in an application server, it is necessary to elaborate on the Question III.2: *Who provides semantic descriptions?* Manual modelling efforts have to be kept as small as possible because the developer does not want to adopt further tasks when he or she already is overburdened by the complexity of the middleware. We have been elaborating on this issue at the beginning of Chapter 4 where Figure 4.1 on page 56 introduces the trade-off between management and modelling efforts.

---

[1]http://www.activebpel.org/
[2]http://bexee.sourceforge.net

It is necessary to identify potential sources which allow us to (semi) automatically obtain semantic descriptions. *Obtaining* comprises: (*i*) reading and parsing of the source, (*ii*) extraction of relevant information and (*iii*) integrating this information as semantic descriptions into the inference engine and ontology. This is quite a simple task given that most descriptors are in XML syntax. Also, the implementation of such mappings has to be undertaken only once. We provide ideas for potential sources as follows:

Manual Modelling The amount of semantic descriptions that are provided manually by the software developer must be minimal because software developers will not be very willing to adopt a large new paradigm at a time when they are just getting used to deployment and WS* descriptors. However, not all aspects can be obtained from existing sources. Additional manual modelling will always be required, e.g., to establish the link between users in an information system and the corresponding natural person. Additional manual modelling is realized by ontology editors and is supplementary to the other possibilities.

Deployment and WS* Descriptors A great deal of semantic descriptions can be obtained from deployment and WS* descriptors. It is a one-off endeavor to code the obtaining of such descriptors (i.e., to code the parsing, the extraction of relevant tags and the mapping from the tags to concepts and associations of our management ontology). In Chapter 9, Section 3, on page 180, we sketch an example for a mapping from WSDL, WS-BPEL and WS-Policy descriptors to concepts and associations of the management ontology.

Source Code Annotations Recently, source code annotations have become a popular method to supplement or even replace XML descriptors. Source-code annotations are of advantage because of the simpler maintenance. XDoclet is an example. It integrates information from different deployment descriptors in JavaDoc comments [Walls and Richards, 2003]. If XDoclet is put in place, the tags can be parsed and integrated instead of the several deployment descriptors they replace.[3] Very similar to the idea of XDoclet, the recent JSR 181, entitled "Web services metadata for the Java platform" [Trezzo and Mihic, 2004], defines a standard way to build and deploy Web Services without learning and implementing generalized API's and deployment descriptors. Proprietary efforts, such as JBoss.Net and also Microsoft's .NET IDE, take a similar approach. Furthermore, Java 5.0 standardized the syntax of JavaDoc annotations, which further simplifies obtaining such information.

---

[3]http://xdoclet.sourceforge.net/xdoclet/index.html

Programme Code Software IDE's internal data models are aware of how exceptions are thrown, invocations across classes, required libraries and a lot more. The IDE's maintain and use this information in their internal datamodels. For an open-source IDE such as Eclipse, it is fairly simple to write a plug-in that obtains such information.

Application Management Descriptors Application Management Systems obtain information about managed applications and resources in the form of Management Information Bases (MIB). MIB's are databases that contain the hierarchical order of all of the managed objects. Each managed object in a MIB has a unique identifier. The identifier includes the type (such as counter, string, gauge or address), access level (such as read/write), size restrictions and range information of the object. Similarly, the Common Information Model (CIM) is a data model of an implementation-neutral schema for describing overall management information in an enterprise environment. Some of the information stored there can also be obtained for our purposes (cf. related work in Chapter 11, Section 1.2, for a detailed discussion).

Semi-automatic Annotation [Patil et al., 2004, Hess and Kushmerick, 2003, Agarwal et al., 2004] introduce frameworks for the semi-automatic generation of semantic descriptions of Web services. For example, they propose a matching algorithm between the XML-Schema types of a WSDL description and a given domain ontology. The approaches are very promising to semi-automatically obtain semantic descriptions.

1.3   How to Integrate the Inference Engine?

In the previous section, we have identified potential sources for obtaining semantic descriptions. The next step is to elaborate on the different ways of using the inference engine. The different possibilities of *how* to integrate the inference engine into the middleware control are discussed in the following paragraphs. They clarify the different usages for building our ontology-based application server. Note that the approaches can be realized in parallel.

Reverse Engineering The reverse engineering approach is non-invasive and does not intervene in the existing infrastructure, i.e., existing descriptor files are still fed into their corresponding engines (e.g., into EJB containers or Web service composition engines). It is still necessary for the developer to familiarize and work with all the descriptor files. However, they are parsed and integrated into the inference engine by a metadata collector (cf. Figure 8.1). Hence, the developer is enabled to query and reason with such information.

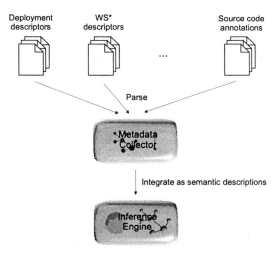

Figure 8.1. The reverse engineering approach applies a metadata collector to obtain semantic descriptions, i.e., to parse potential sources, extract relevant information from them and integrate them into the inference engine and ontology.

Model-Driven Deployment (MDD) In this approach, semantic descriptions are used to generate the component and WS* descriptors. The idea is to have one common information source, viz., the inference engine and ontology, which centralize maintenance instead of having dozens of deployment and WS* descriptor files. The developer and administrator do not have to familiarize and to maintain the descriptor files. The descriptors are generated automatically from the semantic descriptions of components and services. Querying and reasoning with the management ontology for the developer and administrator is possible, too. The descriptor files are still fed into their corresponding engines.

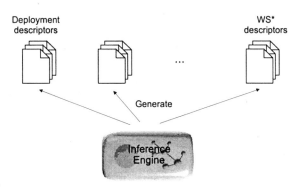

Figure 8.2. The model-driven deployment approach generates the descriptor files out of the inference engine and ontology

We call this approach model-driven deployment as it is similar to the idea of model-driven architectures [Mellor et al., 2004], where a platform-independent conceptual model is used to generate platform-specific code. It is also similar to the approach of XDoclet [Walls and Richards, 2003]. XDoclet is an open source code generation engine. It enables "attribute-oriented programming" for Java. XDoclet parses source files and generates deployment descriptors or source code from them. These files are generated from templates that use the information provided in the source code and its JavaDoc tags.

Ontology Run Time The last approach, labelled ontology run time, disposes the idea of several descriptor files and sets the inference engine and ontology as central information source in an application server. The remaining infrastructure, such as EJB containers or Web service composition engines, has to be adapted accordingly. That means required information is read from the inference engine and ontology and not from deployment descriptors. Putting aside the additional effort of adapting the infrastructure, run time information (e.g., dynamic quality of service parameters) can now be integrated and reasoned with, too.

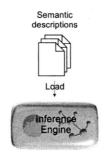

Figure 8.3. The ontology run time approach disposes the idea of descriptor files and puts the inference engine and ontology as central information source in the application server.

2.   Semantic Management of Software Components

So far, we have decided to apply the inference engine in an application server, have identified potential sources for the semantic descriptions and have clarified the different ways of using the inference engine. In this section, we propose a way to realize the semantic management of software components by designing an ontology-based application server. We first identify requirements for such a server in Section 2.1. We continue by deriving the design in a piecemeal manner in 2.2, 2.3 and 2.4. The resulting server is rather generic but provides a number of components to support the application development for the Semantic Web.

2.1   Requirements

Requirements for our ontology-based application server for the Semantic Web are twofold. On the one hand, they are derived from our scenario introduced in Chapter 4, Section 1.1, on page 57. On the other hand, they are derived from the use cases in Chapter 4, Section 2.1, on page 65 that focus on the semantic management of software components.

The scenario introduced in Chapter 4, Section 1.1, deals with the particular situation of application development for the Semantic Web. An infrastructure is required that facilitates plug'n'play engineering of ontology-based software modules and, thus, the development and maintenance of comprehensive Semantic Web applications. We propose the design of an *Application Server for the Semantic Web (ASSW)*, extending the functionality of common application servers by supporting application development for the Semantic Web. The aim is to facilitate the reuse of existing software modules, e.g., ontology stores, editors or reasoners, to coordinate the information flow between such modules, to broadcast events between different modules and to translate between ontology-based data formats.

The requirements derived from the scenario can be grouped as follows: First, such a server should respond to the static aspects of the Semantic Web layer cake (cf. Figure 4.2 on page 58). Second, the Semantic Web's dynamic aspects (also depicted in Figure 4.2 on page 58) result in another group of requirements, viz., finding, accessing, modifying and storing of data, transactions and rollbacks, evolution and versioning, monitoring, as well as inferencing and verification. Third, clients, e.g., portal applications or ontology editors, may want to connect remotely to the server by different protocols and must be properly authorized. Hence, another group deals with connectivity and security. Fourth, the system is expected to facilitate an extensible and reconfigurable infrastructure. This set of requirements, therefore, deals with the flexible handling of modules.

The use cases introduced in Chapter 4, Section 2.1, deal with the semantic enhancement of the server, which poses a fifth group of requirements. In the following sections, we investigate the groups organized in requirements specific to the Semantic Web, common requirements, i.e., requirements that hold for every application server, and requirements that call for the semantic enhancement of the server itself.

Semantic Web Specific Requirements

Requirements Stemming from the Semantic Web's Static Part

The static part of the Semantic Web is introduced in Figure 4.2 on page 58. In essence, the static part defines a stack of languages with increasing modelling capabilities. The requirements below follow straightforwardly from this stack.

- *Language Support* A trivial requirement is the support of all the Semantic Web's ontology and metadata standards. An application server for the Semantic Web has to be aware of RDF, RDFS, OWL, as well as future languages that will be used to specify the logic, proof and trust layers.

- *Semantic Interoperation* We use the term semantic interoperation in the sense of translating between different ontology languages with different semantics. Although the languages of the Semantic Web's static part are standardized and compatible with each other, there remain many widespread proprietary efforts, such as F-Logic [Kifer et al., 1995] or KAON [Maedche et al., 2003], which have to be supported. Hence, an application server for the Semantic Web should enable translation between different languages and semantics [Grosof et al., 2003, Bennett et al., 2002].

- *Ontology Mapping* In contrast to semantic interoperation, ontology mapping translates between different ontologies of the same language. Mapping may become necessary as Web communities usually have their own ontology and could use ontology mapping to facilitate data exchange [Ehrig and Staab, 2004, Noy and Musen, 2000, Handschuh et al., 2003, Euzenat, 2004].

- *Ontology Modularization* Modularization is an established principle in software engineering. It has to be considered also for ontology engineering as the development of large domain ontologies often includes the reuse of several existing ontologies. For example, foundational ontologies might be used as a starting point. Hence, an application server for the Semantic Web should provide means to meet that requirement [Stuckenschmidt and Klein, 2004, Volz et al., 2002, Borgida and Serafini, 2002, Maedche et al., 2003].

Requirements Stemming from the Semantic Web's Dynamic Part

The dynamic part of the Semantic Web is also introduced in Figure 4.2 on page 58. Every dynamic aspect yields a corresponding requirement.

- *Finding, Accessing, Modifying and Storing of Ontologies* Semantic Web applications such as search engines (e.g., http://swoogle.umbc.edu/), editors or portals, have to access, modify and finally store ontological data. In addition, the development of domain ontologies often requires other ontologies as starting points. Examples are the foundational ontologies introduced in Chapter 6, Section 2. Those can be stored and offered by the server to editors.

- *Transactions and Rollbacks* The dynamic aspects transactions and rollbacks lead to further requirements. All updates to the Semantic Web data must be done within transactions assuring the properties of atomicity, consistency, isolation (concurrency) and durability (ACID) [Ullman, 1988]. Although, in general, transactions can be considered as a common requirement, they can become specific as the Semantic Web languages require special handling.

- *Evolution and Versioning* Ontologies are applied in dynamic environments with changing application requirements (cf. [Stojanovic et al., 2002b]). The underlying ontology must be evolved as well to apply the changes. Ontology evolution and versioning has its roots in database research. Evolution is the ability to change a schema of a populated database without loss of data (i.e., providing access to both old and new data through the new schema). Schema versioning is the ability to access all the data (both old and new) through different version interfaces. [Peters and Oezsu, 1997, Banerjee et al., 1987, Stojanovic et al., 2002a, Noy and Klein, 2002, Volz et al., 2003e]

- *Monitoring* Monitoring can be regarded as the process of checking, observing or keeping track of application data for a specific period of time or at specified intervals. An example are web logs of portals which help site administrators to identify traffic, possible bandwidth problems, broken links, etc. However, because the primary focus of this kind of usage recording is technical, an interpretation of URLs in terms of user behavior, interests, and intentions, is not always straightforward. In order to obtain meaningful results, the Web logs must contain the semantics of the pages visited along user paths. [Oberle et al., 2003a]

- *Inferencing and Verification* Inference engines are core components of ontology-based applications and can be used for several tasks such as semantic validation and reasoning. An application server for the Semantic Web should provide access to such engines, which can deliver the reasoning services required. This requirement is not to be confused with the inferencing done in the server itself (cf. the requirements for the semantic enhancement of the server below).

Common Requirements

Common requirements are ones that essentially hold for every application server. We list them here for the sake of completeness.

Connectivity and Security

- *Connectivity* An application server should enable loose coupling, allowing access through standard protocols, as well as close coupling by embedding it into an application. In other words, a client should be able to use the system locally and connect to it remotely.

- *Ease of Use* A developer does not want to expend extra effort in connecting to and using a software component when an application server is applied. A software component ought to be accessed seamlessly.

- *Offering Functionality via Different Communication Protocols* There might be the need to offer a software component's functionality via another communication protocol. For instance, the application server should be able to offer its methods via separate Web services, via peer or agent protocols.

- *Security* Guaranteeing information security means protection against unauthorized disclosure, transfer, modification or destruction, whether accidental or intentional. To realize it, any operation should only be accessible by properly authorized clients. Proper identity must be reliably established by employing authentication techniques. Confidential data must be encrypted for network communication and persistent storage.

Flexible Handling of Modules

- *Extensibility* The need for extensibility applies to most software systems. It is a principle of software engineering to avoid system changes when additional functionality is needed in the future. Hence, extensibility is also desirable for an application server. In addition, our scenario deals with the multitude of layers and data models in the Semantic Web that lead to a multitude of software modules, e.g., XML parsers or validators that support the XML Schema datatypes, RDF stores, tools that map RDFS ontologies to relational databases, ontology stores and OWL reasoners. Therefore, extensibility regarding new data API's and corresponding software components is an important requirement.

- *Integrating Existing Functionality via Different Communication Protocols* A developer might want to integrate different kinds of software entities, e.g., Web services, peers or agents, required to build an application. That enables them to be included in a transaction, for instance, and lifts the responsibility of handling different protocols from the developer.

- *Constraints* The server should enable the expression of constraints among different software components, such as the setting up of event listeners between components. Another example is the management of a dependency, such as "component A is required for component B."

Requirements for the Semantic Enhancement of the Server

In Chapter 4, Section 2.1 we identify several use cases for the semantic management of software components in application servers: *Library Dependencies and Versioning, Licensing, Capability Descriptions, Component Classification and Discovery, Semantics of Parameters, Automatic Generation of Web Service Descriptions, Access Rights, Error Handling, Transactional Settings, Secure Communication.* We combine these requirements into one group because they all call for the semantic enhancement of the server.

The common requirements are met by most of the existing application servers. Semantic Web specific requirements are relevant only for our scenario. The ones that call for the semantic enhancement of the server itself are clearly beyond state-of-the-art and of primary interest. In the following sections, we develop an architecture that is a result of the requirements put forward in this section. Later, in Chapter 9, we present the details of our implementation, called KAON SERVER.

2.2   The Microkernel Design Pattern

This section marks the starting point for the design of our ontology-based application server. The design is expected to meet all the requirements put forward in the previous section. We start with the consideration of the requirement for *Extensibility*, resulting in the first fundamental design decision: the use of the Microkernel design pattern. The pattern applies to software systems that must be able to adapt to changing system requirements. It separates a minimal functional core, i.e., the Microkernel, from extended functionality and application-specific parts. The Microkernel also serves as a socket for plugging in these extensions and coordinating their collaboration [Buschmann et al., 1996].

The Microkernel can be seen as a framework providing basic operations, i.e., the starting, initializing, monitoring, combining, and the stopping of software components, as well as the dispatching of messages between them. The Microkernel acts as a basis for our application server. The basic operations mentioned above are performed on software components. Software components have to conform to the Microkernel's required interfaces in order to be handled by the Microkernel. Conformity is accomplished by *making existing software deployable*, i.e., wrapping existing software in such a way that it implements the Microkernel's required interfaces. In our scenario, ontology-related software modules, such as RDF or ontology stores, have to be made deployable. *Deployment* describes the process of registering a component to the Microkernel with possible initialization and start.

Apart from the cost of making existing software deployable, a drawback of this approach is that performance will suffer slightly in comparison to stand alone use, as a request has to pass through the Microkernel first (and possibly the network). A client that wants to make use of a deployed component's functionality talks to the Microkernel, which in turn dispatches requests.

However, the Microkernel approach delivers several benefits. By making existing software deployable, one is able to handle it in a centralized infrastructure. As a result, we are able to deploy and undeploy components ad hoc, reconfigure, monitor and possibly distribute them dynamically. Proxy components can be developed for software that cannot be made deployable, e.g., because it has been developed for a specific operating system. Furthermore, the Microkernel facilitates the use of interceptors. Interceptors are software entities that monitor a request and modify it before the request is sent to the component. They are a powerful means for increasing flexibility.

2.3   Integration of an Inference Engine

In this section we respond to the group of *Requirements for the Semantic Enhancement of the Server*. All of them implicitly call for the application of our management ontology, providing the means for semantic descriptions of software components. Thus, the second fundamental design decision is to integrate an inference engine that stores and reasons with descriptions of all deployed components. The Microkernel approach requires the integration of an inference engine itself as a component.

From the Microkernel's perspective, every component looks alike. We have to classify the components in order to facilitate development and administration. Such a classification has to be captured by the domain version of our management ontology when applying it in the resulting server. Chapter 10 discusses the application and reuse of the management ontology in more detail. We can identify the following types of components:

System Component Software component providing functionality for the application server itself, e.g., the inference engine.

Functional Component Software component that constitutes application logic. The ontology-related software modules of our scenario become functional components by making them deployable, e.g., RDF stores.

External Module An external module cannot be deployed directly as it may be programmed in a different language or live on a different computing platform. It is equivalent to a functional component from a client perspective by having a proxy component deployed that relays communication to the external module.

Proxy Component Proxy components are special types of functional components that manage the communication to an external module.

Our design leaves open the different ways of using the inference engine (cf. Section 1.3). Depending on the specific implementation and depending on the use case considered, we may realize: (*i*) the reverse engineering approach by obtaining semantic descriptions, (*ii*) model-driven deployment by modelling semantic descriptions and generating specific deployment descriptors and (*iii*) the ontology run time approach, i.e., disposing descriptors in general.

2.4   Architecture

The first two design decisions, i.e., the Microkernel approach and the integration of the inference engine as a component itself, constitute the basis for our architecture. In this section, we complete the design of the server by detailing its overall architecture.

For the Semantic Web scenario we envision the following interplay of design elements: When a client connects to the application server, it either needs to discover the required functional components or to deploy them itself. In the first case, the client uses the inference engine to find a deployed functional component fulfilling its prescriptions. The client retrieves a reference as a response. From then on, the client can seamlessly work with the functional component by surrogates that handle the communication over the network. On the server side, the counterpart to the surrogate is a connector component. It maps requests to the Microkernel's methods. All requests pass the Microkernel, which dispatches them to the appropriate functional component. While dispatching, a request can be modified by interceptors that may deal with auditing, for instance. Finally, the response passes the Microkernel again and finds its way to the client through the connector and the surrogate. The following paragraphs explain the architecture depicted in Figure 8.4.

Surrogates

Surrogates (not shown in Figure 8.4) are objects embedded in the client application that relieve the developer of the communication details similar to stubs in CORBA (cf. requirement *Ease of Use*). They offer the same API as a specific component and relay communication to any connector, which in turn passes the request to the respective functional component through the Microkernel.

Connectors

Connectors are system components. They send and receive requests and responses over the network. Aside from the option to connect locally, further possibilities may exist for remote connection: e.g., ones that offer access via Java Remote Method Invocation (RMI) or ones that offer asynchronous communication. Connectors also allow publishing components' methods as separate Web services. Offering the functionality with peer or agent protocols is also possible (cf. requirement *Offering Functionality via Different Communication Protocols*).

Server Core

The server core comprises the Microkernel (also called kernel), as well as several system components. It is required to deal with the discovery, allocation and loading of components. The inference engine, a system component, man-

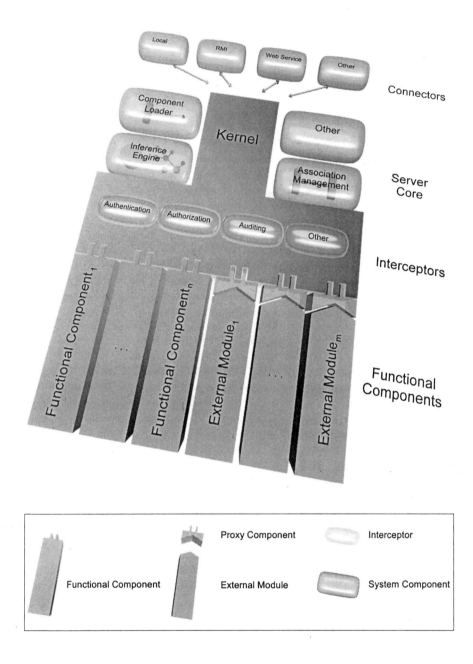

Figure 8.4.   Architecture of the ontology-based application server.

ages descriptions of the components and allows the reasoning with them. The component loader facilitates the deployment process for a client. It takes a semantic description of a component as argument, handles the deployment, integrates the description in the inference engine and ontology and applies the association management if necessary. The latter is another system component that puts ontological constraints among components into action. For example, event listeners can be put in charge so that a component A is notified when B issues an event. Another example might be a component which may only be undeployed if others do not rely on it.

System components can be deployed and undeployed ad hoc, so extensibility is also given for the server core. Further components are possible, e.g., a cascading component that offers seamless access to the components deployed in another application server.

Interceptors

Interceptors are software entities that monitor a request and modify it before the request is sent to the component. Interceptors allow the sharing of generic functionality, such as security, logging, or concurrency control, and require less work than developing individual component implementations. A component can be deployed with a stack of arbitrary interceptors. For example, when a component is restarted, an interceptor can block and queue incoming requests until the component is available again. Another example are security aspects which can be met by interceptors that guarantee that operations offered by functional components in the server are only available to appropriately authenticated and authorized clients.

Functional Components

Functional components are the ones that constitute the application logic. They are of primary interest to the developer whereas system components are a means to an end. In our scenario, RDF stores and ontology stores, etc., are deployed to the kernel as functional components. Proxy components (which are conceptually subsumed by functional components) cannot only be developed for external modules, but also for Web services, peers or agents. That allows a developer to access them conveniently by surrogates instead of handling several other protocols. In addition, interceptors can be applied on top, so that, e.g., a Web service might be part of a transaction along operations of a deployed ontology store.

Table 8.1 shows where the requirements put forward in Section 2.1 are reflected in the architecture. Due to the Microkernel design pattern the architecture basically consists of the Microkernel itself, components, interceptors and surrogates. Components are classified into system, functional and proxy com-

Table 8.1.   Dependencies between requirements (cf. Section 2.1) and design elements.

Requirement \ Design Element	Kernel	Connectors	Inference Engine	Component Loader	Association Management	Functional Components	Proxy Components	Interceptors	Surrogates
Language Support						×			
Semantic Interoperation						×		×	
Ontology Mapping						×			
Ontology Modularization						×		×	
Finding, Accessing, Storing of Ontologies						×			
Transactions and Rollbacks						×		×	
Evolution and Versioning						×		×	
Monitoring						×		×	
Inferencing and Verification						×			
Connectivity		×							
Ease of Use									×
Offering Functionality via Protocols		×							
Security								×	
Extensibility	×	×		×		×	×	×	
Integrating Functionality via Protocols							×		
Constraints					×				
Requirements for Semantic Enhancement			×						

ponents to facilitate their handling and discovery for the application developer. Table 8.1 only shows connectors as subconcept of system component, as well as the inference engine, the component loader and the association management, which are specific system components. Functional and proxy components are represented in one column each.

Most of the Semantic Web specific requirements (*Language Support* to *Inferencing and Verification* in Table 8.1) are met by functional components. We expect that existing software will be made deployable and as such integrated to meet the requirements. In addition, *Semantic Interoperation* can also be realized by interceptors which can translate between Semantic Web ontology languages. For example, if a client wants to talk in frame logic to an OWL ontology store, an interceptor could be registered that automatically translates the request. *Ontology Modularization, Transactions and Rollbacks, Evolution and Versioning*, as well as *Monitoring*, are different in that they all can be implemented within one functional component. A comprehensive ontology store might offer means for transactions, for instance. Interceptors, on the other hand, can realize those mechanisms on top of several components. Akin to what a transaction monitor does with several database systems, an interceptor would be capable of realizing transactions spanning several ontology stores.

The remaining requirements (*Connectivity* to *Requirements for Semantic Enhancement* in Table 8.1) are met as follows: the need for flexible *Connectivity* to the server and the *Offering of Functionality via Different Protocols* is realized by different connector components that can be deployed and undeployed ad hoc. *Ease of Use* particularly affects the surrogate objects, which are objects embedded in the client application to hide to different communication protocols. We expect that *Security* will mainly be realized by interceptors. The requirement of *Extensibility* is met by the Microkernel and component approach as discussed in Section 2.2. Interceptors also foster extensibility because they can be deployed with a component at run time. Proxy components allow the *Integration of Exiting Functionality* and *Constraints* can be handled by the association management system component. Finally, the *Requirements for the Semantic Enhancement* of the server are met by the inference engine.

3. Semantic Management of Web Services

We have discussed in Section 1.1 that application servers typically provide Web service support and, therefore, can also be considered for some of the Web service use cases. Hence, we have decided to use our ontology-based application server also as a platform for the semantic management of Web services. Basically, the realization of semantic management of Web services boils down to an extension of the server. In this section we discuss what this extension looks like.

In Chapter 4, Section 2.2, we have identified several use cases for the semantic management of Web services: *Analyzing Message Contexts*, *Selecting Service Functionality*, *Policy Handling*, *Detecting Loops in Interorganizational Workflows*, *Incompatible Input and Outputs*, *Relating Communication Parameters*, *Monitoring of Changes*, *Aggregating Service Information* and *Quality of Service*. The set of realizable use cases is reduced when choosing an application server as platform: *Detecting Loops in Interorganizational Workflows*, as well as *Aggregating Service Information*, require a Web service composition engine. Furthermore, our relatively simple scenario, called "Web services in SmartWeb" (cf. Chapter 4, Section 1.2, page 62), does not require the *Policy Handling* use case. Regarding the use cases, we can derive the following design elements that have to be integrated in our ontology-based application server:

Metadata Collector Section 1.3 has already indicated that functionality is required to obtain the WS* descriptions of used Web services. We call this functionality metadata collector and integrate it as a system component into our application server. Given the URL of a WS* description, it retrieves the file, parses it, extracts relevant information and integrates the semantic descriptions. Obtaining the descriptions is already sufficient to realize *Monitoring of Changes* and *Incompatible Inputs and Outputs* and serves as a basis for all the other use cases.

Web Service Connector The basic requirement for the *Analyzing Message Context* use case is a SOAP engine, i.e., a Web service connector. The metadata collector can also obtain information from in-and-outcoming SOAP messages. Browsing and querying the inference engine allows the developer to analyze the messages.

Service Matchmaker Manually browsing service capability descriptions or an automatic service matchmaker is required for the use case of *Selecting Service Functionality*. Service matchmakers compare a given service requirement description to several service offering descriptions and choose the best fitting one. Several service matchmaking engines have been prototypically implemented in the area of "Semantic Web Services" (cf. related work in Chapter 11, Section 4). For example, [Li and Horrocks, 2003, Paolucci et al., 2002c, Noia et al., 2003]. Such engines can be integrated as functional components.

Policy Engine For *Policy Handling* and *Relating Communication Parameters* or the even more sophisticated task of automated policy matching, we need a corresponding policy engine. It can be integrated as a component as well, acting on a semantic service description in the inference engine and the policy of an external service. There are some prototypes available in the area of "Semantic Web Services" (cf. related work in Chapter 11, Section 4). For example, [Tonti et al., 2003, Kagal et al., 2003, Agarwal and Sprick, 2004].

Monitoring Interceptor Regarding the use case of *Quality of Service*, an interceptor can be put in place. It allows the monitoring of service requests and, thus, the gathering of statistics on the reliability and availability of business partners' IT infrastructure. Assuming the system is aware of potential endpoints implementing a required service, these endpoints can be pinged regularly. If an actual request arrives, aggregated availability information can be used to direct subsequent requests to one or the other third party service.

Table 8.2 compares the use cases and the design elements that realize them. The metadata collector is necessary for the realization of every use case, emphasizing that semantic management of Web services requires the *Reverse Engineering Approach* because of the standardization of WS* descriptions. *Model-Driven Deployment* is possible in principle, but not required by the use cases considered.

Table 8.2. Dependencies between use cases and design elements.

	Metadata Collector	Web service Connector	Service Matchmaker	Policy Engine	Monitoring Interceptor
		Components			
Use Case \ Design Element					
Analyzing Message Contexts	×	×			
Selecting Service Functionality	×		×		
Policy Handling	×			×	
Incompatible Inputs and Outputs	×				
Relating Communication Parameters	×			×	
Monitoring of Changes	×				
Quality of Service	×				×

4. Summary

In this chapter we have answered the Question III.1: *What is a suitable target platform?* We have opted for an application server, but have come to the conclusion that other platforms would benefit from semantic technology as well. The next question we have answered in this chapter is III.2: *Who provides semantic descriptions?* We have seen that there are many potential sources that allow the (semi) automatic obtaining of semantic descriptions. Therefore, the number of manually provided descriptions can be kept small. We have then moved on to design an ontology-based application server that supports the semantic management of components and services. The resulting architecture is rather generic but provides a number of components to support application development in the Semantic Web (as introduced in our scenario in Chapter 4, Section 1.1). The following chapter presents a possible implementation of this design.

Chapter 9

IMPLEMENTATION

In the last chapter we have designed the architecture of an ontology-based application server that enables the semantic management of components and services. The server provides a number of components to facilitate the development of Semantic Web applications. In this chapter, we implement the architecture, thus answering the Question III.3: *How to implement semantic management?* The recipe for implementation is quite simple: (*i*) reuse an existing application server; i.e., map the design elements of the architecture to concrete implementation elements of the application server and (*ii*) integrate the ontology infrastructure (inference engine, ontology store, ontology editor, etc.) of an existing ontology tool suite.

Regarding (*i*), we choose the open source application server *JBoss*, which is based on the Java Management Extensions (JMX), providing a flexible framework for plugging components in and out at run time. We briefly introduce JBoss in Section 1. Regarding (*ii*), we leverage the wealth of tools provided by the Karlsruhe Ontology and Semantic Web tool suite, *KAON* [Maedche et al., 2003]. A brief overview of KAON is provided in Section 2. We particularly focus on its inference engine, ontology store and ontology editor because we apply them in JBoss. The result of this fruitful combination is called *KAON SERVER* which will be discussed in Section 3. We finish in Section 4 by an example which demonstrates the usefulness of the KAON SERVER for building Semantic Web applications. An assessment of the benefits of its semantic enhancement, as well as the details regarding the application of the management ontology, follow in Chapter 10.

Most of this chapter has been published in conference proceedings, journals and project reports. The KAON SERVER has been outlined and described in several publications [Oberle et al., 2005d, Oberle et al., 2004a, Oberle et al., 2004d, Oberle et al., 2004c, Volz et al., 2003a]. An in-depth discussion of its technical details is given in WonderWeb deliverables [Oberle et al., 2003d, Oberle et al., 2003e, Volz et al., 2003b, Volz et al., 2003c, Volz et al., 2003d, Motik et al., 2002]. The KAON SERVER prototype can be downloaded at `http://kaon.semanticweb.org/server`.

1. The JBoss Application Server

JBoss is an open source J2EE compliant application server.[1] Its core, a JMX implementation called JBossMX, will also act as a basis for our KAON SERVER. In this section, we briefly discuss JMX, JBossMX and the architecture of JBoss.

JMX (Java Management Extensions) is a specification from Sun defining a framework for flexible component-based applications [Lindfors and Fleury, 2002]. JMX defines interfaces of specific software components, called managed beans, or *MBeans* for short.[2] MBeans are hosted by an *MBeanServer*, which allows their manipulation. All operations performed on the MBeans are done through interfaces on the MBeanServer as depicted in Figure 9.1. We would like to point out two important methods of the MBeanServer, namely:

```
registerMBean(Object object, ObjectName name)
```

which, as the name suggests, registers an object as MBean to the MBeanServer; the object has to fulfill a certain contract implementing a prescribed interface, and

```
Object invoke(ObjectName name, String operationName,
              Object[]params, String[] signature)
```

All method invocations are tunnelled through the MBeanServer to the actual MBean by this method. The corresponding MBean is specified by `name`, whereas `operationName, params` and `signature` provide the rest of the information needed. Type checking has to be done by the developer and method calls are centralized. Hence, the architecture responds flexibly to changing requirements and evolving interfaces. Due to this technique, it becomes easy to incorporate the mechanism of interceptors.

An MBean must be a public Java object with at least one public constructor. An MBean must have a statically typed Java interface that explicitly declares the management attributes and operations. The naming conventions used in the MBean interface closely follow the rules set by the JavaBeans component model. To expose the management attributes, one has to declare `get` and `set` methods, similar to JavaBean component properties. The MBeanServer

---

[1]`http://www.jboss.org`
[2]For an introduction to J2EE, components and frameworks, please cf. Chapter 2, Section 3.1.

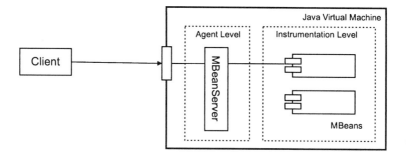

Figure 9.1. JMX Architecture. [Lindfors and Fleury, 2002]

uses introspection on the MBean class to determine which interfaces the class implements. In order to be recognized as a standard MBean, a class x has to implement an interface xMBean. Defining the methods getAttr() and setAttr() will automatically make Attr a management attribute, with read and write access in this case. Only management attributes can be accessed and modified by a client. All the other public methods will be exposed as management operations. Each MBean is accessible by its identifying name, which follows a special syntax.

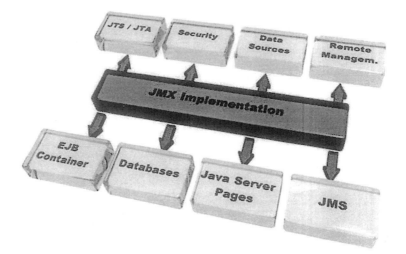

Figure 9.2. Basic architecture of JBoss. The "JMX implementation" represents the MBeanServer of JBossMX. J2EE services, such as "JTS/JTA," "Security," etc., come in the form of MBeans. [http://www.jboss.org]

JMX is only a specification. It can be implemented differently by vendors. There are several implementations available with proprietary extensions. Accordingly, JBoss provides its own implementation of JMX, called *JBossMX*.

JBossMX is the basis of the JBoss application server whose general architecture is depicted in Figure 9.2. JBoss is developed modularly from the ground up. The application server is completely implemented using MBeans. Typical J2EE functionality, such as servlet or EJB containers, are hosted in the form of MBeans.

The modularity benefits the application developer in several ways. The size of JBoss, i.e., the amount of required software libraries, can be further trimmed down to support applications that must have a small footprint. For example, if support for Enterprise JavaBeans is required, the corresponding MBean can be deployed at run time. The MBean can be undeployed on demand when it is not required by an application.

2. The KAON Tool Suite

KAON is an open-source ontology management tool suite targeted at semantics-driven business applications. KAON consists of a number of different tools providing a broad bandwidth of functionalities centered around creation, storage, retrieval, maintenance and application of ontologies. [Maedche et al., 2003, Bozsak et al., 2002, Gabel et al., 2004] The tool suite can be obtained from http://kaon.semanticweb.org. An overview of the tool suite is depicted in Figure 9.3.

We have chosen KAON because its API offers rather advanced features, such as transactions, remote access and client-side caching, which are required for efficient and scalable usage in an application server. For implementing our ontology-based application server, we only use the *API on RDF* implementation of the KAON API as inference engine and ontology store, as well as the *OI-Modeller* as management console. However, it is necessary to shortly introduce the whole toolsuite for a better understanding.

KAON Applications. KAON is distributed with two different applications for ontology creation and management: KAON Workbench and KAON Portal. The *KAON Workbench* provides a graphical environment in turn consisting of three applications: the OI-Modeller, TextToOnto and the Open Registry (a.k.a. Ontology Registry). The *OI-Modeller* is a graphical ontology browser for creating, editing and maintaining ontologies. A screenshot of the OI-Modeller is depicted in Figure 9.4. *TextToOnto* supports the ontology engineering process by text mining techniques. It provides a collection of independent tools for both automatic and semi-automatic ontology extraction. The *Ontology Registry* provides mechanisms for registering and searching ontologies in a distributed context. Finally, *KAON Portal* is a simple tool for multi-lingual, ontology-

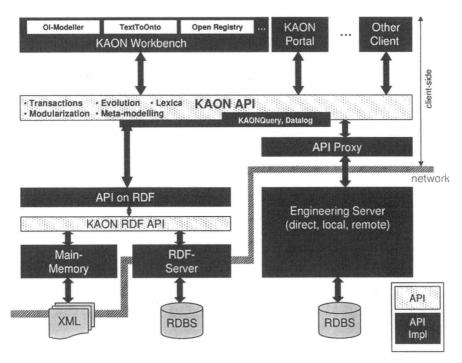

Figure 9.3. KAON tool suite overview. [Gabel et al., 2004]

based Web portals. All of the applications use the KAON API to access and modify ontologies. Other clients can be built accordingly. The KAON API is discussed in the next paragraph.

KAON API. The focal point of the KAON tool suite is its ontology API (*KAON API*), consisting of a set of interfaces for access to ontology entities (OI-models, concepts, associations and instances). The API is based on the KAON language which organizes concepts and associations, as well as instances in *OI-models*. We further discuss the language idiosyncracies in Chapter 10. The API supports advanced features, such as client-side caching and remote access, and incorporates important elements required for the management of OI-models:

- Changes of OI-models are always performed within a *transaction* as a single unit of work. Therefore, the KAON API uses transactions to isolate updates of one user from updates of other users.

- The KAON API supports *modularization* of ontologies by means of ontology inclusion. Each OI-model may include other OI-models, given that they reside in API implementations of the same kind (cf. the discussion

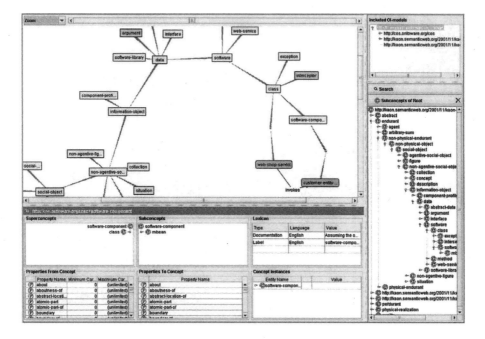

Figure 9.4. KAON OI-Modeller screenshot. Concepts are represented by rectangles, instances by rounded boxes, associations (also called properties in the figure) by labelled edges. Subconcept associations are represented by non-labelled edges. Clicking on "Search" allows the user to enter an arbitrary query.

of different KAON API implementations below). Because the inclusion is implemented as a link, not as a copy, all changes to the included OI-model will immediately affect the including OI-model.

- *Evolution* strategies are responsible for making sure that all changes applied on the ontology leave the ontology in a consistent state; they are also responsible for preventing illegal changes. The evolution strategy also allows the user to customize the evolution process. [Stojanovic, 2004]

- The KAON API supports concept *meta-modelling*, which means that it is possible to treat concepts and associations as instances of meta-concepts. Thus, a concept and an instance with the same URI may exist simultaneously in the same OI-model.

- Concepts, associations and instances are considered as language-neutral by the KAON API. However, *lexica*, referring to different entities in the KAON representation vocabulary, may be defined. The standard lexical description are multilingual labels that may be applied to improve the user's interface.

Another kind of lexical entries are morphologically reduced word stems that may be used by a natural language processing system.

The KAON API relies on a *Datalog* engine to implement lightweight reasoning and querying. Datalog is a database query language that is a syntactic subset of Prolog [Abiteboul et al., 1995]. The emphasis in the KAON API is on conceptual querying, which is different from the traditional query language defined by Datalog, where source and results of queries are always relational. Hence, the KAON API defines its own query language, called *KAON Query*, that considers the idiosyncracies of conceptual querying.

KAON API Implementations.   The KAON API provides abstract interfaces for accessing various types of ontologies independent of the storage mechanism. *API on RDF* and *API Proxy* are two different implementations of the KAON API as discussed below.

API on RDF The *API on RDF* implementation represents an in-memory implementation of the KAON API to access RDF-based data sources via the *KAON RDF API*. Two reference implementations exist for the KAON RDF API: On the one hand, KAON offers a simple *main-memory* implementation, including RDF parser and serializer. On the other hand, we have the *RDF Server* which implements the KAON RDF API remotely and allows for the persistent storage of RDF ontology models in relational databases.

API Proxy The *API Proxy* is an implementation of the KAON API that acts as a client-side proxy for various types of the KAON *Engineering Server*. The Engineering Server provides mechanisms to store KAON ontologies in relational databases, to distribute change notifications (thus allowing for multi-user ontology engineering) and to bulk-load ontology elements.

In the subsequent section, we discuss the application of the *API on RDF*, as well as the *OI-Modeller*, in JBoss. The result of this combination is called *KAON SERVER*, implementing the design proposed in Chapter 8.

3.   KAON SERVER

Our prototype of an ontology-based application server, called *KAON SERVER*, implements the architecture that is presented in the previous chapter. As depicted in Figure 8.4 on page 164, the architecture consists of connectors, the server core, interceptors and functional components. In principle, the KAON SERVER implements the architecture by using JBoss as a basis and by applying the tools of KAON for the semantic enhancement of the server. Regarding the semantic management of Web services, the prototype only provides the Web service connector and the metadata collector.

An in-depth description follows. We start with discussing the server core in 3.1 as it is necessary to understand connectors in 3.2, interceptors in 3.3 and functional components in 3.4. We finish with a look at the management console in 3.5. Figure 9.5 acts as a guide throughout the section, summarizing the mapping between design and implementation elements.

Design Elements		Implementation Elements
Server Core: Kernel	←⟶	JBossMX: MBeanServer
Server Core: Inference Engine	←⟶	KAON: API on RDF as MBean
Server Core: Association Management	←⟶	KAON SERVER: Association Management MBean
Server Core: Component Loader	←⟶	KAON SERVER: Component Loader MBean
Server Core: Metadata Collector	←⟶	KAON SERVER: Metadata Collector MBean
Connectors	←⟶	KAON SERVER: HTTP Adapter, etc.
Interceptors	←⟶	KAON SERVER: Interceptors
Functional Components	←⟶	KAON tools as MBeans and external modules
Functional Components	←⟶	MBeans from JBoss (EJB Container, JTS/JTA, etc.)

Figure 9.5. Mapping from the design elements introduced in Section 2.4 to the implementation elements.

The KAON SERVER applies the *Ontology Run Time* approach (cf. Section 1.3) where components, such as the association management or the component loader, work directly with the inference engine.

3.1   Server Core

The server core consists of the kernel and the following system components: the inference engine, the association management, the component loader and the metadata collector. We outline all of their implementations below.

Kernel

In the case of the KAON SERVER, we use the JBoss implementation of JMX, called JBossMX, as it provides a Microkernel approach, i.e., a flexible framework for deploying and undeploying components at run time. In our setting, the MBeanServer implements the kernel and MBeans implement components. Speaking in terms of JMX, there is no difference between a system component and a functional component. Both are MBeans that are only distinguished in their corresponding semantic descriptions.

Inference Engine

The inference engine is a simple main-memory based ontology store with reasoning capabilities containing component and service descriptions. This information source is built around our management ontology, which specifies the functional aspects of a component, e.g., the libraries required by a component, its name, the class that implements the component itself and so forth. Chapter 10 discusses the adaptation of the management ontology to this specific use.

We wrap the main-memory implementation of the KAON API (API on RDF) as a MBean and use it with an applied version of the management ontology. When a component is deployed, its description (usually stored in an XML file) is represented as an instance of a concept. A client can use the inference engine's surrogate to discover the component it needs or to execute arbitrary KAON queries.

Association Management

The management ontology allows one to express associations between components, such as inter-component dependencies. Therefore, the server has to load all required components and has to be aware of such dependencies when unloading components. Association management tracks the number of clients for a component and will only unload the component if no clients are present.

The JMX specification does not define any type of association management aspect for MBeans. That is the reason why we had to implement this functionality separately as another MBean. Apart from dependencies, it is able to register and manage event listeners between two MBeans A and B, so that B is notified whenever A issues an event.

Component Loader

The MBeanServer offers methods to deploy any MBean at run time; however, the client application of an MBeanServer must explicitly create the MBeans it needs. It must maintain the list of required libraries, and it must integrate the semantic descriptions of newly created MBeans into the inference engine and ontology by itself.

To lift these responsibilities from the individual client, we have developed a special component loader MBean that facilitates the deployment process. MBeans are described by KAON XML serializations according to the management ontology. The component loader uses this description to deploy the MBean, to integrate the MBean component description in the inference engine and ontology and to put associations into action by applying the association management. For example, it deals with the transitive loading of required components. The component loader is able to deploy an MBean from arbitrary URL's; hence, users of the server are not required to install any libraries on the server machine before instantiating a component. The component loader also ensures that shared libraries that are part of the component implementation are only loaded once if multiple components share the same library.

Metadata Collector

Besides the Web service connector, the prototypical KAON SERVER implementation provides a metadata collector responding to the required design elements for semantic management of Web services (cf. Section 3). After providing the URI's of WSDL, WS-BPEL or WS-Policy documents, the metadata collector retrieves the documents and adds them as semantic descriptions to the inference engine. This basically requires a mapping from the documents' tags to concepts and associations of our management ontology. We have already given an example for a resulting service profile of WS-BPEL and WS-Policy documents in Chapter 7, Section 4.3.

In the following, we exemplarily sketch how such a mapping can be achieved in order to provide the general idea. For a detailed description of the mapping algorithm please cf. [Oberle et al., 2003d]. Table 9.1 shows the basic mapping for a selection of WSDL tags and the ontology. Note that the table only sketches the mapping which basically requires a traversal of the document that must also consider attributes of the tags.

Table 9.1.   A selection of WSDL tags and their mapping to concepts and associations of our management ontology.

WSDL Tags	Part of Management Ontology
`<service>`	COWS:ServiceProfile
`<operation>`	CSO:Method
`<input>`	CSO:Input
`<output>`	CSO:Output
`<fault>`	CSO:Exception
`<complexType>`	CSO:dataType
`<simpleType>`	CSO:dataType

In a similar way, Table 9.2 sketches how a mapping from WS-BPEL documents to the management ontology can be achieved. Note that we only consider the workflow information and neglect variables, assignments and correlation. Basically, the WS-BPEL process results in an OoP:Plan with corresponding tasks. The OoP:Plan becomes part of a COWS:ServiceProfile. The OoP:successor association is obtained by considering the nesting of the tags or by explicit BPEL `partnerLinks` (Web service invocations).

The mapping from WS-Policy to the management ontology is sketched in Table 9.3. CSO:PolicyDescriptions of the management ontology model

Table 9.2. A selection of WS-BPEL tags and their mapping to concepts and associations of our management ontology.

WS-BPEL Tags	Part of Management Ontology
`<process>`	OoP:Plan
`<sequence>`	OoP:SequentialTask
`<switch>`	OoP:CaseTask
`<while>`	OoP:LoopTask

WS-Policy assertions. Every COWS:ServiceProfile can contain several CSO:PolicyDescriptions to reflect alternatives (the `<ExactlyOne>` tag). Conjunctions of assertions are represented by nested CSO:PolicyDescriptions (the `All` tag) .

Table 9.3. A selection of WS-Policy tags and their mapping to concepts and associations of our management ontology.

WS-Policy Tags	Part of Management Ontology
Assertions	One CSO:PolicyDescription per assertion
`<ExactlyOne>`	One of the CSO:PolicyDescription in a COWS:ServiceProfile
`<All>`	All of the CSO:PolicyDescription in a CSO:PolicyDescription

3.2 Connectors

The KAON SERVER comes with four MBeans that handle communication. First, there is the HTTP Adapter from Sun, which exposes all of the kernel's methods to a Web frontend. It acts as a JMX console for the administrator. Second and third, we have developed Web service (using the Simple Object Access Protocol) and RMI (Java Remote Method Invocation) connector MBeans. Both export the kernel's methods for remote access. Finally, the Local connector embeds the KAON SERVER locally into the client application.

For the client there is a surrogate object called `RemoteMBeanServer` that implements the `MBeanServer` interface. It is the counterpart to one of the four connector MBeans mentioned above. Similar to stubs in CORBA, the application uses this object to interact with the MBeanServer and is relieved of all communication details. The developer can choose which of the four options (HTTP, RMI, Web Service, Local) shall be used by `RemoteMBeanServer`.

To facilitate all of the above for the client, we have built a `Connector-Factory`, the methods of which return surrogate objects for the inference engine, association management, metadata collector and component loader. In addition, we have developed surrogate objects for functional components. As an example, there exists a `RemoteRDFServer` surrogate, relaying communication to one of the KAON tools (cf. Section 2). Every surrogate has to be provided with the MBean's identifier, which can be discovered in the inference engine.

3.3   Interceptors

As explained in Chapter 8, Section 2.4, interceptors are software entities that monitor a request and modify it before the request is sent to the component [Buschmann et al., 1996].

In the kernel, each MBean can be registered with an invoker and a stack of interceptors. A request received from the client is then delegated to the invoker first before it is relayed to the MBean. The invoker object is responsible for managing the interceptors and sending the requests down the chain of interceptors towards the MBean. For example, a logging interceptor can be activated to implement the auditing of operation requests. An authorization interceptor can be used to check that the requesting client has sufficient access rights for the MBean.

Invokers and interceptors are useful to achieve other goals apart from security. For example, when a component is being restarted, an invoker could block and queue incoming requests until the component is available again or the received requests time out. Alternatively, it could redirect the incoming requests to another MBean which is able to fulfill them. Interceptors may also be used to meet the requirement of *Semantic Interoperation*. Client requests in a specific Semantic Web language can be translated so that they can be understood by a component that might speak another language.

3.4   Functional Components

KAON Tools   There are different implementations that have been made deployable. Among them main-memory based and persistent RDF stores, as well as main-memory based and persistent KAON ontology stores.

External Modules   We have developed several proxy components in order to adapt external modules: Sesame [Volz et al., 2003d], Ontobroker [Volz et al., 2003b], as well as a proxy component for DL reasoners that conform to the DIG interface[3], such as FaCT [Horrocks, 1998] or Racer [Haarslev and Moeller, 2001].

MBeans from JBoss   As already mentioned in Section 1, JBoss is based on a modular design. The application server is completely implemented using

---

[3]Description Logic Implementation Group, `http://dl.kr.org/dig/`

MBeans. Typical J2EE functionality, such as the EJB container or JavaServer Pages, is hosted in the form of MBeans and can be leveraged in the KAON SERVER.

3.5 Management Console

We use the KAON OI-Modeller as a simple management console. It allows the user to browse and edit its contents. The administrator is able to enter KAON Queries to query the inference engine for any concept in the ontology in a separate text box. Using the KAON OI-Modeller as a management console is depicted in Figure 9.6. For starting, stopping and monitoring of components, a common JMX frontend can be used. In our case, we apply the HTTP Adapter from Sun (cf. Section 3.2).

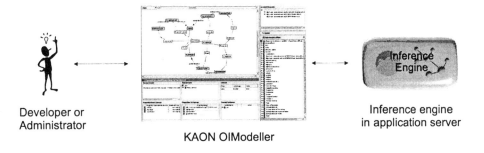

Developer or Administrator

KAON OIModeller

Inference engine in application server

Figure 9.6. The KAON OIModeller ontology editor allows the developer and administrator to browse and query the KAON SERVER's inference engine.

4. Example

This section shows the usefulness of the KAON SERVER with respect to its ability to facilitate the development of Semantic Web applications. An assessment of the benefits of its semantic enhancement follows in Chapter 10. The example shows the reader how the different parts of the KAON SERVER, which so far have only been described in isolation from each other, interact with each other. The first part of the example can be actively followed by downloading the OilEd demonstrator at http://kaon.semanticweb.org/server.

We now refer to the scenario depicted in Figure 4.4 on page 61, which involved concise modelling of the research and academia domain in description logics. The ontology thus created can be used in several research and academia applications. In our scenario, we want to set up a comprehensive portal, which exploits a rule-based system capable of handling large amounts of instances and the deduction of additional information by rules.

In the following sections, we want to show how the scenario can be realized with the KAON SERVER using existing clients and several components. The application version of the domain ontology should be as expressive as possible, formalized in an executable and standardized language in order to facilitate its reuse across applications. Hence, the preferred choice is OWL DL (cf. Chapter 4, Section 1.1). The OilEd ontology editor [Bechhofer et al., 2001] may be used for the construction of such ontologies. OilEd uses the FaCT reasoner [Horrocks, 1998] for consistency checking of ontologies.

For the portal application, OntoEdit [Sure et al., 2002] and its corresponding ontology store Ontobroker [Decker et al., 1998] are well-suited because they are based on frame logics [Kifer et al., 1995] that allow the definition of, and reasoning with, rules, as well as the efficient handling of large amounts of instances.

We assume that an instance of the KAON SERVER is up and running, deployed with: (*i*) RMI and Web service connectors, (*ii*) component loader, inference engine and association management system components, (*iii*) semantic interoperation and ontology repository functional components and (*iv*) proxy components for Ontobroker and FaCT [Horrocks, 1998] (cf. Figure 9.7). The RDF Server will later be deployed by one of the editors.

OilEd's and OntoEdit's interactions with the server are discussed in the following UML-like sequence diagrams [Booch et al., 1998]. Note that these diagrams do not show the exact Java method calls for the sake of brevity. For the same reason, we omit all the details involving connectors.

4.1   Modelling the Ontology

For ontology engineering we use OilEd, an editor that supports the OWL DL language among others. It connects to the KAON SERVER through Java Remote Method Invocation (RMI). As depicted in Figure 9.8, OilEd uses the `ConnectorFactory` to retrieve surrogate objects for the `MBeanServer` itself, the component loader and the inference engine in the acquisition phase (1).

In step (2), a successful discovery of the ontology repository functional component follows.[4] A reference to the repository MBean is returned to OilEd, which in turn loads the DOLCE top-level ontology from the ontology repository as the starting point for modelling the domain ontology. The corresponding method invocation, `invoke(MBean-ref, load, DOLCE)`, is directly routed through the MBeanServer without using a surrogate object. This is achieved by the `invoke()` method (cf. Section 1), which takes an MBean reference,

---

[4]Interactions from surrogate objects (i.e., Remote*x*, where *x* is the name of a component) to the KAON SERVER are not shown in the diagrams. Each surrogate has to be created on the client's side and relay its method calls over the network to a connector's `invoke()` method, which eventually calls the MBeanServer's `invoke()`.

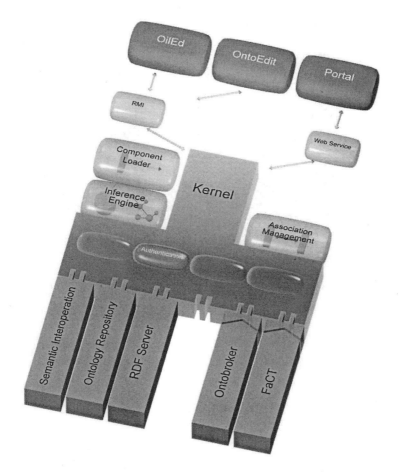

Figure 9.7. An instance of KAON SERVER where OilEd, OntoEdit and the portal application act as clients.

the name of the operation and its parameters as arguments. After that, the editor looks up the MBean reference for the semantic interoperation functional component. OilEd uses it to transform the DOLCE ontology into the OWL DL language. This method invocation is also routed through the MBeanServer without any surrogate objects.

At this point, the user is able to start editing the research and academia ontology (3). When finished, a verification on the ontology is usually done by applying the FaCT reasoner [Horrocks, 1998]. OilEd tries to discover such a reasoner. In our scenario, we assume that there is a proxy component deployed, and, thus a reference is returned. The editor creates a RemoteFaCT object, which hides the communication details. In our case, since the ontology is consistent, the user proceeds with saving.

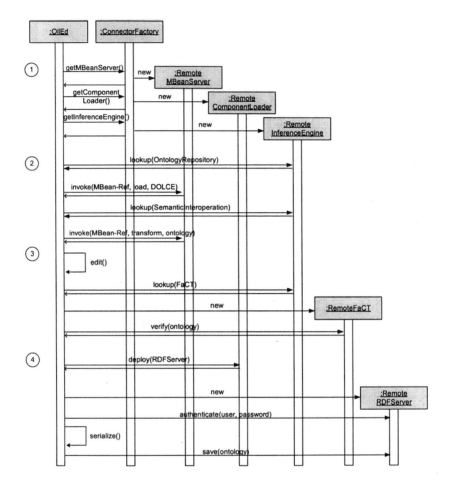

Figure 9.8.   Sequence diagram — OilEd with KAON SERVER.

For storing the ontology, an instance of KAON's RDF Server along an authentication interceptor is created by using the component loader (4). OilEd
is relieved from starting and initializing. It retrieves a reference to the newly
created MBean from the component loader. Only then it is able to create an
instance of RemoteRDFServer, which, like all other surrogates, hides the communication details and handles possible interceptors. For the latter, Remote-
RDFServer has to be first provided with the credentials. After serializing the
ontology into RDF, it is finally saved by the persistent RDF Server.

4.2   Definition of Rules

In our portal, we want to be able to handle large amounts of instances.
Furthermore, we want to apply complex rules for deducing additional facts,

e.g., *if a Person A works in Project X and X's topic is Z, then Person A is familiar with the topic Z*. OntoEdit and its corresponding ontology store Ontobroker are well-suited for such purposes because they are based on frame logics. Frame logics allow the definition of rules and the efficient handling of large amounts of instances. We assume that the semantic interoperation functional component allows the translation of the concept hierarchy and the associations from OWL DL to frame logics. Note that we do neglect the details of translating between different logics for the sake of a simple scenario. The translation allows using OntoEdit, which provides a graphical user interface for editing ontologies and rules.

Figure 9.9 depicts the sequence diagram for OntoEdit's communication with the server. RemoteMBeanServer and RemoteInferenceEngine objects are created in phase (1), similar to OilEd's interactions. We assume that the user is aware of the RDF Server and the ontology just created. He/she can provide enough information to perform a successful discovery for the store, as well as the required credentials (2). An instance of RemoteRDFServer is responsible for communication and handling the authentication interceptor on the server's side. The invocation of getOntology(...) on RemoteRDFServer yields an RDF-stream that is to be transformed into frame logic, i.e., OntoEdit's ontology language, by the semantic interoperation functional component. OntoEdit discovers the latter and calls the respective method directly, without creating any special surrogate object, through RemoteMBeanServer. The user is now able to add rules and instances and to perform adaptations on the ontology, as only the concept hierarchy and associations have been translated from the OWL DL ontology (3).

OntoEdit uses Ontobroker for ontology storage and reasoning, as well as semantic validation of the ontology (analogous to OilEd and FaCT). Ontobroker exploits a relational database system for persistence. We have already assumed that a proxy component for Ontobroker is deployed to the KAON SERVER. Instead of loading a new one, OntoEdit tries to discover such a component and retrieves a reference to the respective MBean (4). Before loading the frame logic ontology into Ontobroker, the editor ensures that the proxy component is not unloaded by other clients or unloaded for server performance reasons. It, therefore, retrieves a reference to the association management via the inference engine and invokes a corresponding method. Frame logic ontology, instances and rules can now be loaded into Ontobroker.

4.3 Setting up the Portal

After translation into frame logic, possible adaptations and addition of rules with OntoEdit, the portal application just needs to reuse the deployed Ontobroker residing within the KAON SERVER. It already holds the required ontology together with the rules. The application has to connect to the KAON SERVER,

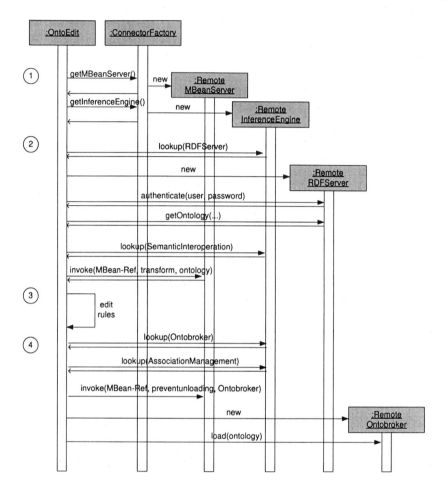

Figure 9.9.   Sequence diagram — OntoEdit with KAON SERVER.

in this scenario by a Web service connector, discover Ontobroker and start displaying and changing the ontology's instances by a Web front-end. Without the KAON SERVER, all of the above would lead to a one-off effort of combining software modules without the possibility for much reuse and extensibility.

5.   Summary

In this chapter we have responded to the Question III.3: *How to implement semantic management?* We have reused the open source application server *JBoss* and have leveraged the wealth of tools provided by the Karlsruhe Ontology and Semantic Web tool suite, *KAON* [Maedche et al., 2003]. KAON's inference engine, ontology store and ontology editor have been applied to semantically enhance JBoss. The result of this fruitful combination is called

KAON SERVER, whose usefulness for building Semantic Web applications has been demonstrated by an example. The example has shown that without the KAON SERVER, application development for the Semantic Web leads to a one-off effort of combining software modules without the possibility for much reuse and extensibility. An assessment of the benefits of semantic management, as well as details regarding the application of the management ontology, follow in Chapter 10.

Chapter 10

APPLYING THE MANAGEMENT ONTOLOGY

In the last chapter we have been concerned with implementing the design of an ontology-based application server. We have reused the existing application server JBoss and applied the tools of KAON for the semantic enhancement of the server. However, we have not detailed the steps necessary to reuse our management ontology in the resulting KAON SERVER.

In this chapter, we fill the gap by responding to the Question III.4: *How to reuse the ontology?* We have designed the management ontology in such a way as to be platform-independent and as specific as possible at the same time. For reuse in the KAON SERVER, one needs to take the following three steps (cf. Figure 10.1): (*i*) we have to specialize the core concepts and associations to reflect the idiosyncracies of the platform. For example, we have to introduce MBeans as a special kind of COSC:SoftwareComponent. The result of this step is a *domain*, *reference* and *heavyweight* version of our management ontology. Step (*ii*) removes concepts and associations that have been introduced merely for reference purposes. An example are ComputationalObjects and ComputationalActivities because both were introduced for a better explanation of other terms, such as Software or Data. The result is a *domain*, *application* and *heavyweight* version. Finally, step (*iii*) requires the adaptation of the axiomatization to the KAON language, which is less expressive than the management ontology's language (i.e., modal logic S5). The resulting ontology, viz., a *domain*, *application* and *lightweight* version of the management ontology, is actually applied in the KAON SERVER and can be obtained from http://cos.ontoware.org.

Sections 1 to 3 discuss the three steps in detail. Finally, Section 4 assesses the benefits of semantic management by comparing efforts with and without semantic technology on a per-use-case basis.

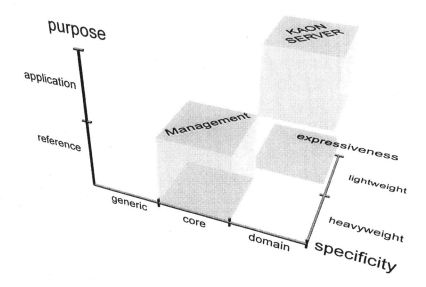

Figure 10.1. Reuse of the management ontology in the KAON SERVER requires (*i*) special-ization of the core entities to reflect domain knowledge, (*ii*) shifting from reference to application purpose and (*iii*) reduction from heavyweight to lightweight axiomatization.

1. From Core to Domain

The first step in reusing our management ontology is to specialize and extend its concepts and associations so that they reflect the idiosyncracies of the KAON SERVER. That means moving from *core* to *domain* on the specificity axis of our classification (cf. Figure 10.1). The result of this step is a *domain*, *reference* and *heavyweight* version of our management ontology. That means, we keep the representation formalism of the management ontology, i.e., modal logic S5, in this step. The resulting taxonomy is depicted in the Appendix on page 253.

This step requires an analysis of the typical concepts prevailing in the KAON SERVER. As KAON SERVER is based on J2EE, and, more specifically, on JMX, we find terms such as "MBean" or "JAR" (Java ARchive). Furthermore, Chapter 7, Section 2.3, page 162, introduced a classification taxonomy of "func-tional components," "proxy components," and "system components." Such concepts must be aligned to the concepts of the management ontology. That means choosing an appropriate superconcept and axiomatizing their meaning by applying concepts and associations of the management ontology. Hence, the following sections introduce MBeans as a special kind of COSC:Software-Component and additional kinds of profiles to capture the classification tax-onomy. Component providers can further extend the ontology by introducing customized profiles to categorize specific components.

1.1 MBeans

The KAON SERVER is based on JBoss, which in turn relies on JMX (the Java Management Extensions). JMX is a specification from Sun defining a framework for flexible component-based applications. JMX defines interfaces of specific software components, called managed beans or *MBeans*. The goal of this section is to formalize MBeans as a specialization of COSC:Software-Component. For this reason, we analyze the contents of MBean deployment descriptors, called MLETs [Lindfors and Fleury, 2002]. MLETs define MBeans by the following attributes:

code This attribute specifies the full Java class name, including the package name, of the MBean described.

object This attribute specifies the .ser file that contains a serialized representation of the MBean described. Either code or object must be present.

archive This mandatory attribute specifies one or more .jar files containing MBeans or other resources used by the MBean described.

codebase This optional attribute specifies the codebase URL of the MBean to be obtained. It identifies the directory that contains the .jar files specified by the archive attribute.

name This optional attribute specifies the object name to be assigned to the MBean instance when it is registered to the MBeanServer.

version This optional attribute specifies the version number of the MBean and associated .jar files to be obtained. The version number can be used to update .jar files that are loaded by the MBeanServer.

arglist This optional attribute specifies a list of one or more parameters for the MBean to be instantiated. This list describes the parameters to be passed to the MBean's constructor.

The definitions and axioms below capture such an MBean description by means of our management ontology.[1] We use the nomenclature above as names of the corresponding associations although it is mnemonically misleading. Note that we omit the definitions of associations with simple XML-Schema datatypes, such as xsd:string or xsd:integer, as range. These are code, object, codebase, name and version.

---

[1]Note that the symbol ⊕ represents the logical xor (exclusive or) connective.

(D39) $\text{MBean}(x) =_{def} \text{COSC:SoftwareComponent}(x) \wedge \exists y(\text{code}(x,y) \oplus \text{object}(x,y)) \wedge \exists a, cb, n, v, al(\text{archive}(x,a) \wedge \text{codebase}(x,cb) \wedge \text{name}(x,n) \wedge \text{version}(x,v) \wedge \text{arglist}(x,al))$

(A31) $\text{MBean}(x) \rightarrow$
$\text{COSC:conforms}(x, JMX) \wedge \text{COSC:FrameworkSpecification}(JMX)$

(D40) $\text{JARCollection}(x) =_{def}$
$\text{DOLCE:Collection}(x) \wedge \forall y(\text{DOLCE:member}(x,y) \rightarrow \text{JAR}(y))$

(D41) $\text{JAR}(x) =_{def} \text{COSC:SoftwareLibrary}(x) \wedge$
$\forall c((\text{DOLCE:properPart}(x,c) \wedge \text{CSO:Class}(c)) \rightarrow$
$(\text{OIO:orderedBy}(c, Java) \wedge$
$\text{OIO:InformationEncodingSystem}(Java)))$

(D42) $\text{Argument}(x) =_{def} \text{CSO:Data}(x) \wedge \exists t, v(\text{type}(x,t) \vee \text{value}(x,v))$

(A32) $\text{archive}(x,y) \rightarrow \text{MBean}(x) \wedge \text{JARCollection}(y)$
(A33) $\text{arglist}(x,y) \rightarrow \text{MBean}(x) \wedge \text{Argument}(y)$
(A34) $\text{nextArgument}(x,y) \rightarrow \text{Argument}(x) \wedge \text{Argument}(y)$
(A35) $\text{type}(x,y) \rightarrow \text{Argument}(x) \wedge (y = java.lang.Boolean \vee y = java.lang.Byte \vee y = java.lang.Short \vee y = java.lang.Long \vee y = java.lang.Integer \vee y = java.lang.Float \vee y = java.lang.Double \vee y = java.lang.String)$

(D39) and (A31) characterize an MBean as a COSC:SoftwareComponent conforming to the JMX framework specification with all the attributes introduced above. While code, object, codebase, name and version are simple attributes, archive and arglist require more attention. As defined in (A32), the range of archive points to a JARCollection, viz., a DOLCE:Collection, consisting of JARs (Java ARchives). JARs are COSC:SoftwareLibraries whose CSO:Classes are represented in the Java language (cf. (D40 and D41)). The range of arglist points to an Argument (cf. (A33)), which is simply defined as a special kind of CSO:Data with type and value attributes. (A35) defines type by enumeration. We omit the definition of value because it is a simple attribute. In order to preserve the ordering of Arguments, each Argument may point to its successor via nextArgument as defined in (D42) and (A34).

1.2 Profiles

Section 2.3 in Chapter 8 on page 162 introduced a particular classification of components in our ontology-based application server. MBeans can act as functional, system or proxy components. This section is concerned with formalizing this classification. The definitions and axioms below capture the terms as special kinds of COSC:ComponentProfile.

Functional components are MBeans deployed in the ontology-based application server that constitute the application logic. In the scenario of application development for the Semantic Web, ontology-related software modules, e.g., RDF stores, become functional components by making them deployable (that means wrapping them as MBeans). An arbitrary stack of interceptors can be deployed with each functional component, and the developer can define individual dependencies between them. Accordingly, we define FunctionalComponent-Profiles and the associations to interceptors and to other profiles in (D43), (A36) and (A37) below.

System components are software components providing functionality for the server itself. In the KAON SERVER, we have a fixed number of system components, namely ones for the inference engine, the association management, the metadata collector, the component loader, as well as several connector components. Consequently, we define SystemComponentProfiles by enumeration in (D44) below.

Finally, proxy components are special types of functional components that manage the communication to an external module. External modules cannot be deployed directly as they may be programmed in a different language, live on a different computing platform, etc. Thus, ProxyComponentProfiles are characterized as FunctionalComponentProfiles whose COSC:described MBeans have a dependence on some kind of software (cf. (D45) below).

(D43) FunctionalComponentProfile(x) $=_{def}$
COSC:ComponentProfile$(x) \wedge \forall y($COSC:describes$(x, y) \rightarrow$
MBean$(y))$

(D44) SystemComponentProfile(x) $=_{def}$ COSC:ComponentProfile$(x) \wedge$
$(x = IEProfile \vee x = AssociationManagementProfile \vee x =$
$MetadataCollectorProfile \vee x = ComponentLoaderProfile \vee x =$
$HTTPConnectorProfile \vee x = RMIConnectorProfile \vee x =$
$WebServiceConnectorProfile \vee x = LocalConnectorProfile)$

(D45) ProxyComponentProfile(x) $=_{def}$
FunctionalComponentProfile$(x) \wedge \forall y($COSC:describes$(x, y) \rightarrow$
$\exists z($MBean$(y) \wedge$ DOLCE:specificallyConstantlyDependsOn$(y, z) \wedge$
CSO:Software$(z)))$

(D46) Interceptor(x) $=_{def}$
CSO:Class$(x) \wedge \exists m($CSO:invokes$(x, m) \wedge$ MBean$(m))$

As discussed in Chapter 8, Section 2.4, interceptors are software entities that monitor component requests and modify them. According to this definition, (D46) introduces the concept of an Interceptor as specialization of a CSO:-Class that CSO:invokes an MBean. It is possible to define a whole sequence of interceptors that act on a component. In order to capture the sequence, (A37), (A38), and (A39) introduce the unique firstInterceptor association on the profiles, as well as the transitive nextInterceptor.

(A36) profileDepends(x, y) → FunctionalComponentProfile(x) ∧
       FunctionalComponentProfile(y) ∧
       DOLCE:specificallyConstantlyDependsOn(x, y)

(A37) firstInterceptor(x, y) → FunctionalComponentProfile(x) ∧
       Interceptor(y) ∧ ¬∃z(Interceptor(z) ∧ $y \neq z$)

(A38) nextInterceptor(x, y) → Interceptor(x) ∧ Interceptor(y) ∧
       CSO:invokes(x, y) ∧ ¬∃z(Interceptor(z) ∧ $y \neq z$)

(A39) nextInterceptor(x, y) ←
       nextInterceptor(x, z) ∧ nextInterceptor(z, y)

2.   From Reference to Application

The second step requires moving from *reference* to *application* on the purpose axis of our classification (cf. Figure 10.1 on page 192). That means removing concepts and associations that have been introduced merely for reference purposes. The result is a *domain*, *application* and *heavyweight* version of the management ontology. In this section we basically revisit all definitions and axioms and single out ones that are introduced for reference purposes (cf. Tables 10.1 and 10.2). On the one hand, the main reason for removing a definition is as follows:

Explanation Concepts and associations might be introduced merely to catch the intended meanings of other concepts more precisely, i.e., they are required for a better *explanation* of other concepts but not for reasoning purposes. Examples are CSO:ComputationalObjects and CSO:-ComputationalActivities. They are introduced to capture the notion of Data and Software more precisely. CSO:ComputationalObjects are a special kind of OIO:InformationRealization and captures specific contents in main memory. CSO:ComputationalActivities are the DOLCE:-Perdurants that represent actual CPU operations. Both concepts neither have subconcepts, nor do we expect to model such information in an application ontology.

On the other hand, we can identify different reasons for keeping specific definitions and axioms. Note that there might be more than one reason for a definition at the same time. The tables below only list the primary reason in each case.

Taxonomy We expect that only specializations of core concepts, such as COSC:SoftwareComponent, will be instantiated in a concrete application. For example, the domain version introduced MBean as specific kind of COSC:SoftwareComponent. Hence, there will only be instances of MBean in the application ontology. However, we keep core concepts, such as COSC:SoftwareComponent, in the application version of our ontology in order to have a meaningful taxonomy.

Application Finally, we can find definitions or axioms, which are required for the application version because they are introduced to enable run time reasoning. Most definitions but also axioms for transitivity or symmetry of associations make up this category. As an example, consider (A39) on page 196, which defines the nextInterceptor association as transitive. Furthermore, domain and range restrictions on associations belong in this category. We opt to keep such axioms also in the application ontology. For example, Definition (D9) on page 119 specifies the domain and range of CSO:identifies as CSO:AbstractData and DOLCE:Particular.

The executable target language constrains how much of the axiomatization can be captured. Consider the definition of Software (cf. (D5) on page 117) as an example. If we choose KAON as target language, we can only keep the information that CSO:Software is a specialization of OIO:Information-Object. If we choose a typical description logic, we are able to capture the whole expression. We elaborate on this issue in the next section which deals with step (*iii*), i.e., moving from heavyweight to lightweight axiomatization.

Table 10.1: Definitions kept or removed from the management ontology.

No.	Description	Keep	Reason	Page
(D1)	CSO:ComputationalObject	No	Explanation	116
(D2)	CSO:ComputationalActivity	No	Explanation	116
(D3)	DOLCE:spec.Const.Dep.On	No	Explanation	116
(D4)	DOLCE:presentAt	No	Explanation	117
(D5)	CSO:Software	Yes	Taxonomy	117
(D6)	CSO:ComputationalTask	Yes	Application	117
(D7)	CSO:Data	Yes	Taxonomy	118
(D8)	CSO:AbstractData	Yes	Taxonomy	119
(D9)	CSO:identifies	Yes	Application	119
(D10)	CSO:Class	Yes	Application	120
(D11)	CSO:Method	Yes	Application	120
(D12)	CSO:Exception	Yes	Application	120
(D13)	DOLCE:properPart	No	Explanation	120
(D14)	CSO:Interface	Yes	Application	121
(D15)	CSO:executes	Yes	Application	123
(D16)	CSO:accesses	Yes	Application	123
(D17)	CSO:invokes	Yes	Application	123
(D18)	CSO:contextUser	Yes	Application	123
(D19)	CSO:Input	Yes	Application	124
(D20)	CSO:Output	Yes	Application	124
(D21)	CSO:User	Yes	Application	125
(D22)	CSO:UserGroup	Yes	Application	125
(D23)	CSO:PolicySubject	Yes	Application	125

(D24)	CSO:PolicyObject	Yes	Application	126
(D25)	CSO:TaskCollection	Yes	Application	126
(D26)	CSO:Constraint	Yes	Application	126
(D27)	CSO:PolicyDescription	Yes	Application	126
(D28)	COSC:FrameworkSpecification	No	Explanation	129
(D29)	COSC:conforms	No	Explanation	129
(D30)	COSC:SoftwareComponent	Yes	Taxonomy	129
(D31)	COSC:SoftwareLibrary	Yes	Taxonomy	130
(D32)	COSC:License	Yes	Taxonomy	130
(D33)	COSC:Profile	Yes	Taxonomy	132
(D34)	COSC:ComponentProfile	Yes	Taxonomy	132
(D35)	COSC:Characteristic	Yes	Taxonomy	132
(D36)	COWS:WebService	Yes	Application	137
(D37)	COWS:ServiceProfile	Yes	Application	137
(D38)	COWS:QualityOfService	Yes	Taxonomy	137
(D39)	MBean	Yes	Application	193
(D40)	JARCollection	Yes	Application	194
(D41)	JAR	Yes	Application	194
(D42)	Argument	Yes	Application	194
(D43)	FunctionalComponentProfile	Yes	Application	195
(D44)	SystemComponentProfile	Yes	Application	195
(D45)	ProxyComponentProfile	Yes	Application	195
(D46)	Interceptor	Yes	Application	195

Table 10.1 shows the definitions which are kept or removed from the management ontology. We have already explained the removal of Computational-Objects and ComputationalActivities above. DOLCE:presentAt is used in the definition of DOLCE:specificallyConstantlyDependsOn. The DOLCE:specificallyConstantlyDependsOn and DOLCE:properPart association are only used for a more precise explanation of other concepts. Finally, COSC:FrameworkSpecification and COSC:conforms are there to specify COSC:SoftwareComponent.

Table 10.2: Axioms kept or removed from the management ontology.

No.	Description	Keep	Reason	Page
(A1)	CSO:methodRequires	Yes	Application	120
(A2)	CSO:methodYields	Yes	Application	120
(A3)	CSO:methodThrows	Yes	Application	120
(A4)	CSO:dataType	Yes	Application	120
(A5)	CSO:interfaceRequires	Yes	Application	122
(A6)	CSO:implements	Yes	Application	122
(A7)	Transitivity of CSO:invokes	Yes	Application	123
(A8)	Axiom for CSO:executes	Yes	Application	123
(A9)	Axiom for CSO:invokes	Yes	Application	123
(A10)	CSO:inputFor	Yes	Application	124
(A11)	CSO:outputFor	Yes	Application	124
(A12)	Axioms for CSO:Input, CSO:Output	No	Explanation	124

(A13)	Axioms for CSO:Input, CSO:Output	No	Explanation	124
(A14)	CSO:comp.RightTowards	Yes	Application	126
(A15)	Axiom for CSO:comp.RightTowards	Yes	Application	126
(A16)	Axiom for group memberships	Yes	Application	126
(A17)	COSC:libraryDependsOn	Yes	Application	130
(A18)	Transitivity of COSC:libraryDependsOn	Yes	Application	130
(A19)	COSC:libraryConflictsWith	Yes	Application	130
(A20)	Symmetry of COSC:libraryConflictsWith	Yes	Application	130
(A21)	Axiom for COSC:libraryConflictsWith	Yes	Application	130
(A22)	COSC:releasedUnder	Yes	Application	130
(A23)	COSC:licenseIncompatibleWith	Yes	Application	130
(A24)	Symmetry of COSC:licenseIncompatibleWith	Yes	Application	130
(A25)	COSC:describes	Yes	Application	132
(A26)	COSC:profiles	Yes	Application	132
(A27)	COSC:directlyAccessibleResource	Yes	Application	134
(A28)	COSC:indirectlyAccessibleResource	Yes	Application	134
(A29)	Axiom for COWS:WebService	No	Explanation	137
(A30)	COWS:invokesWebServiceWithPolicy	Yes	Application	139
(A31)	Axiom for MBean	No	Explanation	194
(A32)	archive	Yes	Application	194
(A33)	arglist	Yes	Application	194
(A34)	nextArgument	Yes	Application	194
(A35)	type	Yes	Application	194
(A36)	profileDepends	Yes	Application	195
(A37)	firstInterceptor	Yes	Application	196
(A38)	nextInterceptor	Yes	Application	196
(A39)	Transitivity of nextInterceptor	Yes	Application	196

Table 10.2 shows the axioms which are kept or removed from the management ontology. (A12) and (A13) are removed because they are only introduced to capture the difference between CSO:Inputs and CSO:Outputs. In a similar vein, (A29) and (A31) help to explain COWS:WebService and MBean, respectively. Hence, they are not required for reasoning purposes.

3. From Heavyweight to Lightweight

After removing definitions and axioms for reference purposes in step (*ii*), the remaining ones have to be adapted manually to an executable language. That means moving from *heavyweight* to *lightweight* on the expressiveness axis (cf. Figure 10.1 on page 192) because executable languages are typically less expressive than the management ontology's language (i.e., modal logic S5). As discussed in Chapter 9, Section 2, page 174, we have chosen the KAON toolsuite and, thus, we are bound to the KAON language.

We already mentioned in the previous section, that the choice of the executable language constrains how much of the axiomatization can be captured. In essence, each definition and axiom has to be adapted manually to fit the target language. We considered the definition of Software. If we choose a typical description logic, such as OWL DL, we are able to capture the whole expression. If we choose KAON as target language, we can only keep the information that CSO:Software is a specialization of OIO:InformationObject. In general, KAON only allows expressing concept and association hierarchies, domain, range and cardinality restrictions on associations, and inverse, symmetry, as well as transitivity axioms. The resulting ontology, viz., a *domain, application* and *lightweight* version of the management ontology, is actually applied in the KAON SERVER and can be obtained from http://cos.ontoware.org.

3.1   The KAON Language

As discussed in Chapter 9, Section 2, page 174, we have chosen the KAON toolsuite as the semantic technology in the KAON SERVER because the KAON API offers a comprehensive set of features in order to control the application server with an ontology. Therefore, we are bound to the KAON language, which is a proprietary extension of RDFS (cf. Chapter 4, Section 1.1). It follows the object-oriented modelling paradigm as closely as possible and extends it with simple deductive features by keeping in mind some practical aspects. KAON is primarily based on deductive database techniques, such as magic sets [Beeri and Ramakrishnan, 1987], which have proven to be indispensable for achieving inferencing tractability and practicability. The language allows modelling concept and association hierarchies, domain, range and cardinality restrictions on associations and inverse, symmetry, as well as transitivity axioms.[2] The information is structured in *OI-models*, containing concepts, associations,[3] *and* instances at the same time. Unlike most logics, KAON does not introduce a specific syntax, but an abstract structure of OI-models instead. The following definitions are taken from [Maedche et al., 2003]. For the sake of brevity, we only present the OI-model structure, the ontology structure and the modularization constraints.

Definition 10.1 (OI-model Structure)
An OI-model (ontology-instance-model) structure is a tuple OIM := (E, INC) where

- *E is the set of entities of the OI-model,*

- *INC is the set of included OI-models.*

An OI-model represents a self-contained unit of structured information that may be reused. It consists of entities and may include a set of other OI-models

---

[2]At the time of writing the book, KAON2 is just being developed. KAON2 is based on a more expressive description logic and offers much more reasoning capabilities than its predecessor. http://kaon2.semanticweb.org

[3]Note that associations are called *properties* in KAON.

(represented through the set *INC*. Different OI-models can talk about the same entity, so the sets of entities E of these OI-models do not need to be disjoint.

Definition 10.2 (Ontology Structure)

An ontology structure of an OI-model is a structure $O(OIM) := (C, P, R, S, T, INV, H_C, H_P, domain, range, mincard, maxcard)$ where

- $C \subseteq E$ *is a set of concepts,*

- $P \subseteq E$ *is a set of properties,*

- $R \subseteq P$ *is a set of relational properties (properties from the set $A = P \setminus R$ are called attribute properties),*

- $S \subseteq R$ *is a subset of symmetric properties,*

- $T \subseteq R$ *is a subset of transitive properties,*

- *$INV \subseteq R \times R$ is a symmetric relation that relates inverse relational properties: if $(p_1, p_2) \in INV$, then p_1 is an inverse relational property of p_2,*

- *$H_C \subseteq C \times C$ is an acyclic relation called concept hierarchy: if $(c_1, c_2) \in H_C$ then c_1 is a subconcept of c_2 and c_2 is a superconcept of c_1,*

- *$H_P \subseteq P \times P$ is an acyclic relation called property hierarchy: if $(p_1, p_2) \in H_P$ then p_1 is a subproperty of p_2 and p_2 is a superproperty of p_1,*

- *function $domain : P \rightarrow 2^C$ gives the set of domain concepts for some property $p \in P$,*

- *function $range : R \rightarrow 2^C$ gives the set of range concepts for some relational property $p \in R$,*

- *function $mincard : C \times P \rightarrow \mathbb{N}_0$ gives the minimum cardinality for each concept-property pair,*

- *function $maxcard : C \times P \rightarrow (\mathbb{N}_0 \cup \{\infty\})$ gives the maximum cardinality for each concept-property pair.*

Each OI-model has an ontology structure associated with it, consisting of concepts (to be interpreted as sets of elements) and properties (to be interpreted as extensional relations between elements). Each property can have domain concepts. In addition, relational properties can have range concepts. Domain and range concepts constrain the types of instances to which the properties may be applied. If these constraints are not satisfied, the ontology is inconsistent. Relational properties may be marked as transitive and/or symmetric, and it is possible to say that two relational properties are inverse to each other. For each concept-property pair it is possible to specify the minimum and maximum cardinalities. Concepts (properties) can be arranged in a hierarchy, as specified by the H_C (H_P) relation, whose reflexive transitive closure follows from the semantics defined in [Maedche et al., 2003].

Definition 10.3 (Modularization Constraints)
If an OI-model OIM imports some other OI-model OIM_1 (with elements marked with subscript 1), that is, if $OIM_1 \in INC(OIM)$, then the following modularization constraints must be satisfied:

- $E_1 \subseteq E$, $C_1 \subseteq C$, $P_1 \subseteq P$, $R_1 \subseteq R$, $T_1 \subseteq T$, $INV_1 \subseteq INV$, $H_{C_1} \subseteq H_C$, $H_{P_1} \subseteq H_P$,

- $\forall p \in P_1$ $domain_1(p) \subseteq domain(p)$,

- $\forall p \in P_1$ $range_1(p) \subseteq range(p)$,

- $\forall p \in P_1, \forall c \in C_1$ $mincard_1(c, p) = mincard(c, p)$,

- $\forall p \in P_1, \forall c \in C_1$ $maxcard_1(c, p) = maxcard(c, p)$,

- $I_1 \subseteq I$, $L_1 \subseteq L$,

- $\forall c \in C_1$ $instconc_1(c) \subseteq instconc(c)$,

- $\forall p \in P_1, i \in I_1$ $instprop_1(p, i) \subseteq instprop(p, i)$.

According to Definition 10.3, reuse is supported by allowing an OI-model to include other OI-models, thus obtaining the union of the definitions from all included models. Cyclical inclusions are not allowed; that is, a graph whose nodes are OI-models and whose arcs point from including to included models must not contain a cycle. Inclusion is performed by reference. The models are virtually merged, but the information about the origin of each entity is represented explicitly.[4]

3.2   Adaptation of Definitions and Axioms

In this section we formulate all ontology modules by means of one KAON OI-model per ontology module. OI-models include others according to the dependency graph depicted in Figure 7.1 on page 108. We start with the KAON SERVER module, which formalizes the domain knowledge discussed in Section 1. The KAON SERVER OI-model includes the Core Ontology of Web Services, which in turn includes the Core Ontology of Software Components and so forth.

---

[4]Please cf. [Maedche et al., 2003] for the definition of *instconc* and *instprop*.

We preserve as much of the axiomatization as possible. Because of the limited expressiveness of the KAON language, we can only capture concept and association hierarchies, domain, range and cardinality restrictions on associations, and inverse, symmetry, as well as transitivity axioms.

Defining the OI-models basically requires to revisit all definitions and axioms. Let us give an example. Consider Axioms (A38) and (A39) on page 196, which define the nextInterceptor association. In a first step, we have to insert nextInterceptor into $E_{KAONSERVER}$ because it is one of the entities of the KAON SERVER ontology discussed in this chapter. In the second step, we have to include it in P and in R since it is a "relational property," i.e., an association with a concept as range. Third, nextInterceptor is defined as being transitive in (A39). Hence, it becomes an element of T. Fourth, (A38) specified nextInterceptor as a special kind of CSO:invokes. As a consequence, we add (nextInterceptor, CSO:invokes) to H_P. Fifth, nextInterceptor links two Interceptors, and, therefore, its domain and range point to Interceptor. Finally, (A38) lets us derive that there is at most one nextInterceptor per Interceptor. Accordingly, we set $mincard$ and $maxcard$ to 0 and 1, respectively.

KAON SERVER

The OI-model $KAONSERVER = (E_{KAONSERVER}, INC_{KAONSERVER})$ is the one that will finally be applied in the application server. It includes the concepts and associations of all other OI-models (including DOLCE and its modules) because of the transitive inclusions of OI-models. $E_{KAONSERVER}$ and $INC_{KAONSERVER}$ are defined as follows:[5]

$E_{KAONSERVER} =$ {MBean, JARCollection, JAR, Argument, code, object, codebase, name, archive, version, arglist, nextArgument, type, value, FunctionalComponentProfile, SystemComponentProfile, ProxyComponentProfile, Interceptor, profileDepends, firstInterceptor, nextInterceptor} and $INC_{KAONSERVER} = \{E_{COWS}\}$.

$O_{KAONSERVER}(KAONSERVER)$ consists of the following:

- $C =$ {MBean, JARCollection, JAR, Argument, FunctionalComponentProfile, SystemComponentProfile, ProxyComponentProfile, Interceptor}

- $P =$ {code, object, codebase, name, archive, arglist, nextArgument, version, type, value, profileDepends, firstInterceptor, nextInterceptor}

---

[5]We assume that for any property there exists an inverse. For the sake of brevity, we omit the definition of *INV* in the remainder of this section.

- $R = \{$archive, arglist, nextArgument, profileDepends, firstInterceptor, nextInterceptor$\}$

- $S = \varnothing$

- $T = \{$nextInterceptor$\}$

- $H_C = \{$(MBean, COSC:SoftwareComponent), (Argument, CSO:Data), (JARCollection, DOLCE:Collection), (JAR, COSC:SoftwareLibrary), (FunctionalComponentProfile, COSC:ComponentProfile), (SystemComponentProfile, COSC:ComponentProfile), (ProxyComponentProfile, FunctionalComponentProfile), (Interceptor, CSO:Class)$\}$

- $H_P = \{$(nextInterceptor, CSO:invokes)$\}$

- $domain(\text{code}) = \{$MBean$\}$
  $domain(\text{object}) = \{$MBean$\}$
  $domain(\text{codebase}) = \{$MBean$\}$
  $domain(\text{name}) = \{$MBean$\}$
  $domain(\text{archive}) = \{$MBean$\}$
  $range(\text{archive}) = \{$JARCollection$\}$
  $domain(\text{arglist}) = \{$MBean$\}$
  $range(\text{arglist}) = \{$Argument$\}$
  $domain(\text{nextArgument}) = \{$Argument$\}$
  $range(\text{nextArgument}) = \{$Argument$\}$
  $domain(\text{version}) = \{$MBean$\}$
  $domain(\text{type}) = \{$Argument$\}$
  $domain(\text{value}) = \{$Argument$\}$
  $domain(\text{profileDepends}) = \{$FunctionalComponentProfile$\}$
  $range(\text{profileDepends}) = \{$FunctionalComponentProfile$\}$
  $domain(\text{firstInterceptor}) = \{$FunctionalComponentProfile$\}$
  $range(\text{firstInterceptor}) = \{$Interceptor$\}$
  $domain(\text{nextInterceptor}) = \{$Interceptor$\}$
  $range(\text{nextInterceptor}) = \{$Interceptor$\}$

- $mincard(\text{MBean}, \text{code}) = 0$
  $maxcard(\text{MBean}, \text{code}) = 1$
  $mincard(\text{MBean}, \text{object}) = 0$
  $maxcard(\text{MBean}, \text{object}) = 1$
  $mincard(\text{MBean}, \text{codebase}) = 0$
  $maxcard(\text{MBean}, \text{codebase}) = 1$
  $mincard(\text{MBean}, \text{name}) = 0$
  $maxcard(\text{MBean}, \text{name}) = 1$
  $mincard(\text{MBean}, \text{archive}) = 0$

$maxcard(\text{MBean}, \text{archive}) = 1$
$mincard(\text{MBean}, \text{arglist}) = 0$
$maxcard(\text{MBean}, \text{arglist}) = 1$
$mincard(\text{Argument}, \text{nextArgument}) = 0$
$maxcard(\text{Argument}, \text{nextArgument}) = 1$
$mincard(\text{MBean}, \text{version}) = 0$
$maxcard(\text{MBean}, \text{version}) = 1$
$mincard(\text{Argument}, \text{type}) = 0$
$maxcard(\text{Argument}, \text{type}) = 1$
$mincard(\text{Argument}, \text{value}) = 0$
$maxcard(\text{Argument}, \text{value}) = 1$
$mincard(\text{FunctionalComponentProfile}, \text{profileDepends}) = 0$
$maxcard(\text{FunctionalComponentProfile}, \text{profileDepends}) = \infty$
$mincard(\text{FunctionalComponentProfile}, \text{firstInterceptor}) = 0$
$maxcard(\text{FunctionalComponentProfile}, \text{firstInterceptor}) = 1$
$mincard(\text{FunctionalComponentProfile}, \text{nextInterceptor}) = 0$
$maxcard(\text{FunctionalComponentProfile}, \text{nextInterceptor}) = 1$

Core Ontology of Web Services (COWS)

The OI-model of the Core Ontology of Web Services $COWS = (E_{COWS}, INC_{COWS})$ includes the OI-model of the Core Ontology of Software Components (COSC).

$E_{COSC} = \{\text{WebService, ServiceProfile, QualityOfService, invokesWebServiceWithPolicy}\}$ and $INC_{COWS} = \{E_{COSC}\}$.

$O_{COWS}(COWS)$ consists of the following:

- $C = \{\text{WebService, ServiceProfile, QualityOfService}\}$

- $P = \{\text{invokesWebServiceWithPolicy}\}$

- $R = P = \{\text{invokesWebServiceWithPolicy}\}$

- $S = \varnothing$

- $T = \varnothing$

- $H_C = \{(\text{WebService, CSO:Software}), (\text{ServiceProfile, COSC:Profile}), (\text{QualityOfService, COSC:Characteristic})\}$

- $H_P = \{(\text{invokesWebServiceWithPolicy, CSO:invokes})\}$

- $domain(\text{invokesWebServiceWithPolicy}) = \{\text{WebService}\}$
  $range(\text{invokesWebServiceWithPolicy}) = \{\text{WebService}\}$

- $mincard(\text{WebService}, \text{invokesWebServiceWithPolicy}) = 0$
  $maxcard(\text{WebService}, \text{invokesWebServiceWithPolicy}) = \infty$

Core Ontology of Software Components (COSC)

The OI-model of the Core Ontology of Software Components $COSC = (E_{COSC}, INC_{COSC})$ includes the OI-model of the Core Software Ontology (CSO).

E_{COSC} = {SoftwareComponent, SoftwareLibrary, License, libraryDependsOn, libraryConflictsWith, releasedUnder, licenseIncompatibleWith, Profile, ComponentProfile, describes, profiles, Characteristic, informationTimestamp, informationSource} and $INC_{COSC} = \{E_{CSO}\}$.

$O_{COSC}(COSC)$ consists of the following:

- C = {SoftwareComponent, SoftwareLibrary, License, Profile, ComponentProfile, Characteristic}

- P = {libraryDependsOn, libraryConflictsWith, releasedUnder, licenseIncompatibleWith, describes, profiles, informationTimestamp, informationSource}

- R = {libraryDependsOn, libraryConflictsWith, releasedUnder, licenseIncompatibleWith, describes, profiles}

- S = {libraryConflictsWith, licenseIncompatibleWith}

- T = {libraryDependsOn}

- H_C = {(SoftwareComponent, CSO:Class), (SoftwareLibrary, CSO:Data), (Profile, OIO:InformationObject), (ComponentProfile, Profile), (Characteristic, DnS:Parameter) }

- H_P = {(libraryDependsOn, DOLCE:specificallyConstantlyDependsOn), (releasedUnder, OIO:expresses), (describes, OIO:about), (profiles, DnS:defines), (profiles, DnS:unifies), (profiles, OIO:about), (profiles, OIO:expressedBy)}

- $domain(\text{libraryDependsOn}) = \{\text{SoftwareLibrary}\}$
  $range(\text{libraryDependsOn}) = \{\text{SoftwareLibrary}\}$
  $domain(\text{libraryConflictsWith}) = \{\text{SoftwareLibrary}\}$
  $range(\text{libraryConflictsWith}) = \{\text{SoftwareLibrary}\}$
  $domain(\text{releasedUnder}) = \{\text{SoftwareLibrary}\}$
  $range(\text{releasedUnder}) = \{\text{License}\}$

domain(licenseIncompatibleWith) = {License}
range(licenseIncompatibleWith) = {License}
domain(describes) = {Profile}
range(describes) = {CSO:Software}
domain(profiles) = {OIO:InformationObject}
domain(profiles) = {DnS:SituationDescription}
range(profiles) = {CSO:Data}
range(profiles) = {DnS:ConceptDescription}
range(profiles) = {DOLCE:Collection}
domain(informationTimestamp) = {CSO:PolicyDescription}
domain(informationTimestamp) = {COSC:SoftwareLibrary}
domain(informationTimestamp) = {CSO:Interface}
domain(informationTimestamp) = {OoP:Plan}
domain(informationTimestamp) = {COSC:Characteristic}
domain(informationSource) = {CSO:PolicyDescription}
domain(informationSource) = {COSC:SoftwareLibrary}
domain(informationSource) = {CSO:Interface}
domain(informationSource) = {OoP:Plan}
domain(informationSource) = {COSC:Characteristic}

- *mincard*(SoftwareLibrary, libraryDependsOn) = 0
  maxcard(SoftwareLibrary, libraryDependsOn) = ∞
  mincard(SoftwareLibrary, libraryConflictsWith) = 0
  maxcard(SoftwareLibrary, libraryConflictsWith) = ∞
  mincard(SoftwareLibrary, releasedUnder) = 0
  maxcard(SoftwareLibrary, releasedUnder) = ∞
  mincard(License, licenseIncompatibleWith) = 0
  maxcard(License, licenseIncompatibleWith) = ∞
  mincard(Profile, describes) = 1
  maxcard(Profile, describes) = ∞
  mincard(CSO:PolicyDescription, informationTimestamp) = 0
  maxcard(CSO:PolicyDescription, informationTimestamp) = 1
  mincard(COSC:SoftwareLibrary, informationTimestamp) = 0
  maxcard(COSC:SoftwareLibrary, informationTimestamp) = 1
  mincard(CSO:Interface, informationTimestamp) = 0
  maxcard(CSO:Interface, informationTimestamp) = 1
  mincard(OoP:Plan, informationTimestamp) = 0
  maxcard(OoP:Plan, informationTimestamp) = 1
  mincard(COSC:Characteristic, informationSource) = 0
  maxcard(COSC:Characteristic, informationSource) = 1
  mincard(CSO:PolicyDescription, informationSource) = 0

$maxcard(\text{CSO:PolicyDescription}, \text{informationSource}) = 1$
$mincard(\text{COSC:SoftwareLibrary}, \text{informationSource}) = 0$
$maxcard(\text{COSC:SoftwareLibrary}, \text{informationSource}) = 1$
$mincard(\text{CSO:Interface}, \text{informationSource}) = 0$
$maxcard(\text{CSO:Interface}, \text{informationSource}) = 1$
$mincard(\text{OoP:Plan}, \text{informationSource}) = 0$
$maxcard(\text{OoP:Plan}, \text{informationSource}) = 1$
$mincard(\text{COSC:Characteristic}, \text{informationSource}) = 0$
$maxcard(\text{COSC:Characteristic}, \text{informationSource}) = 1$

Core Software Ontology (CSO)

The OI-model of the Core Software Ontology $CSO = (E_{CSO}, INC_{CSO})$ includes the OI-model of the Ontology of Information Objects (OIO), as well as the OI-model of the Ontology of Plans (OoP).

$E_{cso} = \{$Software, ComputationalTask, Data, AbstractData, identifies, Class, Method, Exception, dataType, methodRequires, methodYields, methodThrows, Interface, interfaceRequires, implements, executes, accesses, invokes, contextUser, Input, Output, inputFor, outputFor, User, UserGroup, PolicySubject, PolicyObject, TaskCollection, computationalRightTowards, PolicyDescription, Constraint$\}$ and $INC_{cosc} = \{E_{OIO}, E_{OoP}\}$.

$O_{CSO}(CSO)$ consists of the following:

- $C = \{$Software, ComputationalTask, Data, AbstractData, Class, Method, Exception, Interface, Input, Output, User, UserGroup, PolicySubject, PolicyObject, TaskCollection, PolicyDescription, Constraint$\}$

- $P = \{$identifies, dataType, methodRequires, methodYields, methodThrows, interfaceRequires, implements, executes, accesses, invokes, contextUser, inputFor, outputFor, computationalRightTowards$\}$

- $R = P$

- $S = \varnothing$

- $T = \{$invokes$\}$

- $H_C = \{$(Software, Data), (ComputationalTask, OoP:Task), (Data, OIO:InformationObject), (AbstractData, Data), (Class, Software), (Method, Software), (Exception, Class), (Interface, Data), (Input, DnS:Role), (Output, DnS:Role), (User, AbstractData), (UserGroup,

DOLCE:Collection), (PolicySubject, DnS:AgentiveRole),
(PolicyObject, DnS:NonAgentiveRole), (TaskCollection,
DOLCE:Collection), (PolicyDescription, DnS:SituationDescription),
(Constraint, DnS:Parameter)}

- $H_P = \{$(identifies, OIO:about), (interfaceRequires,
  DOLCE:properPart), (methodThrows, methodYields),
  (interfaceRequires, DOLCE:properPart),
  (computationalRightTowards, DnS:rightTowards), (contextUser,
  DnS:attitudeTowards), (inputFor, DnS:modalTarget), (outputFor,
  DnS:modalTarget),

- *domain*(identifies) = {AbstractData}
  range(identifies) = {DOLCE:Particular}
  domain(dataType) = {Data}
  range(dataType) = {DOLCE:Region}
  range(dataType) = {Data}
  domain(methodRequires) = {Method}
  range(methodRequires) = {Data}
  domain(methodYields) = {Method}
  range(methodYields) = {Data}
  domain(methodThrows) = {Method}
  range(methodThrows) = {Exception}
  domain(interfaceRequires) = {Interface}
  range(interfaceRequires) = {Method}
  domain(implements) = {Class}
  range(implements) = {Interface}
  domain(executes) = {Software}
  range(executes) = {ComputationalTask}
  domain(accesses) = {ComputationalTask}
  range(accesses) = {Data}
  domain(invokes) = {Software}
  range(invokes) = {Data}
  domain(contextUser) = {User}
  range(contextUser) = {ComputationalTask}
  domain(inputFor) = {Input}
  range(inputFor) = {ComputationalTask}
  domain(outputFor) = {Output}
  range(outputFor) = {ComputationalTask}
  domain(computationalRightTowards) = {PolicySubject}
  range(computationalRightTowards) = {ComputationalTask}
  range(computationalRightTowards) = {TaskCollection}

- $mincard(\mathsf{Data}, \mathsf{identifies}) = 0$
  $maxcard(\mathsf{Data}, \mathsf{identifies}) = 1$
  $mincard(\mathsf{Data}, \mathsf{dataType}) = 0$
  $maxcard(\mathsf{Data}, \mathsf{dataType}) = 1$
  $mincard(\mathsf{Method}, \mathsf{methodRequires}) = 0$
  $maxcard(\mathsf{Method}, \mathsf{methodRequires}) = \infty$
  $mincard(\mathsf{Method}, \mathsf{methodYields}) = 0$
  $maxcard(\mathsf{Method}, \mathsf{methodYields}) = 1$
  $mincard(\mathsf{Method}, \mathsf{methodThrows}) = 0$
  $maxcard(\mathsf{Method}, \mathsf{methodThrows}) = \infty$
  $mincard(\mathsf{Interface}, \mathsf{interfaceRequires}) = 1$
  $maxcard(\mathsf{Interface}, \mathsf{interfaceRequires}) = \infty$
  $mincard(\mathsf{Class}, \mathsf{implements}) = 0$
  $maxcard(\mathsf{Class}, \mathsf{implements}) = \infty$
  $mincard(\mathsf{Software}, \mathsf{executes}) = 0$
  $maxcard(\mathsf{Software}, \mathsf{executes}) = \infty$
  $mincard(\mathsf{ComputationalTask}, \mathsf{accesses}) = 0$
  $maxcard(\mathsf{ComputationalTask}, \mathsf{accesses}) = \infty$
  $mincard(\mathsf{Software}, \mathsf{invokes}) = 0$
  $maxcard(\mathsf{Software}, \mathsf{invokes}) = \infty$
  $mincard(\mathsf{Input}, \mathsf{inputFor}) = 0$
  $maxcard(\mathsf{Input}, \mathsf{inputFor}) = \infty$
  $mincard(\mathsf{Output}, \mathsf{outputFor}) = 0$
  $maxcard(\mathsf{Output}, \mathsf{outputFor}) = \infty$
  $mincard(\mathsf{User}, \mathsf{contextUser}) = 0$
  $maxcard(\mathsf{User}, \mathsf{contextUser}) = 1$
  $mincard(\mathsf{User}, \mathsf{computationalRightTowards}) = 0$
  $maxcard(\mathsf{User}, \mathsf{computationalRightTowards}) = \infty$
  $mincard(\mathsf{UserGroup}, \mathsf{computationalRightTowards}) = 0$
  $maxcard(\mathsf{UserGroup}, \mathsf{computationalRightTowards}) = \infty$

Modelling Basis (DOLCE, DnS, OoP, OIO)

Finally, each ontology module of our modelling basis (DOLCE, Descriptions & Situations, the Ontology of Plans and the Ontology of Information Objects) becomes a separate OI-model. However, Descriptions & Situations and the Ontology of Information Objects mutually depend on each other (cf. Figure 7.1 on page 108). Hence, we have to put both in one OI-model.

For the sake of brevity, we do not present the respective ontology structures here. All the modules are available in a description logic (OWL DL). The entirety of this application version is called *DOLCE Lite Plus (DLP)*. Their axiomatization underwent a similar process such as our contributed modules, i.e., the axiomatization was adapted to application purposes. For example, temporally indexed (and, thus, ternary) associations were decomposed by newly introduced temporal associations. For this work, we have obtained the KAON OI-models from the description logic files by means of RDFS exports and imports, respectively. Creating the KAON version then boils down to manually maintaining symmetry, transitivity, inverses, and cardinality restrictions. The KAON version of the modelling basis is also available at `http://cos.ontoware.org`.

4. Assessment

This section responds to the Cardinal Question: *Can ontologies be used to facilitate the development and management of middleware-based applications for developers and administrators?*). Demonstrating that we have achieved our goal of facilitating the management of middleware proves to be problematic for two reasons.

First, the complexity of application servers makes it very difficult to single out, measure, and evaluate improvements of any kind. As explained in Chapter 2, Section 3.1, page 18, an application server consists of many interwoven parts. Often an application server subsumes several other types of middleware in one product.

Second, it is usually difficult to substantiate the advantages of ontology-based applications in numbers. The best way to demonstrate their benefits is to have a modularized application and to perform a controlled experiment. Modules providing the same functionality with and without the usage of ontologies have to be applied and the application evaluated each time. Such experiments are difficult to set up and in many cases the nature of the application makes it impossible. This is the case with semantic management because its usage is spread throughout the target platform. Furthermore, the developer and administrator have to familiarize with ontologies and semantic technology in general, much like they have or had to familiarize with deployment and WS* descriptors. In both cases, it would be necessary to compare the effort of familiarization with the savings of management efforts and to each other. In addition, we have to take into account efforts for maintaining the ontology (because ontologies typically evolve over time).

Because it is very difficult to find measures for a sensible comparison, we take a qualitative approach for assessing the benefits of semantic management. We basically revisit the use cases introduced in Chapter 4, Section 2, starting on page 65, and compare management and modelling efforts with and without semantic management.

While the modelling efforts are independent of the underlying semantic technology, we encounter a trade-off between management efforts and reasoning capabilities. Our use cases require a whole bandwidth of reasoning capabilities: one requires subsumption reasoning; another uses the reified satisfaction of Descriptions & Situations; others require browsing and querying; and so forth. As a consequence, some use cases cannot be realized with KAON or require management efforts that could have been saved with more powerful reasoning. This is due to KAON's limited reasoning capabilities. In essence, there is not much more than subsumption, transitivity and symmetry. A description logic reasoner is far more powerful and might save management efforts accordingly. We will consider this issue when inspecting the use cases in the following sections.

4.1   Application Server Use Cases

We start our assessment with an effort comparison for the similar *Library Dependencies and Versioning* and *Licensing* use cases in Table 10.3. Without our approach, no modelling efforts have to be expended, but the developer has to check for conflicting libraries each time the classpath is changed. Expert knowledge is required to avoid run time failures, e.g., when a lib1.jar conflicts with a lib2.jar. In a system that supports semantic management, we have to model COSC:libraryConflictsWith and COSC:licenseIncompatibleWith between COSC:SoftwareLibraries and COSC:Licenses, respectively. A check then boils down to a simple query with KAON, as well as with a DL reasoner. KAON Query suffices because this use case only requires transitivity and symmetry reasoning.

Table 10.3.   Effort comparison for the *Library Dependencies and Versioning* and *Licensing* use cases.

Effort	Without semantic management	Using semantic management
Management	For n libraries in the classpath: $\binom{n}{2}$ manual comparisons	n simple queries for COSC:libraryConflictsWith
Modelling	None	Model COSC:libraryConflictsWith or COSC:licenseIncompatibleWith libraries or licenses

The *Capability Descriptions* use case deals with the fact that components often adhere to standard interfaces, but differ in their capabilities. In this case, the developer has to react to all possible cases in the code anytime the interface is accessed. Semantic management allows obtaining such information manually or automatically from the COSC:ComponentProfile by browsing or querying, respectively. We compare the efforts in Table 10.4. KAON's limited reasoning capabilities might require more or less management efforts depending on the complexity of the query. That means, the result might have to be (partially) obtained by coding in comparison to a much more powerful DL reasoner.

Component Classification and Discovery and *Semantics of Parameters* address the problem of searching or comparing functionality over a large number of component API's at development time. Such tasks are very tedious without

Table 10.4. Effort comparison for the *Capability Descriptions* use case.

Effort	Without semantic management	Using semantic management
Management	Code extensive distinction of cases and exception handling to avoid run time failures	Browse or query COSC:Component-Profile to obtain the component's COSC:Characteristics
Modelling	None	Model COSC:Component-Profile once

our approach because they require source code analyses and coding of possible cases when the semantics of parameters are not specified. As shown in Table 10.5, semantic management requires modelling the components' CSO:-Interfaces, but allows convenient browsing and querying possibilities at development time. Like with the previous use case, the management effort with KAON might be higher depending on the complexity of the query.

Table 10.5. Effort comparison for the *Component Classification and Discovery* and *Semantics of Parameters* use cases.

Effort	Without semantic management	Using semantic management
Management	Tedious source code analyses, extensive coding of possible cases and exception handling	Browsing or simple querying the CSO:Interfaces in the COSC:ComponentProfiles
Modelling	None	Model CSO:Interfaces once

The benefits of the next use case, viz., *Automatic Generation of Web Service Descriptions*, are a desirable side effect of semantic management. Given the savings of management efforts of all the other use cases, this use case proposes to generate specific WS* descriptions from the ontology automatically.[6] WS-BPEL documents could be generated from a corresponding OoP:Plan, for instance. No additional modelling efforts have to be expended if the OoP:Plan already exists (cf. Table 10.6).

For the *Access Rights* use case, we return to our motivating example on page 23, which discusses the indirect permission of the WebShopServlet to the Customer table via a context switch. We have already seen that discovering such situations is a very costly task. Using semantic management, we can conveniently evaluate or query for COSC:indirectlyAccessibleResource with no additional modelling efforts when we use a DL reasoner. While KAON is

---

[6]This is a use case for *model-driven deployment* as proposed in Chapter 8, Section 1.3.

Table 10.6. Effort comparison for the *Automatic Generation of Web Service Descriptions* use cases.

Effort	Without semantic management	Using semantic management
Management	Compare other use cases	Compare other use cases
Modelling	Modelling the Web service descriptions, e.g., WS-BPEL	No additional efforts required if information exists in the ontology, e.g., OoP:Plan

able to reason with the transitivity of CSO:invokes, it cannot handle its decomposition into CSO:executes and CSO:accesses. Additional coding is necessary to obtain the result. Table 10.7 depicts the management effort in the DL case.

Table 10.7. Effort comparison for the *Access Rights* use case with a DL reasoner.

Effort	Without semantic management	Using semantic management
Management	For i servlets, j EJBs, k tables: compare i web.xml files and code, j ejb-jar.xml files and k table metadata	i evaluations of COSC:indirectlyAccessible-Resource
Modelling	Creating and maintaining i web.xml, j ejb-jar.xml descriptors and k metadata tables	Same as without semantics because semantic descriptions are automatically obtained

Table 10.8 compares the efforts for the *Exception Handling* use case. We can see that semantic management avoids the tedious manual surveying of exceptions in the source code by justifiable modelling efforts. The savings in management effort depend on the reasoning capability. Complex queries require additional efforts when using KAON.

Table 10.8. Effort comparison for the *Exception Handling* use case.

Effort	Without semantic management	Using semantic management
Management	Survey calling stack and component dependencies and check if exceptions are caught	Browsing or simple querying of the API descriptions (i.e., CSO:Methods and CSO:Exceptions)
Modelling	None	Modelling API descriptions

Finally, the similar *Transactional Settings* and *Secure Communication* use cases require a manual check of the transactional or security settings of a chain of calls across components without our approach. Modelling of workflow information, as well as the transactional and security settings, are necessary to check the validity by a simple query. We encounter the same dilemma between management efforts and reasoning capabilities as with the *Access Rights* use case.

Table 10.9. Effort comparison for the *Transactional Settings* and *Secure Communication* use cases using a DL reasoner.

Effort	Without semantic management	Using semantic management
Management	For a chain of calls: compare transactional or security settings for participating components	One query involving OoP:Plan and COSC:ComponentProfiles
Modelling	None	Modelling of workflow information via OoP:Plan and settings via COSC:ComponentProfiles

4.2 Web Services Use Cases

The first Web services use case considered in Chapter 4, Section 2, page 70, was *Analyzing Message Contexts*, which is very similar to the application server use cases *Access Rights*, *Transactional Settings*, and *Secure Communication*. Hence, we refer the reader to Tables 10.7 and 10.9 for the comparison.

The use case of *Selecting Service Functionality* is similar to one of the application server use cases, viz., *Component Classification and Discovery*, whose efforts are compared in Table 10.5.

For the similar *Policy Handling* and *Relating Communication Parameters* use cases, we demonstrate the benefits by our motivating example in Chapter 2, Section 3.2, page 30, which discusses the integration of WS-BPEL and WS-Policy descriptors. We have learned that discovering external service invocations with attached policy remains a pure manual task. Using semantic management, we can simply query with no additional modelling efforts (cf. Table 10.10). The dilemma between management efforts and reasoning capabilities is similar to the *Access Rights* use case in the previous section.

Table 10.11 compares management and modelling efforts for the *Detecting Loops in Interorganizational Workflows* use case. The use case proposes the parsing and integration of WS-BPEL descriptors to enable a check for cycles in the invocation chain across WS-BPEL documents, for instance. Without our approach, this check has to be done by hand, what can be rather expensive considering large numbers of processes. Semantic management only requires a simple query with no additional modelling efforts. We encounter the same dilemma between management efforts and reasoning capabilities as with the *Access Rights* application server use case.

Table 10.10.   Effort comparison for the *Policy Handling* and *Relating Communication Parameters* use cases using a DL reasoner.

Effort	Without semantic management	Using semantic management
Management	For each process in a WS-BPEL document: Check for external Web service invocation and existence of WS-Policy document	One query to retrieve ext. Web service invocations with attached policies
Modelling	creating and maintaining the WS-BPEL and WS-Policy documents	Same as without semantics because semantic descriptions are automatically obtained

Table 10.11.   Effort comparison for the *Detecting Loops in Interorganizational Workflows* use case with a DL reasoner.

Effort	Without semantic management	Using semantic management
Management	Check whether external service invocations lead to loops in one or more WS-BPEL documents	One query on an OoP:Plan to retrieve cyclic invocations
Modelling	Creating and maintaining the WS-BPEL documents	Same as without semantics because semantic descriptions are automatically obtained

Regarding the use case of *Incompatible Inputs and Outputs*, we refer the reader to the *Semantics of Parameters* use case in Table 10.5 in the previous section. Both use cases are similar with comparable modelling and management efforts.

Monitoring of Changes addresses the problem of changing interfaces in a loosely coupled environment. Changes of used services have to be detected and depending services have to be identified and adapted. Without our approach this remains a manual effort. In contrast, semantic management supports the developer in detecting such changes and identifying the depending service (cf. Table 10.12). KAON is capable of handling such queries. Hence, the management efforts are the same compared to a DL reasoner.

The *Aggregating Service Information* use case discusses the automatic calculation of first-cut quality of service parameters for composite services. In order to obtain such numbers automatically, service parameters have to be modelled for each of the composed services. The alternative is to obtain such information manually, which is particularly tedious if the composite service contains a large number of composed services. Table 10.13 compares the efforts in both cases. The limited reasoning capabilities of KAON might require more or less management efforts depending on the complexity of the query.

Table 10.12. Effort comparison for the *Monitoring of Changes* use case.

Effort	Without semantic management	Using semantic management
Management	Manual monitoring of changes, detecting and adapting each depending component or service	One query for detecting the change, one query to detect depending components or service, adaptation
Modelling	None	None because semantic descriptions are automatically obtained

Table 10.13. Effort comparison for the *Aggregating Service Information* use case.

Effort	Without semantic management	Using semantic management
Management	For each composite service: Obtain first-cut data manually	For each composite service: One query to obtain first-cut data
Modelling	None	QualityOfService parameters for composed services

Finally, the *Quality of Service* use case suggests the gathering of one's own data about the reliability or availability of used services in the ontology. The semantic descriptions can be exploited to route service requests to the most reliable service endpoint, for instance. When applying semantic management, the most reliable service can be obtained by a simple query. Otherwise, the application logic has to be hard-coded, leading to an inflexible system with higher maintenance, and, thus management efforts. Table 10.14 compares the efforts in both cases. Like with the previous use case, the management effort with KAON might be higher depending on the complexity of the query.

Table 10.14. Effort comparison for the *Quality of Service* use case.

Effort	Without semantic management	Using semantic management
Management	Code and maintain the best fitting service manually	One query to select the best fitting service
Modelling	None	QualityOfService parameters for each service

5. Summary

In this chapter we have answered the Question III.4: *How to reuse the ontology?* by taking the following steps: (*i*) we have specialized the core concepts and associations of the management ontology to reflect the idiosyncracies of the KAON SERVER. (*ii*) We have removed concepts and associations that were introduced merely for reference purposes and (*iii*) we have adapted the axiomatization to the KAON language. The resulting *domain*, *application* and *lightweight* version of the management ontology is actually applied in the KAON SERVER and can be obtained from `http://cos.ontoware.org`.

Finally, we have assessed the benefits of semantic management thus answering the Cardinal Question from the Introduction: *Can ontologies be used to facilitate the development and management of middleware-based applications for developers and administrators?* We have taken a qualitative approach for assessment by revisiting the use cases introduced in Chapter 4, Section 2 and comparing management and modelling efforts with and without semantic management. The assessment demonstrated that the rather modest modelling efforts are clearly outplayed by the savings in management efforts.

PART IV

FINALE

Chapter 11

RELATED WORK

This chapter provides an overview of related work by classifying relevant literature according to research communities and areas, rather than by classifying according to the organization of the book.

Generally speaking, this work applies the methodologies and tools of the Semantic Web research community to solve some of the problems of the Middleware community. Both communities put forth some technologies and approaches relevant for our work. First, we find the established technology of *Enterprise Application Management* (Section 1). Enterprise application management comprises the processes that are used to monitor and control the software elements that make up application systems. It is a very broad field that starts at network management and ends at automatic software distribution to the desktop. Second, the paradigm of *Model-Driven Architectures (MDA)* has gained wide-spread influence in software engineering (Section 2). The principal idea of MDA is to separate conceptual concerns from implementation-specific concerns. MDA achieves this separation by factorizing the two concerns, specifying them separately via models and compiling them into an executable. Methodologies and tools of UML are used to capture the models. Third, we relate some approaches that show the bias towards integrating WS* descriptions in Section 3, although we already introduced the reader to Web services in Chapter 2, Section 3.2. Fourth, *Semantic Web Services* are a field of research opting for a wide-reaching formalization that allows full automation of the Web service management tasks, such as discovery and composition (Section 4). Finally, we relate miscellaneous efforts and technologies that cannot be classified in the aforementioned categories (Section 5).

1.   Enterprise Application Management

Application management can be considered as the task of monitoring and controlling the software elements that make up application systems. It includes people, policies, procedures and tools to manage the millions of software elements and configurations that exist in a corporate computing network. This can include practices that take place when new desktop systems are purchased, such as reformatting of the hard drive or installing standard configurations. It may also include the use of automated tools that analyze and update the configuration of systems. It may consist of traditional practices, such as manual inventories of software installed on desktop systems, software distribution, sophisticated performance measurement, and control systems using policy-based service-level agreements. [Sturm and Bumpus, 1998, Cho and Ejiri, 2004]

Enterprise application management is related to our work in two ways. First, corresponding management systems share some of our use cases simply because the management of middleware-based applications is a part of application management. Hence, it is a worthy challenge to semantically enhance also such management systems (as already discussed in Chapter 8, Section 1.1). We discuss such systems in Section 1.1. Second, the schemas of enterprise application management, such as MIB or CIM are (semi-formal) conceptual models that can be a source for semantic descriptions (cf. Chapter 8, Section 1.2). We discuss the management schemas in Section 1.2.

1.1   Application Management Systems

Enterprise application management can be seen as the task of monitoring and controlling applications in an enterprise so that they can be made resilient to failures, configurable to changing needs of the business, accountable for billing and auditing, capable of performing under varying workloads and secure to intended or unintended attacks. There have been several attempts at standardizing such tasks in the context of conventional middleware. For example, CORBA (cf. Chapter 2, Section 3) specifies lifecycle interfaces for configuration management, and the Java Management Extensions specify a framework for defining management interfaces on Java objects [Lindfors and Fleury, 2002]. One of the first efforts, however, stems from the International Standards Organisation (ISO), which introduced the Simple Network Management Protocol (SNMP) defining a set of objects called application Management Information Bases (MIB's) [Kalbfleisch et al., 1999]. Furthermore, Application Response Measurement (ARM) is a standard for managing performance events from applications.[1]

---

[1]http://www.opengroup.org/management/arm.htm

All the management standards that have been described aim at defining interfaces between the management system and managed applications. Some of these interfaces are useful in sending data from the application to the management system (e.g., SNMP, CIM, ARM). These are called *data interfaces* or *instrumentation interfaces*. Others are used by the management system to execute control actions on the application (e.g., JMX, CORBA lifecycle interfaces, SNMP, CIM). These are called *control interfaces*.

The infrastructure that manages applications using these interfaces is called an enterprise application management system. Examples of commonly used application management systems are HP OpenView,[2] Computer Associates Unicenter,[3] and IBM Tivoli.[4]

Enterprise application management systems share some of our use cases because the management of middleware-based applications can be considered a part of application management. As already discussed in Chapter 8, Section 1.1, such systems can thus be regarded as a possible platform for semantic management.

Web Services Management

Application management is currently extended to Web services. The Organization for the Advancement of Structured Information Standards (OASIS) is standardizing a *Web Services Distributed Management (WSDM)* specification.[5] Its first part, *MUWS (Management Using Web Services)*, defines how an information technology resource connected to a network can provide manageability interfaces so that the IT resource can be managed locally and remotely using Web services technologies. It is the foundation of enabling management applications to be built using Web services and allows resources to be managed by many applications with one set of instrumentation.

Its second part, *MOWS (Management of Web Services)*, is closely related to our work. It defines the manageability model for managing Web services as a resource and specifies how to describe and access that manageability using MUWS. MOWS can be seen as an extension of enterprise application management and has two sides: management of applications within an enterprise and management of relationships with other Web services across enterprises. The challenges in and approaches to dealing with the first side of Web services management are very similar to those in traditional application management. However, Web services simplify certain aspects of application management through their standardized abstractions. The second side of Web services man-

---

[2]http://www.managementsoftware.hp.com/
[3]http://ca.com/unicenter
[4]http://www.tivoli.com
[5]http://www.oasis-open.org/committees/tc_home.php?wg_abbrev=wsdm

agement (i.e., managing relationships with other Web services) raises a completely new set of challenges, since cross-enterprise interactions were not dealt with before in application management. These are some of the challenges we have addressed in our use cases (Chapter 4, Section 2.2). Applying semantic technology can be leveraged in corresponding Web service management systems to make them even more powerful by reasoning capabilities. Accordingly, we have proposed such management systems as a possible platform for semantic management in Chapter 8, Section 1.1. Besides WSDM, there are also proprietary efforts, e.g., [Tosic et al., 2004].

Management of Application Servers

In contrast to the standardization efforts of application management, and also of Web services management, the management of application servers remains a proprietary effort. In principle, every application server defines its own management model, with proprietary tools and graphical user interfaces. Some provide integration with application management systems, e.g., IBM WebSphere with IBM Tivoli.[6] Like Web service management systems, the management of application servers can be improved by semantic technology as we proposed in this thesis.

1.2   Application Management Schemas

The effort of developing a unified model for systems management emerged from the Distributed Management Task Force (DMTF). This model is being referred to as the Common Information Model (CIM) — an industry effort to develop a common object model for management. The Applications Management Working Committee of the DMTF has been working to unify the IETF, POSIX, DMTF, and the Tivoli AMS models of application management. It is interesting to note the similarities between these models and the different terms that have been developed to represent the same concepts. For example, what the POSIX model refers to as "file set," the DMTF refers to as "software element."

The DMTF realized the importance of developing a common model of an application and of using a common terminology because future management technologies will leverage standard models and nomenclatures. It is becoming increasingly difficult for management application vendors to provide agents, infrastructure and user interfaces for all of the complex networked elements. Using a common model enables greater interoperability. Management applications developers may also leverage the information that is available. [Sturm and Bumpus, 1998]

---

[6]http://www-306.ibm.com/software/tivoli/features/websphere/integration.html

On the one hand, CIM is comparable to our work in conceptually harmonizing the different existing schemas for application management. However, the CIM schemas are semi-formal and do not allow reasoning as a consequence. On the other hand, the CIM schemas have been considered as a potential source for obtaining semantic descriptions (cf. Chapter 8, Section 1.2). For example, there is a CIM schema for J2EE application servers as depicted in Figure 11.1

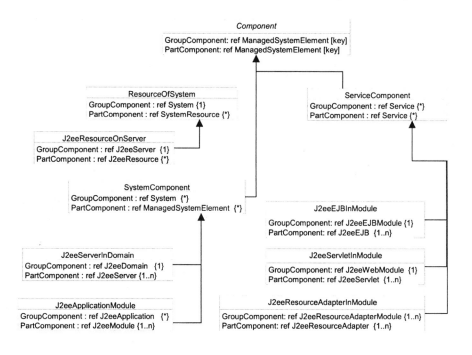

Figure 11.1. CIM for J2EE Application Servers. [http://www.dmtf.org]

Very similar approaches are application Management Information Bases (MIB's) and the MOWS schema for Web service management. The first approach stems from the International Standards Organization (ISO), which introduced the Simple Network Management Protocol (SNMP) defining a set of objects called Management Information Bases (MIB's) for managing applications. There is a plethora of MIB's for different purposes, e.g., MIB's for printers, routers, FTP servers, or for information modelling to support service and network management integration [Daho et al., 2004]. The second approach is the MOWS (Management of Web Services) Schema from OASIS, which defines states and properties of managed Web services.[7]

---

[7]http://docs.oasis-open.org/wsdm/2004/12/wsdm-mows-1.0.pdf

2.   Model-Driven Architectures

Throughout the history of computing systems, we have witnessed a remarkable evolution regarding the level of software reuse. Several kinds of software building blocks were developed with ever increasing abstraction and encapsulation of functionality. In the earliest computer systems, *functions* were the predominant software building blocks, returning the same result for a given input every time. However, functions are not suitable as soon as outputs depend on knowledge of previous deductions. In order to respond to this shortcoming, *subroutines and libraries* were introduced in the sixties and seventies. It quickly became apparent that sharing data between subroutines was desirable. However, coordinating concurrent and competing access to a global data structure between different libraries proved to be a maintenance problem. Thus, the *object* was born, encapsulating data and functionality (often called behavior in this case). Objects are still small-scale compared to the size of the systems we build today. It soon became apparent that there is benefit in reusing a collection of related objects together. The result was yet another software building block, viz., *software components*, enabling reuse at a higher level.

Even with these advances in the level of reuse, it is nonetheless difficult to reuse applications. There are more and more reimplementations of existing functionality because the underlying platforms change (e.g., updates of the operating system) or because of improving and progressing technology (e.g., new versions of Java). It is this shortcoming that the concept of Model-Driven Architectures (MDA) addresses [Mellor et al., 2004]. The principal idea of MDA is to separate *conceptual concerns* from *implementation-specific concerns*. MDA achieves this separation by factorizing the two concerns, specifying them separately and compiling them into an executable application. Methodologies and tools of UML are exploited to capture the concerns by models. Platform-independent models specify the conceptual concerns, whereas platform-specific models specify the implementation-specific concerns. Transformation rules define how to obtain different platform-dependent models from platform-independent ones. Thus, *models* become the unit of reuse and can be considered an asset resilient to changing platforms and technologies.

There are approaches that apply MDA for middleware-based applications [Gokhale et al., 2004, Brambilla et al., 2005], or application management [Debusmann et al., 2004]. However, in contrast to our work, MDA uses the models mainly to specify development aspects with focus on distinguishing platform-independent from platform-specific aspects, as well as on the definition of transformation rules between them. While something similar can be done also for the management of middleware, the main use case of MDA is to generate an executable application out of the platform-independent model. Our approach focuses on run time relevant characteristics of component and service management, such as which version of an application interface requires which versions of libraries. We exploit the logic-based semantics of ontologies for querying the inference engine in an application server whether configurations are valid or whether further components are needed. Ontologies are best-suited for this purpose.

While UML has not been based on ontologies initially, there is a tendency to bring the two worlds closer together. In 2003, the Object Management Group (OMG), the institution responsible for MDA, issued a request for the proposal of an *Ontology Definition Metamodel (ODM)*. This was done in order to support the development of ontologies using UML modeling tools, the implementation of ontologies in the W3C Web Ontology language OWL, as well as forward and reverse engineering for ontologies. Several proposals have been issued so far, e.g., [Hart et al., 2004]. It remains to be seen whether ODM would allow realizing our approach with UML and MDA technologies.

3. Web Services

We have already introduced the reader to Web services in Chapter 2, Section 3.2. We have seen that developers must face the multitude of descriptor files introduced by WSDL [Christensen et al., 2001], WS-BPEL [Andrews et al., 2005], WS-Security [Atkinson et al., 2002], WS-Transaction [Cabrera et al., 2004], WS-Trust [BEA Systems et al., 2004], WSCI [Arkin et al., 2002], WSCL [Banerji et al., 2002], WS-Coordination [Cabrera et al., 2003], UDDI [UDDI Coalition, 2000], etc. Because of their sheer number and disjointness, managing Web services with the *WS* specification* creates high costs for the developer. However, several approaches clearly demonstrate that there is a tendency to integrate all the disjoint information. The late JSR 181 [Trezzo and Mihic, 2004], e.g., defines a standard way to build and deploy Web services without learning and implementing generalized API's and deployment descriptors. The new Java 1.5 source code metadata annotation mechanism is used to flexibly define corresponding tags. Proprietary efforts like JBoss.Net and also Microsoft's .NET IDE take a similar approach. The development is facilitated because a familiarization with all the descriptor files is no longer necessary.

[Tai et al., 2004a] investigate the combination of WS-BPEL with WS-Coordination, WS-AtomicTransaction and WS-BusinessActivity using WS-Policy to support the definition of production workflows for Web services. They introduce coordination policies and specific WS-BPEL coordination policy attachments to compose Web services that require coordination protocols for interaction. They define the semantics of the proposed policy-based composition model and discuss the methods, the programming model, and the middleware support required for defining and executing composed and coordinated services. In [Tai et al., 2004b], they discuss a new approach to policy-based transactional coordination of services. They propose attaching policies to WSDL and WS-

BPEL definitions. The policies can be applied to the Web services specifications WS-Coordination, WS-Transaction, and WS-ReliableMessaging.

These are just *some* of the approaches that show the tendency to integrate the so far separated aspects of WS* descriptions. However, the missing coherent formal model of WS* makes it difficult to ask for, possibly undesirable, conclusions that arise from integrating several WS* descriptions. In contrast, our approach uses ontologies as explicit conceptual model whose underlying logic provides concise formal semantics and allows reasoning with such descriptions.

An exception are [Agarwal et al., 2005], who find that the main approaches taken thus far to standardize and compose Web services are piecemeal and insufficient. The business world has adopted a distributed programming approach in which Web service instances are described using WSDL, composed into flows with a language, such as WS-BPEL, and invoked with the SOAP protocol. The field of Semantic Web Services (cf. Section 4) propounds the approach of formally representing Web service capabilities in ontologies, and reasoning with their composition using goal-oriented inferencing techniques from planning. This new approach presents the first integrated work in composing Web services end to end from specification to deployment by synergistically combining the strengths of the above approaches.

4.   Semantic Web Services

The principal objective of Semantic Web Services is a wide-reaching formalization that allows *full automation* of the Web service management tasks, such as discovery and composition [McIlraith et al., 2001]. This field of research has articulated the shortcomings of WS* standardizations and has been presenting interesting proposals to counter some of them. The core of their proposals lies in creating *semantic* standards for the markup of Web services. The potential advantage is the reduction of management efforts to a minimum. The disadvantages, however, are also apparent. It is not clear, what kind of powerful machinery could constitute a semantic model that would allow for full automation, nor does it appear to be possible that real-world software developers could specify a semantic model of Web services that would be fine-grained enough to allow for full automation anytime soon. Therefore, our approach of semantic management of Web services does not propose to tackle full automation of *all* Web service management tasks. We claim that the full breadth of Web Service management requires an understanding of the world that is too deep to be modelled explicitly. Instead, we have presented a more passive role for semantic management of Web services — one that is driven by the needs of the developers who must cope with the complexity of Web service integration and WS* descriptions.

We now discuss several existing ontologies and frameworks for Semantic Web Services. We can summarize the differences to all of them as follows: (*i*) the ontologies are of low quality with respect to the ontology quality criteria introduced in Chapter 3, Section 1, page 41. They are hardly axiomatized and, thus, cover many unintended models leading to conceptual ambiguity, loose design and narrow scope (as demonstrated by the example of OWL-S in Chapter 5, Section 3). This is in conflict with our goals of having a high-quality ontology with heavyweight axiomatization and reference characteristic. (*ii*) The frameworks altogether aim at full automation of all management tasks incurring high modelling efforts. In contrast, our approach arrives at a minimum of management and modelling efforts as discussed at the beginning of Chapter 4. In addition, we do not propose a semantic standard for Web service description, such as some of the approaches do. The reverse engineering approach does not intervene with existing WS* specifications (which have yet to gain acceptance besides WSDL and WS-BPEL). We apply semantic technology within an application server and, thus, within the scope of an organizational unit, to facilitate some of the typical management tasks.

4.1   OWL-S

As discussed in Chapter 5, Section 1, OWL-S [Martin et al., 2004] is one of the first core ontologies explicitly aiming at automatic discovery, automatic invocation, automatic composition and interoperation, as well as automatic execution of Web services. We have inspected OWL-S and have come to the conclusion that it is a big step forward with design principles suitable also for our purposes. However, OWL-S exhibits shortcomings that stand in conflict with our goals of high quality, heavyweight axiomatization, and reference purpose. Our Core Ontology of Web Services can be seen as an improvement of OWL-S. Along the same lines, previous efforts responded to some of the problems of OWL-S. We briefly discuss the two initiatives we are aware of by describing their motivation, the parts of OWL-S they focus on, the techniques they use, as well as some initial results.

The first initiative [Narayanan and McIlraith, 2003] is motivated by the need of formal semantics to describe, simulate, automatically compose, test and verify Web service compositions. It focuses solely on the OWL-S Service-Model, which provides all the constructs for specifying composition. The authors establish a situation calculus semantics for the main elements in the OWL-S ServiceModel (e.g., atomic and composite processes, conditional effects and outputs), and then translate it to the operational semantics provided by Petri nets. This knowledge representation formalism has a rich theoretical and tool support for the various composition tasks. Indeed, the semantics of this knowledge representation mechanisms allows reusing an existing simulation and modelling environment. Further, the authors were able to identify more tractable subsets of OWL-S (less expressive but more efficient analysis for verification, composition and model checking).

The second effort [Ankolekar et al., 2002] also focuses only on the OWL-S ServiceModel and proposes a concurrent operational semantics that incorporates subtype polymorphism. The motivation for this work is to provide an initial reference semantics that would discover any possible ambiguity in the developed language. It would also serve for developing techniques for automated verification of OWL-S models. Finally, if other Web standards would provide a similar semantics, it would be much easier to compare them and to understand their strengths and weaknesses. The authors of both efforts mutually acknowledge the similarity between the two proposed semantics, except some minor details discussed in [Ankolekar et al., 2002].

Both approaches limit their attention to the OWL-S ServiceModel. From a methodological perspective, the approaches provide independent reconstructions of OWL-S, while we embed the information represented in the OWL-S ServiceModel in the larger context offered by the foundational ontology. Therefore we can deduce, e.g., that OWL-S does not address the difference between a real-life object (e.g., a book), and its representational counterpart in an information system (e.g., an ISBN number), an important ontological distinction. Finally, the semantics established by the approaches are not reflected in their OWL formalization. In contrast, our ontologies inherit the axiomatization from DOLCE and provide further axioms. Besides aiming at increased formal axiomatization, it has been our goal to explain the concepts as precisely as possible. The analysis of OWL-S in Chapter 5, Section 3, also brings to surface several shortcomings of OWL-S. Furthermore, one of the long term benefits of having an ontology with reference characteristics is that it allows a comparison among other ontologies (a goal also stated in [Ankolekar et al., 2002]).

The actions on OWL-S are continued by the Semantic Web Services Initiative Architecture committee (SWSA),[8] whose objective is to develop architectural and protocol abstractions forming a reference architecture to support Semantic Web Service technologies. One of their proposals is the framework discussed next: METEOR-S.

4.2 METEOR-S

The METEOR-S project at the LSDIS Lab, University of Georgia, aims to extend WS* specifications with Semantic Web technologies to achieve greater dynamism and scalability.[9] More specifically, METEOR-S focuses on adding semantics to WSDL and UDDI, on adding semantics to WS-BPEL and on a semi-automatic approach for annotating Web services described in WSDL. The endeavor is to define and support the complete lifecycle of Semantic Web

---

[8] http://www.daml.org/services/swsa/
[9] http://lsdis.cs.uga.edu/Projects/METEOR-S/

Services processes. Like with all other approaches, METEOR-S aims at full automation of all management tasks, while our approach aims at facilitating some management tasks by keeping the modelling efforts minimal. An introduction to the parts of the METEOR-S project follows.

Semantic Annotation of Web Services

The METEOR-S Web Service Annotation Framework (MWSAF) [Patil et al., 2004] is a graphical tool that allows annotating existing Web service descriptions with semantic descriptions according to an arbitrary ontology. The tool facilitates the parsing of WSDL files and ontologies, enabling the user to annotate Web service descriptions semi-automatically by a matching algorithm. The matching algorithm works on the XML-Schema types of a WSDL description and a given domain ontology. Such an approach is very promising also for our work because it allows obtaining semantic descriptions semi-automatically (cf. Chapter 8, Section 1.2).

WSDL-S

WSDL-S [Akkiraju et al., 2005] is an evolutionary and compatible upgrade of the existing WSDL descriptions. Semantic descriptions are attached to WSDL descriptions whereby the expressiveness of WSDL is augmented with semantics. This is done by employing concepts analogous to those in OWL-S, while being agnostic to the semantic representation language. The advantage of adding semantics to WSDL in such an evolutionary way is multi-fold. First, users can, in an upwardly compatible way, describe both the semantics and operation level details in WSDL — a language with which the developer community is familiar with. Second, by externalizing the semantic domain models, WSDL-S takes an agnostic approach to ontology representation languages. This allows Web service developers to annotate their Web services with their choice of the ontology language (such as UML or OWL). This is significant since the ability to reuse existing domain models expressed in modelling languages, such as UML, can greatly alleviate the need to separately model semantics. Moreover, this approach realizes the need for the existence of multiples ontologies, either from the same or different domains. Finally, it is relatively easy to update the existing tooling around the WSDL specification to accommodate such an incremental approach. According to the authors, this work is being provided as input for the next version of WSDL that will support semantic representation.

Abstract Process Creation

The METEOR-S Web Service Composition Framework (MWSCF) [Sivashanmugam et al., 2004] considers the fact that the activity of creating Web processes using Web services has been handled mostly at the syntactic level. Current composition standards focus on building the processes based on the interface description of the participating services. The limitation of such a rigid approach is that it does not allow businesses to dynamically change partners and services. MWSCF enhances the current Web process composition techniques by using "Semantic Process Templates" to capture the semantic requirements of the process. The semantic process templates can act as configurable modules for common industry processes maintaining the semantics of the participating activities, control flow, intermediate calculations, conditional branches and exposing it in an industry accepted interface. The templates are instantiated to form executable processes according to the semantics of the activities in the templates. The use of ontologies in template definitions allows a much richer description of activity requirements and a more effective way of locating services to carry out the activities in the executable Web process. During the discovery of services, the framework considers not only functionality, but also the quality of service of the corresponding activities. The framework combines the expressive power of the present Web service composition standards and the advantages of the Semantic Web techniques for process template definition and Web service discovery.

Semantic Discovery of Web Services

The METEOR-S Web Service Discovery Infrastructure (MWSDI) [Verma et al., 2005] supports Web service publication and discovery among multiple registries. This work uses an ontology-based approach to organize registries, enabling semantic classification of all Web services based on specific domains. Each of these registries supports semantic publication of the Web services, which is used during the discovery process. Two algorithms for semantic publication and one algorithm for semantic discovery of Web services have been implemented. According to the authors, this semantic approach will significantly improve Web services publication and discovery involving a large number of registries.

Composition of Web Services

Automatically selecting new services which best fit a specific requirement necessitates the quantifying of criteria for selection. In addition, there are challenging issues of correctness and optimality. The "Constraint Driven Web Service Composition" tool in METEOR-S [Aggarwal et al., 2004] allows process designers to bind Web services to an abstract process, based on business and process constraints, and generate an executable process. The approach is to reduce much of the service composition problem to a constraint satisfaction problem. It uses a multi-phase approach for constraint analysis.

4.3 WSMO

The Web Service Modeling Ontology (WSMO) along with its related efforts WSML and WSMX (see below) presents a complete framework for Semantic Web Services, combining Semantic Web and Web service technologies. The Web Service Modeling Framework (WSMF) [Fensel and Bussler, 2002] is taken as a starting point, refined and extended by developing a formal ontology and language. WSMF consists of four different main elements for describing Semantic Web Services: (1) ontologies that provide the terminology used by other elements, (2) goals that define the problems that should be solved by Web services, (3) Web services descriptions that define various aspects of a Web service and (4) mediators, which bypass interoperability problems. [Roman et al., 2005]

The Web Service Modeling Language (WSML) provides a formal syntax and the semantics for the Web Service Modeling Ontology. WSML is based on different logical formalisms, namely, description logics, first-order logic and logic programming, which are useful for the modeling of Semantic Web Services. WSML consists of a number of variants based on these different logical formalisms, namely WSML-Core, WSML-DL, WSML-Flight, WSML-Rule and WSML-Full. [de Bruijn et al., 2005]

Finally, The Web Services Execution Environment (WSMX) is an execution environment for dynamic discovery, selection, mediation and invocation of Semantic Web Services. WSMX is developed as a reference implementation of an execution environment for Web services. It manages a repository of Web services, ontologies and mediators. According to the authors, WSMX can achieve a user's goal by dynamically selecting a matching Web service, mediating the data that needs to be communicated to this service and invoking it. [Aiken and Zaremba, 2005]

WSMO is no exception in that its goal is the full automation of all management tasks. Our approach, in contrast, aims at facilitating only some of the typical Web service management tasks by a justifiable amount of semantic modelling.

4.4 IRS

IRS–II (Internet Reasoning Service) is a framework whose main goal is to support the publication, location, composition and execution of heterogeneous Web services, augmented with semantic descriptions of their functionalities. IRS–II has three main classes of features, which distinguish it among other works on Semantic Web Services. First, it supports one-click publishing of stand-alone software: IRS–II automatically creates the appropriate wrappers, given pointers to the stand-alone code. Second, it explicitly distinguishes between tasks (what to do) and methods (how to achieve tasks), and, as a result supports capability-driven service invocation, flexible mappings from services to problem specifications and dynamic, knowledge-based service selection. Finally, IRS–II services are Web service compatible. Standard Web services can be trivially published through the IRS–II and any IRS–II service automatically appears as a standard Web service to other Web service infrastructures [Motta et al., 2003]. Like with all other approaches, IRS aims at full automation of all management tasks. Our approach of semantic management of Web services, however, aims at facilitating some management tasks by keeping the modelling efforts minimal.

4.5   KDSWS

The Knowledge-based Dynamic Semantic Web Services (KDSWS) framework presents an agent-based approach to managing the brokering of Semantic Web Services for use within a virtual organization. The framework provides a formal model-based approach to implementing Web services that defines the modelling, specification, design, implementation and deployment of systems composed of Semantic Web Services. The goal of the framework is to support the automatic discovery, composition, execution and management of Web services for the virtual organization in a protocol-independent manner. This research is still at an abstract level and a proof of concept implementation of the framework is planned to demonstrate and mature the facets of the research. [Howard and Kerschberg, 2004] KDSWS' goal is the full automation of all Web service management tasks, such as all other approaches. Our approach, in contrast, aims at facilitating only some of the management tasks by a justifiable amount of semantic modelling.

4.6   Other Approaches

There are several other approaches (as opposed to complete frameworks) that try to exploit semantic technologies in existing Web services middleware. Two approaches try to incorporate semantic technology in UDDI, for instance. The first, [Voskob, 2004], stems from the OASIS[10] itself and proposes a taxonomy support for semantics in UDDI registries. The primary aim is to enable a better discovery and matchmaking by leveraging the ontological descriptions. The second tries to achieve similar goals by incorporating OWL-S profiles into the UDDI registry [Paolucci et al., 2002a].

[Mandell and McIlraith, 2003] take into account that most semantic efforts have been disconnected from the emerging WS* standards. Hence, they propose a "bottom-up" approach of enriching WS-BPEL by semantics.

---

[10]http://www.oasis-open.org

Furthermore, there are *semantic service matchmakers* that compare a given service requirement description to several service offering descriptions and choose the best fitting one. Several service matchmaking engines have been prototypically implemented, e.g., [Li and Horrocks, 2003, Paolucci et al., 2002c, Noia et al., 2003]. Even the sophisticated task of *automated policy matching* is currently approached in the field of Semantic Web Services. Corresponding policy engines act on semantic policy descriptions and try to match them. There are several prototypes available, e.g., [Tonti et al., 2003, Kagal et al., 2003, Agarwal and Sprick, 2004, Uszok et al., 2004]. It remains to be seen whether the problems related to semantic interpretations of documents can be solved in the full generality required for real-life service and policy matching. Instead, we want to provide developers with some tool support in browsing, selecting and handling services and policies at *development* time. Hence, we propose to support the developers in their management tasks and not to replace them.

5. Miscellaneous

The final section groups related approaches that cannot be classified in the aforementioned categories. We discuss *software reuse systems* (Section 5.1), the *DL IDL* approach (Section 5.2), Microsoft's *System Definition Model* (Section 5.3), the *integration of software specifications* (Section 5.4), as well as *ontologies* comparable to our work (Section 5.5).

5.1 Software Reuse Systems

Classical software reuse systems are comparable to our work in that they also need to describe software modules appropriately for efficient and precise retrieval. Techniques, such as the faceted classification [Diaz, 1991], concentrate on representing the features of the software providers. Techniques, such as the analogical software reuse [Massonet and van Lamsweerde, 1997], share a representation of modules that is based on goals achieved by the software, roles and conditions. [Zaremski and Wing, 1997] describe a specification language and matching mechanism for software modules. They allow for multiple degrees of matching, but consider only syntactic information. UPML, the Unified Problem-solving Method Development Language [Fensel et al., 1999], has been developed to describe and implement intelligent broker architectures and components to facilitate semi-automatic reuse and adaptation. It is a framework for developing knowledge-intensive reasoning systems based on libraries of generic problem-solving components that are represented by inputs, outputs, preconditions and effects of tasks. However, none of these approaches focuses on the aspects that have to be described for management purposes. Most of them are also not based on logics, disallowing reasoning and querying.

5.2   DL IDL

[Borgida and Devanbu, 1999] show how description logics can be used to augment CORBA IDL specifications so that the compatibility testing of IDL specifications, local consistency checking, and more thorough treatment of exceptions is possible. However, this approach just augments the syntactic part of an API's description. That means DL IDL does not allow to model the meaning or behavior of methods and parameters, such as our Core Software Ontology. Given such information, our approach allows more powerful searches over a large unfamiliar API, for instance. However, DL IDL could be extended in this direction.

5.3   Microsoft SDM

The Dynamic Systems Initiative (DSI) is an industry effort led by Microsoft to enhance the Windows platform and to deliver a coordinated set of solutions that simplify and automate how businesses design, deploy and operate distributed systems. The System Definition Model (SDM)[11] is a key technology component of the DSI product roadmap that provides a common language (called meta-model) used to create models that capture the organizational knowledge relevant to entire distributed systems.

SDM takes a similar approach to ours because it tries to include heterogeneous information (in this case about software, hardware and network) in a unified system model. SDM targets design, deployment and operation. The first actual software tool implementing this strategy is the Visual Studio development environment. SDM illustrates the trend of representing different system aspects in a common framework, although it seems to rely solely on XML without any underlying logic-based semantics.

5.4   Integration of Software Specifications

[Grosse-Rhode, 2004] addresses the model-based development of software systems, which uses different views on a system specified in appropriate modelling languages and techniques. These range from formal specification techniques, such as process calculi, Petri nets and rule-based formalisms to semi-formal software modelling languages, such as those in the UML family. Because of the unavoidable heterogeneity of the models, a semantic integration is required to establish the correspondences of the models and to allow the checking of the relative consistency.

The proposed integration approach is based on a common semantic domain of abstract systems, their composition and development. Its applicability is shown through semantic interpretations and compositional comparisons of dif-

---

[11]http://www.microsoft.com/windowsserversystem/dsi/sdm.mspx

ferent specification approaches. Algebraic reference models are used to integrate the different specification formalisms. Their operational semantics can be faithfully rephrased in terms of algebraic transformation systems. This common semantic interpretation yields the possibility of formal comparisons of heterogeneous specifications given in different languages even with different underlying paradigms.

The initial problem that is addressed by this work is very similar to ours. Grosse-Rhode tries to harmonize the different views of software development, such as UML class diagrams or Petri nets, in a common model. However, our focus is not on development, but rather on management. In addition, we concentrate on typical middleware systems with their descriptor files. We use an ontology with logic-based semantics as opposed to the algebraic approach. We do so because we exploit the reasoning capabilities of corresponding inference engines to support developers and administrators in their daily tasks.

5.5 Other Ontologies

There have been several efforts to define ontologies that overlap with the ideas presented in Chapter 7. For example, the COHSE Java ontology[12] offers a formal schema for turning a Java software project into an ontology. The open source project Introspector[13] is a back-end to the popular GNU compiler collection gcc,[14] which generates an RDF defined ontology out of gcc compiled source code. Thus, it works with all languages supported by gcc, for example, C, C++, Java, Fortran and others. [Welty, 1995] offers a more profound and sound ontology-based foundation to these levels of detail, analyzing the constructs available when programming. All these works provide support for using ontologies in the area of software development but on a much finer grained level than the work presented here.

An example of a higher level software component ontology in use is provided by [Ankolekar et al., 2003]. Instead of the technological management of software components as provided by the middleware layer and described herein, her work focuses on the social and project-level management of open source software projects. As we can see by these numerous examples, the use of Semantic Web technologies in the area of software engineering is gaining momentum. A task force within the Semantic Web Best Practises group has been formed in order to organize and bring together these various efforts.[15]

---

[12]http://cohse.semanticweb.org/software.html
[13]http://introspector.sourceforge.net
[14]http://gcc.gnu.org
[15]http://www.w3.org/2001/sw/BestPractices/SE/

Chapter 12

CONCLUSION & OUTLOOK

The contribution of this work is to solve some of the problems of the Middleware community by applying the technologies of the Semantic Web community. More specifically, the book positively answers its Cardinal Question: *Can ontologies be used to facilitate the development and management of middleware-based applications for developers and administrators?* In this final chapter, we provide a summary of the book in Section 1. In essence, we have subdivided the Cardinal Question into three Main Questions. In each part of the document we have been concerned with answering one of the Main Questions. Furthermore, we detail the contributions separately in Section 2. First, our approach of semantic management allows the automation of *some* typical management tasks prevailing in application servers and Web services middleware. Second, we explicitly build our approach on the observation that there is a trade-off between management and modelling efforts. Third, we provide a set of ontologies which are well-designed, avoiding the typical shortcomings of commonly built ontologies. Open issues and possible directions for future research are discussed in Section 3.

1. Summary

We have subdivided the Cardinal Question into the three Main Questions. Below, we give a brief summary of how the three Main Questions have been answered.

I *How to find a good trade-off between modelling and management efforts?*
In Part I, we have claimed that the full breadth of management requires an understanding of the world that is too deep to be modelled explicitly. There is a *trade-off* between expending efforts for management and expending efforts for semantic modelling. The trade-off point was approached by

identifying a set of use cases. Each of them responded to the questions *who uses the semantic descriptions?*, *what are they used for?* and *when do they occur?* The use cases also yielded a set of modelling requirements for choosing which aspects our ontology should formalize.

II *How to build a suitable management ontology?* The modelling requirements that were derived in Part I serve as an input to Part II, where we have analyzed whether existing ontologies can be reused and adapted for our purposes. In order to answer the question *can an existing ontology be reused for our purposes?*, we have had a closer look at potential core ontologies for the description of Web services and software components. The conclusion was that existing ontologies exhibit severe problems that conflict with our goals of having a high-quality management ontology. Hence, we have decided to model an appropriate management ontology anew. Appropriateness required answering the questions: *how to ensure high quality?*, and *how to decrease modelling efforts and enable reuse?* We have achieved these goals by: (*i*) axiomatizing the intended models of our universe of discourse as closely as possible and (*ii*) capturing the idiosyncracies of components and services *and* by being platform-independent at the same time. The resulting management ontology can be downloaded at http://cos.ontoware.org.

III *How to realize semantic management of middleware?* It was the purpose of Part III to elaborate on all issues of realization. The ontology is merely a passive object which has to be applied in an inference engine in order to realize all the querying and reasoning tasks introduced in our use cases. The first question that arose was: *what is a suitable target platform?* We have chosen an application server because many use cases can be realized. The next question, *who provides semantic descriptions?*, addressed the problem that the number of manually provided descriptions must be kept as small as possible because developers and administrators do not want to expend additional efforts. Hence, we have elicited further options on how to arrive at semantic descriptions of components and services. We have continued by designing an ontology-based application server in a piecemeal manner. In order to respond to *how to implement semantic management?*, we have reused an existing application server and have leveraged the wealth of tools provided by an existing ontology tool suite. Another significant body of work elaborated on the steps necessary to reuse and apply our management ontology in this specific implementation (*how to reuse the ontology?*). Our prototypical implementation, the KAON SERVER, can be obtained from http://kaon.semanticweb.org/server.

2. Contributions

The book proposes the semantic management of middleware-based applications to support the developer and administrator. That means using an ontology to make the underlying conceptual model of middleware elements explicit by formal logic-based semantics. Therefore, semantic descriptions of such middleware-elements may be queried, may foresight required actions or may be checked to avoid inconsistent system configurations. The contributions can be factorized as follows:

State-of-the-art Ontology Engineering Commonly and often naively built ontologies suffer from conceptual ambiguity, poor axiomatization, loose design and narrow scope. They are often reduced to simple taxonomies and leave open many interpretations of their concepts and associations. We have responded to such shortcomings by adopting the advanced theory of Guarino and have introduced a new classification of ontologies in order to explain their different uses. We have carefully chosen an appropriate foundational ontology on the basis of specific ontological choices. The foundational ontology was used as a modelling basis and extended by highly axiomatized core ontologies.

We have shown how to develop *and* use the ontological foundations of this work in a concrete software environment. This was done in a way that the usage of the resulting middleware infrastructure seems amenable to a sophisticated software developer even though the development of a complex foundational ontology may have to be left to some few specialists.

Finally, the extensive axiomatization of the management ontology and, thus, its reference characteristic, makes evident that there are only minor differences between modelling software components and modelling Web services.

Reduction of Management Efforts Another novelty of our approach is to use, adapt, extend and apply semantic technology to automate some of the management tasks of application server and Web services middleware. Such middleware solutions are very complex software products that are hard to tame because of the intricacies of building distributed systems. So far, their functionalities have mostly been developed and managed with the help of administration tools and corresponding configuration files, recently in XML. Though this constitutes a very flexible way of developing and administrating a distributed application, the disadvantage is that the conceptual model underlying the different configurations is *only implicit*. Hence, its bits and pieces are difficult to retrieve, survey, check for validity and maintain. To remedy such problems, we contribute an ontology-based approach to support the development and administration of middleware-based applications. The ontology captures properties of, relationships between and behaviors of the components and services that are required for development and administration purposes. The ontology is an *explicit* conceptual model with formal logic-based semantics. Therefore, its descriptions may be queried and reasoned with. Thus, the ontology-based approach retains the original flexibility in configuring and running the middleware, but it adds new capabilities for the developer and user of the system. The proposed scheme is prototypically implemented in an open-source application server.

Consideration of Modelling Efforts Our approach is one of the first that acknowledges and explicitly builds on the observation that the use of declarative specifications, such as those in Web services, or formal declarative specifications, such as in Semantic Web Services, comes with economic modelling costs that need to be justified by savings in other places.

This lets us presume that formal specifications with the objective of fully automatic Web service composition and orchestration remain a valid research topic, but one that will find its applications in niches rather than in wide-spread adoption by software developers.

3.   Open Issues

Every solution raises new problems, and our work is no exception here. First, the scope of this work could be extended to other middleware platforms. Second, its prototypical implementation could be extended to a full-fledged solution. Third, further research is required for a concise comparison of management efforts vs. reasoning capabilities. Fourth, the assessment of the benefits could be extended to a comprehensive economic analysis. Last but not least, the realization of semantic managements will hopefully culminate in industry adoption.

Scope Although the name of the book is "semantic management of middleware" we have limited its focus on application servers and Web services. Consequently, the solution we provide concentrates on the semantic management of software components and Web services. Even within the limited *scope* we have only scratched the surface with the identified use cases. All of them are subject to be discussed in much more detail. Some of them might even require separate treatment. In addition, there are probably dozens of other use cases where semantic technology can be fruitfully applied.

The diversity of current middleware products gives rise to other solutions and middleware elements. We have already considered other platforms, as well, which could benefit from semantic technology, e.g., software IDE's or Web service composition engines, let alone the more recent developments in the areas of grid or peer-to-peer computing [Haase et al., 2004].

Implementation The implementation of the proposed design, the KAON SERVER, is a prototype, which realizes only a subset of the use cases. This is not surprising, because the breadth and depth of the presented use cases are large and each use case might be extended to a whole book. It is therefore required to expend much more manpower into *implementation* details.

Also, the semantic management of Web services necessitates many more details than presented in this book. Although the problems are similar to the semantic management of software components, the situation here is more complex due to the mere fact of distribution, which entails network delays, reliability, trust or additional security issues. Considering all these issues, easily fills additional books. Furthermore, we have only prototypically realized a subset of the required design elements for semantic management of Web services, viz., the Web service connector and the metadata collector.

Management Efforts vs. Reasoning Capabilities The KAON toolsuite is used as the semantic technology in our prototype because its API offers a comprehensive set of features in order to control the application server with an ontology. However, it must be said that KAON's reasoning capabilities are quite limited. In essence, there is not much more than subsumption, transitivity and symmetry. The use cases require a whole bandwidth of reasoning capabilities: one requires subsumption reasoning; another uses the reified satisfaction of Descriptions & Situations; others require browsing and querying; and so forth. As a consequence, some use cases cannot be realized with KAON or require management efforts that could have been saved with more powerful reasoning. Further research is necessary for a concise comparison of *management efforts vs. reasoning capabilities*. For example, the currently developed successor of KAON, viz., KAON2,[1] is based on a more expressive description logic, and even allows the definition of rules.

Economic Analysis of Semantic Management Our assessment of the benefits of semantic management is based on a qualitative comparison between modelling and management efforts with and without semantic management. However, a full assessment will need to include further crucial factors (cf. [Wolff et al., 2005] for an initial, extended assessment): (*i*) the application requirements, such as the number and size of applications, the frequency of changes, or the required service level. (*ii*) the organizational factors, e.g., the number of developers and administrators, their skills, their turnover, the learning curves for using deployment descriptors or for using semantic tech-

---

[1]http://kaon2.semanticweb.org

nology, etc. (*iii*) the service characteristics, i.e., the number of Web services, as well as their diversity and complexity. Future research should, therefore, strive for a comprehensive *economic analysis of the semantic management* approach.

Industry Adoption The ideal platform for bringing this research more towards industry is the JBoss application server, of course. This is not only because our prototype builds on JBoss, but also because JBoss is open-source and, thus, leaves more room for experiments.

The success of such an approach heavily depends on usability and *industry adoption* by software developers and administrators, who will not be very willing to familiarize with a large new paradigm when they are just getting used to deployment and WS* descriptors. The working with ontologies must be as seamless and intuitive as ever possible. Hence, additional efforts have to be invested to adopt the administration console, which is merely an ontology browser at the moment. It should hide the ontology idiosyncracies and adapt to the typical administrator to be more intuitive.

Appendix A
Taxonomies

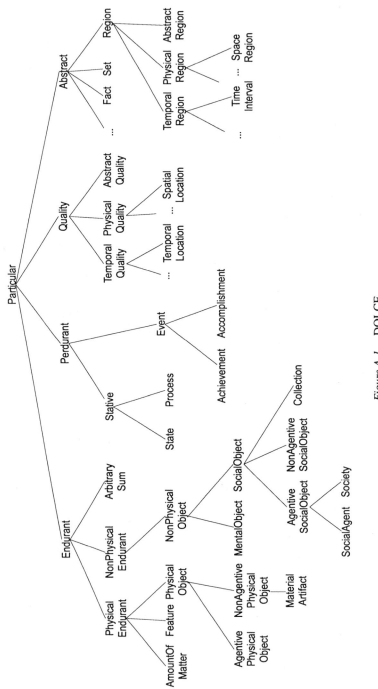

Figure A.1. DOLCE.

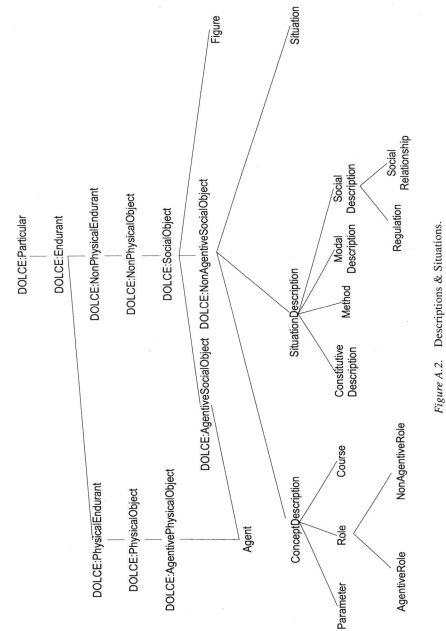

Figure A.2. Descriptions & Situations.

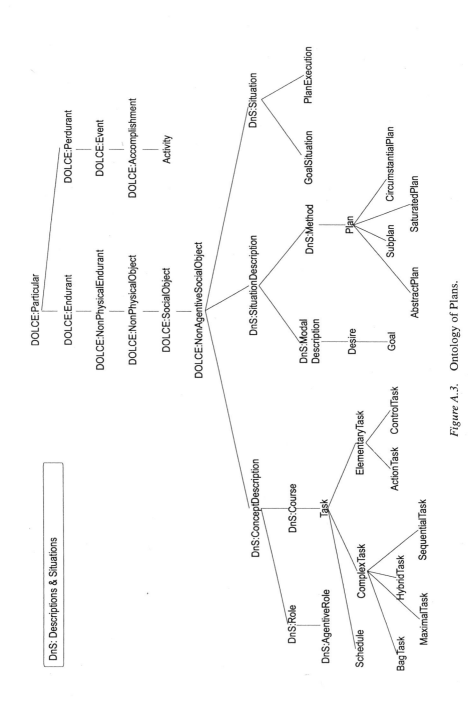

Figure A.3.   Ontology of Plans.

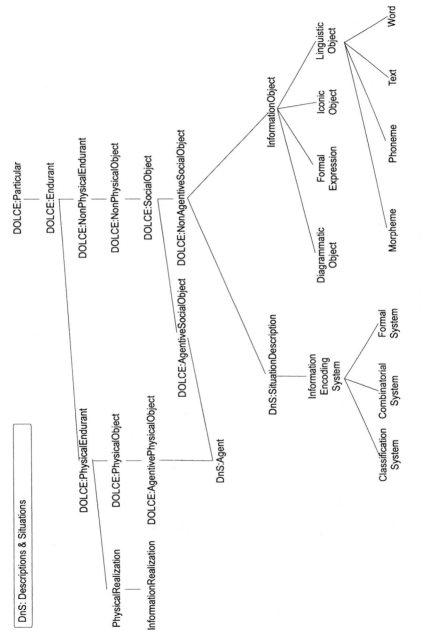

Figure A.4. Ontology of Information Objects.

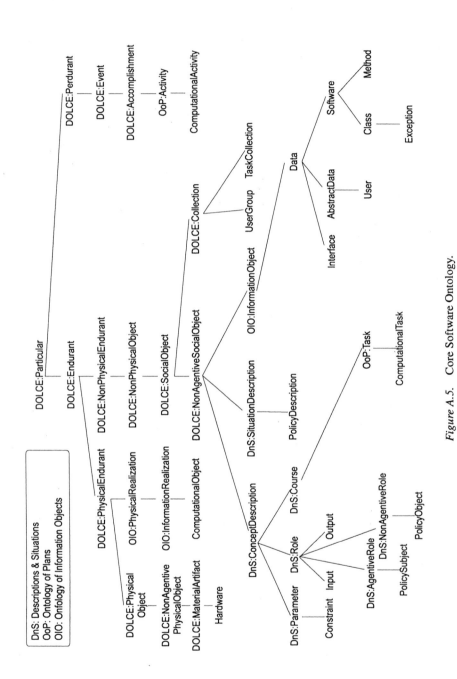

Figure A.5. Core Software Ontology.

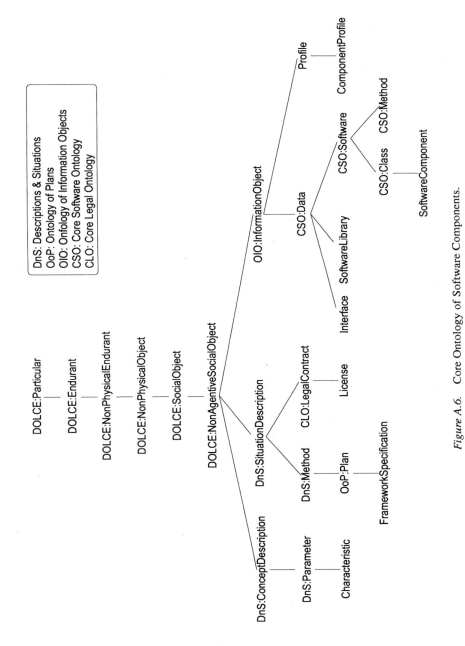

Figure A.6. Core Ontology of Software Components.

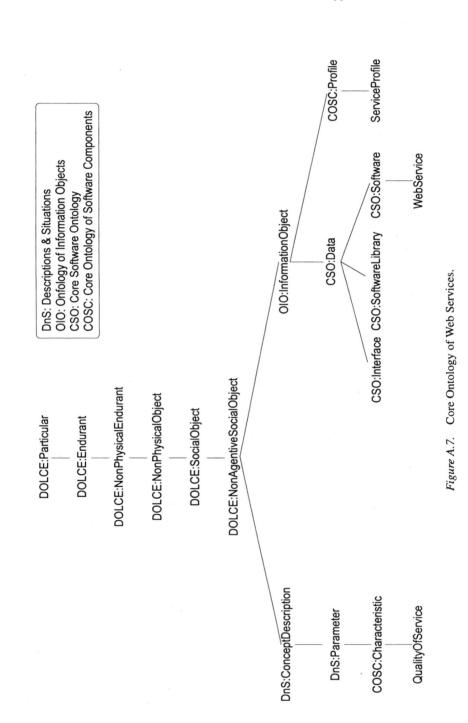

Figure A.7. Core Ontology of Web Services.

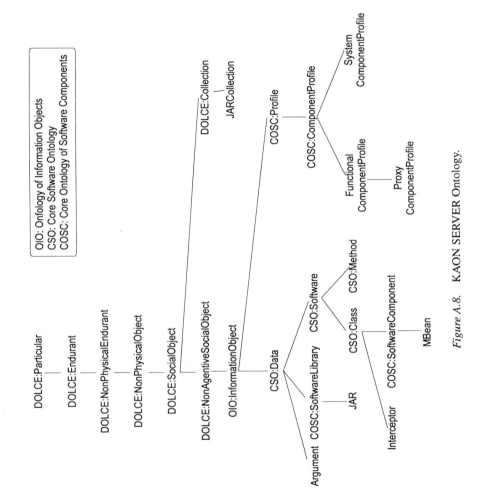

Figure A.8. KAON SERVER Ontology.

References

Abiteboul, Serge, Hull, Richard, and Vianu, Victor (1995). *Foundations of Databases*. Addison-Wesley.

Agarwal, Sudhir, Handschuh, Siegfried, and Staab, Steffen (2004). Annotation, Composition and Invocation of Semantic Web Services. *Journal of Web Semantics*, 2(1):31–48.

Agarwal, Sudhir and Sprick, Barbara (2004). Access Control for Semantic Web Services. In *Proceedings of the IEEE International Conference on Web Services (ICWS'04), June 6-9, 2004, San Diego, California, USA*, pages 770–773. IEEE Computer Society.

Agarwal, Vikas, Dasgupta, Koustuv, Karnik, Neeran, Kumar, Arun, Kundu, Ashish, Mittal, Sumit, and Srivastava, Biplav (2005). A Service Creation Environment Based on End to End Composition of Web Services. In Ellis, Allan and Hagino, Tatsuya, editors, *Proceedings of the 14th International Conference on World Wide Web, WWW 2005, Chiba, Japan, May 10-14, 2005*, pages 128–137. ACM.

Aggarwal, Rohit, Verma, Kunal, Miller, John, and Milnor, William (2004). Constraint Driven Web Service Composition in METEOR-S. In *Proceedings, 2004 IEEE International Conference on Services Computing (SCC'04)*, pages 23–30. IEEE Computer Society.

Aiken, David and Zaremba, Maciej (2005). WSMX Documentation. WSMX Working Draft D22.0v0.2, SDK WSMX working group.

Akkiraju, Rama, Farrell, Joel, Miller, John, Nagarajan, Meenakshi, Schmidt, Marc-Thomas, Sheth, Amit, and Verma, Kunal (2005). Web Service Semantics - WSDL-S. Technical report, IBM Research and LSDIS Lab, University of Georgia.

Allen, James (1984). Towards a General Theory of Action and Time. *Artificial Intelligence*, 23:123–154.

Alonso, Gustavo, Casati, Fabio, Kuno, Harumi, and Machiraju, Vijay (2004). *Web Services*. Springer.

Andrews, Tony, Curbera, Francisco, Dholakia, Hitesh, Goland, Yaron, Leymann, Johannes Klein Frank, Liu, Kevin, Roller, Dieter, Smith, Doug, Thatte, Satish, Trickovic, Ivana, and Weerawarana, Sanjiva (2005). Business Process Execution Language for Web Services Version 1.1. Specification. http://www-128.ibm.com/developerworks/library/specification/ws-bpel/.

Ankolekar, Anupriya, Herbsleb, James, and Sycara, Katia (2003). Addressing Challenges to Open Source Collaboration With the Semantic Web. In Feller, Joseph, Fitzgerald, Brian, Hissam, Scott, and Lakhani, Karim, editors, *Proceedings of Taking Stock of the Bazaar: The 3rd Workshop on Open Source Software Engineering, the 25th International Conference on Software Engineering (ICSE)*, Washington, D.C. IEEE Computer Society.

Ankolekar, Anupriya, Huch, Frank, and Sycara, Katia (2002). Concurrent Execution Semantics for DAML-S with Subtypes. In Horrocks, Ian and Hendler, James A., editors, *1st International Semantic Web Conference (ISWC), Proceedings*, volume 2342 of *LNCS*. Springer.

Aristotle (350 B.C.). Metaphysics Book IV Part 2. `http://classics.mit.edu/Aristotle/`. Translated by W.D. Ross.

Arkin, Assaf, Askary, Sid, Fordin, Scott, Jekeli, Wolfgang, Kawaguchi, Kohsuke, Orchard, David, Pogliani, Stefano, Riemer, Karsten, Struble, Susan, Takacsi-Nagy, Pal, Trickovic, Ivana, and Zimek, Sinisa (2002). Web Service Choreography Interface (WSCI). W3C Note. `http://www.w3.org/TR/wsci`.

Atkinson, Bob, Della-Libera, Giovanni, Hada, Satoshi, Hondo, Maryann, Hallam-Baker, Phillip, Klein, Johannes, LaMacchia, Brian, Leach, Paul, Manferdelli, John, Maruyama, Hiroshi, Nadalin, Anthony, Prafullchandra, Nataraj Nagaratnam Hemma, Shewchuk, John, and Simon, Dan (2002). Web Services Security (WS-Security). Specification. `http://www-106.ibm.com/developerworks/webservices/library/ws-secure/`.

Baader, Franz, Horrocks, Ian, and Sattler, Ulrike (2003). *Description Logics*, volume Handbook on Ontologies in Information Systems of *International Handbooks on Information Systems*, chapter I: Ontology Representation and Reasoning, pages 3–31. Steffen Staab and Rudi Studer, Eds., Springer.

Baida, Ziv, Gordijn, Jaap, Omelayenko, Borys, and Akkermans, Hans (2004). A Shared Terminology for Online Service Provisioning. In *Proceedings of the Sixth International Conference on Electronic Commerce (ICEC04), Delft, The Netherlands*.

Bajaj, Siddharth, Box, Don, Chappell, Dave, Curbera, Francisco, Daniels, Glen, Hallam-Baker, Phillip, Hondo, Maryann, Kaler, Chris, Langworthy, Dave, Malhotra, Ashok, Nadalin, Anthony, Nagaratnam, Nataraj, Nottingham, Mark, Prafullchandra, Hemma, von Riegen, Claus, Schlimmer, Jeffrey, Sharp, Chris, and Shewchuk, John (2004). Web Services Policy Framework (WS-Policy). Specification. `http://www-128.ibm.com/developerworks/library/specification/ws-polfram`.

Banerjee, Jay, Kim, Won, Kim, Hyoung-Joo, and Korth, Henry F. (1987). Semantics and Implementation of Schema Evolution in Object-oriented Databases. In *SIGMOD '87: Proceedings of the 1987 ACM SIGMOD international conference on Management of data*, pages 311–322, New York, NY, USA. ACM Press.

Banerji, Arindam, Bartolini, Claudio, Beringer, Dorothea, Chopella, Venkatesh, Govindarajan, Kannan, Karp, Alan, Kuno, Harumi, Lemon, Mike, Pogossiants, Gregory, Sharma, Shamik, and Williams, Scott (2002). Web Services Conversation Language (WSCL). W3C Note. `http://www.w3.org/TR/wscl10/`.

BEA Systems, Computer Associates International, IBM Corporation, Layer 7 Technologies, Microsoft Corporation, Netegrity, Oblix, OpenNetwork Technologies, Ping Identity Corporation, Reactivity, RSA Security, VeriSign, and Westbridge Technology (2004). Web Services Trust Language (WS-Trust). Specification. `http://www-106.ibm.com/developerworks/library/specification/ws-trust/`.

Bechhofer, S., Horrocks, I., Goble, C., and Stevens, R. (2001). OilEd: A reason-able ontology editor for the Semantic Web. In *Proceedings of the Joint German Austrian Conference on Artificial Intelligence*, volume 2174 of *Lecture Notes In Artificial Intelligence*, pages 396–408. Springer.

Beeri, Catriel and Ramakrishnan, Raghu (1987). On the Power of Magic. In *Proceedings of the Sixth ACM SIGACT—SIGMOD—SIGART Symposium on Principles of Database Systems, March 23-25, 1987, San Diego, California*, pages 269–283. ACM.

Bennett, Brandon, Dixon, Clare, Fisher, Michael, Hustadt, Ullrich, Franconi, Enrico, Horrocks, Ian, and de Rijke, Maarten (2002). Combinations of Modal Logics. *Artificial Intelligence Review*, 17(1):1–20.

Berners-Lee, Tim (1998). Semantic Web Roadmap. http://www.w3.org/DesignIssues/ Semantic.html.

Berners-Lee, Tim (2000). Semantic Web — XML 2000. http://www.w3.org/2000/Talks/ 1206-xml2k-tbl/Overview.html.

Bernstein, Philip A. (1996). Middleware: A Model for Distributed System Services. *Communications of the ACM*, 39(2):86–98.

Biron, Paul V. and Malhotra, Ashok (2001). XML Schema part 2: Datatypes. W3C Recommendation. http://www.w3.org/TR/xmlschema-2/.

Birrell, Andrew D. and Nelson, Bruce Jay (1984). Implementing Remote Procedure Calls. *ACM Transactions on Computer Systems*, 2(1):39–59.

Booch, Grady, Jacobson, Ivar, and Rumbaugh, James (1998). *The Unified Modeling Language User Guide*, volume 1. Addison-Wesley.

Booth, David, Haas, Hugo, McCabe, Francis, Newcomer, Eric, Champion, Michael, Ferris, Chris, and Orchard, David (2004). Web Services Architecture. http://www.w3.org/TR/ws-arch/.

Borgida, Alex and Devanbu, Premkumar (1999). Adding more "DL" to IDL: Towards more Knowledgeable Component Inter-operability. In *Proceedings of the 21st International Conference on Software engineering*, pages 378–387. IEEE Computer Society Press.

Borgida, Alexander and Serafini, Luciano (2002). Distributed Description Logics: Directed Domain Correspondences in Federated Information Sources. In Meersman, Robert and Tari, Zahir, editors, *On the Move to Meaningful Internet Systems, 2002 - DOA/CoopIS/ODBASE 2002 Confederated International Conferences DOA, CoopIS and ODBASE 2002 Irvine, California, USA, October 30 - November 1, 2002, Proceedings*, volume 2519 of *Lecture Notes in Computer Science*, pages 36–53. Springer.

Borgo, Stefano, Gangemi, Aldo, Guarino, Nicola, Masolo, Claudio, and Oltramari, Alessandro (2002). Ontology RoadMap. WonderWeb Deliverable D15. http://wonderweb. semanticweb.org.

Borgo, Stefano, Guarino, Nicola, and Masolo, Claudio (1996). A Pointless Theory of Space Based on Strong Connection and Congruence. In *Proceedings of the Fifth International Conference on Principles of Knowledge Representation and Reasoning (KR'96), Cambridge, Massachusetts, USA, November 5-8, 1996*, pages 220–229. Morgan Kaufmann.

Bozsak, E., Ehrig, Marc, Handschuh, Siegfried, Hotho, Andreas, Maedche, Alexander, Motik, Boris, Oberle, Daniel, Schmitz, Christoph, Staab, Steffen, Stojanovic, Ljiljana, Stojanovic, Nenad, Studer, Rudi, Stumme, Gerd, Sure, York, Tane, Julien, Volz, Raphael, and Zacharias, Valentin (2002). KAON - Towards a large scale Semantic Web. In Bauknecht, Kurt, Tjoa, A. Min, and Quirchmayr, Gerald, editors, *E-Commerce and Web Technologies, Third International Conference, EC-Web 2002, Aix-en-Provence, France, September 2-6, 2002, Proceedings*, volume 2455 of *Lecture Notes in Computer Science*, pages 304–313. Springer.

Brambilla, Marco, Ceri, Stefano, Fraternali, Piero, Acerbis, Roberto, and Bongio, Aldo (2005). Model-driven Design of Service-enabled Web Applications. In *Proceedings of the ACM SIGMOD/PODS 2005 Conference, Baltimore, Maryland*. ACM Press.

Buschmann, Frank, Meunier, Regine, Rohnert, Hans, Sommerlad, Peter, and Stal, Michael (1996). *Pattern-Oriented Software Architecture, Volume 1: A System of Patterns*, volume 1. John Wiley and Son Ltd.

Cabrera, Felipe, Copeland, George, Cox, Bill, Klein, Tom Freund Johannes, Storey, Tony, and Thatte, Satish (2004). Web Services Transaction (WS-Transaction). Specification. http: //www-128.ibm.com/developerworks/library/specification/ws-tx/.

Cabrera, Luis Felipe, Copeland, George, Cox, William, Feingold, Max, Freund, Tom, Johnson, Jim, Kaler, Chris, Klein, Johannes, Langworthy, David, Nadalin, Anthony, Orchard, David, Robinson, Ian, Shewchuk, John, and Storey, Tony (2003). Web Services Coordination (WS-Coordination). Specification. `http://www-106.ibm.com/developerworks/library/ws-coor/`.

Campbell, A., Coulson, G., and Kounavis, M. (1999). Managing Complexity: Middleware Explained. *IT Professional, IEEE Computer Society*, 1(5):22–28.

Cardoso, J., Sheth, Amit P., Miller, John A., Arnold, Jonathan, and Kochut, Krys J. (2004). Modeling Quality of Service for Workflows and Web Service Processes. *Journal of Web Semantics*, 1(3):281–308.

Casati, Roberto and Varzi, Achille C. (1995). *Holes and other Superficialities*. MIT Press.

Chen, Peter Pin-Shan (1976). The Entity-Relationship Model — Toward a Unified View of Data. *ACM Transactions on Database Systems*, 1(1):9–36.

Cho, Young-Hyun and Ejiri, Masayoshi, editors (2004). *Managing Next Generation Convergence Networks and Services: Proceedings of the 2004 IEEE/IFIP Network Operations and Management Symposium (NOMS), 2004, IEEE/IFIP, Seoul, Korea, April, 2004*. IEEE.

Christensen, Erik, Curbera, Francisco, Meredith, Greg, and Weerawarana, Sanjiva (2001). Web Services Description Language (WSDL). W3C Note. `http://www.w3.org/TR/wsdl`.

Curry, Edward (2004a). Adaptive and Reflective Middleware. In [Mahmoud, 2004], chapter 2, pages 29–52.

Curry, Edward (2004b). Message-Oriented Middleware. In [Mahmoud, 2004], chapter 1, pages 1–28.

Daho, Z.B., Simoni, N., Chevanne, M., and Betge-Brezetz, S. (2004). An Information model for Service and Network Management Integration: From Needs Towards Solutions. In [Cho and Ejiri, 2004], pages 527–540.

Das, Subrata Kumar (1992). *Deductive Databases and Logic Programming*. Addison Wesley.

de Bruijn, Jos, Lausen, Holger, Krummenacher, Reto, Polleres, Axel, Predoiu, Livia, Kifer, Michael, and Fensel, Dieter (2005). Web Service Modeling Language (WSML). WSML Final Draft D16.1v0.2, SDK WSML working group.

Debusmann, M., Kroger, R., and Geihs, K. (2004). Unifying Service Level Management Using an MDA-based Approach. In [Cho and Ejiri, 2004], pages 801–814.

Decker, Stefan, Erdmann, Michael, Fensel, Dieter, and Studer, Rudi (1998). Ontobroker: Ontology Based Access to Distributed and Semi-Structured Information. In *Database Semantics - Semantic Issues in Multimedia Systems*, volume 138 of *IFIP Conference Proceedings*, pages 351–369. Kluwer.

Diaz, Ruben Prieto (1991). Implementing Faceted Classification for Software Reuse. *Communications of the ACM*, 34(5):88–97.

Dumbill, Edd (2001). Building the Semantic Web. `http://www.xml.com/pub/a/2001/03/07/buildingsw.html`. Knowledge Technologies Conference 2001, March 4-7, Austin Convention Center, Austin, TX, USA, Keynote presentation.

Eberhart, Andreas (2004). Ad-hoc Invocation of Semantic Web Services. In *Proceedings of the IEEE International Conference on Web Services (ICWS'04), June 6-9, 2004, San Diego, California, USA*, pages 116–123. IEEE Computer Society.

Ehrig, Marc and Staab, Steffen (2004). QOM - Quick Ontology Mapping. In McIlraith, Sheila A., Plexousakis, Dimitris, and van Harmelen, Frank, editors, *Proceedings of the Third International Semantic Web Conference*, volume 3298 of *LNCS*, pages 683–697, Hiroshima, Japan. Springer.

Elrad, Tzilla, Filman, Robert E., and Bader, Atef (2001). Aspect-oriented Programming: Introduction. *Communications of the ACM*, 44(10):29–32.

Euzenat, Jérôme (2004). An API for Ontology Alignment. In McIlraith, Sheila A., Plexousakis, Dimitris, and van Harmelen, Frank, editors, *The Semantic Web - ISWC 2004: Third International Semantic Web Conference, Hiroshima, Japan, November 7-11, 2004. Proceedings*, volume 3298 of *Lecture Notes in Computer Science*, pages 698–712. Springer.

Fensel, Dieter, Benjamins, Richard, Motta, Enrico, and Wielinga, Bob J. (1999). UPML: A Framework for Knowledge System Reuse. In Dean, Thomas, editor, *Proceedings of the Sixteenth International Joint Conference on Artificial Intelligence, IJCAI 99, Stockholm, Sweden, July 31 - August 6, 1999. 2 Volumes, 1450 pages*, pages 16–23. Morgan Kaufmann.

Fensel, Dieter and Bussler, Christoph (2002). The Web Service Modeling Framework WSMF. *Electronic Commerce: Research and Applications*, 1:113–137.

Gabel, Thomas, Sure, York, and Völker, Johanna (2004). KAON — An Overview. Technical report, University of Karlsruhe, Institute AIFB & FZI — Research Center for Information Technologies, Karlsruhe, Germany. http://kaon.semanticweb.org.

Gangemi, A., Catenacci, C., and Battaglia, M. (2004a). Inflammation Ontology Design Pattern: an Exercise in Building a Core Biomedical Ontology with Descriptions and Situations. In Pisanelli, D.M., editor, *Ontolgies in Medicine*, pages 64–80. IOS Press.

Gangemi, Aldo, Borgo, Stefano, Catenacci, Carola, and Lehmann, Jos (2004b). Task Taxonomies for Knowledge Content. Metokis Deliverable D07.

Gangemi, Aldo, Fisseha, Frehiwot, Keizer, Johannes, Lauser, Boris, Lehmann, Jos, Liang, Anita, Pettman, Ian, Sim, Margherita, and Taconet, Mac (2002). An Overview of the FOS Project: Towards a Fishery Semantic Web. Internal project report, ISTC-CNR, Laboratory for Applied Ontology, Rome, Italy.

Gangemi, Aldo, Guarino, Nicola, Masolo, Claudio, and Oltramari, Alessandro (2003a). Sweetening WordNet with DOLCE. *AI Magazine*, 24(3):13–24.

Gangemi, Aldo and Mika, Peter (2003). Understanding the Semantic Web through Descriptions and Situations. In *DOA/CoopIS/ODBASE 2003 Confederated International Conferences DOA, CoopIS and ODBASE, Proceedings*, LNCS. Springer.

Gangemi, Aldo, Mika, Peter, Sabou, Marta, and Oberle, Daniel (2003b). An Ontology of Services and Service Descriptions. Technical report, Laboratory for Applied Ontology (ISTC-CNR), Viale Marx, 15, 00137 Roma.

Gangemi, Aldo, Sagri, Maria-Teresa, and Tiscornia, Daniela (2004c). A Constructive Framework for Legal Ontologies. Internal project report, EU 6FP METOKIS Project, Deliverable. http://metokis.salzburgresearch.at.

Genesereth, M. R. and Fikes, R. E. (1992). Knowledge Interchange Format Version 3.0 Reference Manual. Report Logic 92-1, Logic Group, Stanford University, California, USA.

Genesereth, Michael R. and Nilsson, N. J. (1987). *Logical Foundations of Artificial Intelligence*. Morgan Kaufmann, Los Altos, California, USA.

Georgakopoulos, Dimitrios, Hornick, Mark F., and Sheth, Amit P. (1995). An Overview of Workflow Management: From Process Modeling to Workflow Automation Infrastructure. *Distributed and Parallel Databases*, 3(2):119–153.

Gokhale, Aniruddha, Schmidt, Douglas C., Natarajan, Balachandran, Gray, Jeff, and Wang, Nanbor (2004). Model Driven Middleware. In [Mahmoud, 2004], chapter 7, pages 163–187.

Gray, Jim and Reuter, Andreas (1993). *Transaction Processing: Concepts and Techniques*. Morgan Kaufmann.

Grosof, B., Horrocks, I., Volz, R., and Decker, S. (2003). Description Logic Programs: Combining Logic Programs with Description Logic. In *Proceedings of the Twelfth International World Wide Web Conference, WWW2003, Budapest, Hungary, 20-24 May 2003*, pages 48–57. ACM.

Grosse-Rhode, Martin (2004). *Semantic Integration of Heterogeneous Software Specifications*. Monographs in Theoretical Computer Science. Springer.

Gruber, Thomas R. (1995). Toward Principles for the Design of Ontologies Used for Knowledge Sharing. *International Journal of Human Computer Studies*, 43(5-6):907–928.

Grüninger, Michael and Menzel, Christopher (2003). The Process Specification Language (PSL) Theory and Applications. *AI Magazine*, 24(3):63–74.

Guarino, N. (1998). Formal Ontology in Information Systems. In Guarino, N., editor, *Formal Ontology in Information Systems. Proceedings of FOIS'98, Trento, Italy, June 6-8, 1998,* pages 3–15, Amsterdam. IOS Press.

Guarino, N., Carrara, M., and Giaretta, P. (1994). Formalizing Ontological Commitment. In *Proceedings of National Conference on Artificial Intelligence (AAAI-94),* pages 560–567, Seattle. Morgan Kaufmann.

Guarino, N. and Giaretta, P. (1995). Ontologies and Knowledge Bases: Towards a Terminological Clarification. In Mars, N., editor, *Towards Very Large Knowledge Bases: Knowledge Building and Knowledge Sharing,* pages 25–32, Amsterdam. IOS Press.

Guarino, Nicola and Welty, Christopher A. (2002). Evaluating Ontological Decisions with OntoClean. *Communications of the ACM,* 45(2):61–65.

Gudgin, Martin, Hadley, Marc, Mendelsohn, Noah, Moreau, Jean-Jacques, and Nielsen, Henrik Frystyk (2003). SOAP Version 1.2 Part 1: Messaging Framework. http://www.w3.org/TR/soap12-part1/. W3C Recommendation.

Guha, R. V. and Lenat, D.B. (1990). Cyc: A Mid-term Report. *AI Magazine,* 11(3):32–59.

Haarslev, V. and Moeller, R. (2001). RACER System Description. In *Proceedings of Automated Reasoning, First International Joint Conference, IJCAR,* volume 2083 of *Lecture Notes in Computer Science,* pages 701–706. Springer.

Haase, Peter, Broekstra, Jeen, Ehrig, Marc, Menken, Maarten, Mika, Peter, Plechawski, Michal, Pyszlak, Pawel, Schnizler, Björn, Siebes, Ronny, Staab, Steffen, and Tempich, Christoph (2004). Bibster - A Semantics-Based Bibliographic Peer-to-Peer System. In McIlraith, Sheila A., Plexousakis, Dimitris, and van Harmelen, Frank, editors, *Proceedings of the Third International Semantic Web Conference, Hiroshima, Japan, 2004,* volume 3298 of *LNCS,* pages 122–136. Springer.

Handschuh, Siegfried, Staab, Steffen, and Volz, Raphael (2003). On Deep Annotation. In *Proceedings of the Twelfth International World Wide Web Conference, WWW2003, Budapest, Hungary, 20-24 May 2003,* pages 431–438. ACM.

Hart, Lewis, Emery, Patrick, Colomb, Robert, Raymond, Kerry, Chang, Dan, Ye, Yiming, Kendall, Elisa, and Dutra, Mark (2004). Usage Scenarios and Goals for Ontology Definition Metamodel. In Zhou, Xiaofang, Su, Stanley, and Papazoglou, Mike P., editors, *Proceedings of the Third International Semantic Web Conference,* volume 3306 of *LNCS,* pages 596–607. Springer.

Hartmann, Jens and Sure, York (2004). An Infrastructure for Scalable, Reliable Semantic Portals. *IEEE Intelligent Systems,* 19(3):58–65.

Hess, Andreas and Kushmerick, Nicholas (2003). Automatically Attaching Semantic Metadata to Web Services. In Kambhampati, Subbarao and Knoblock, Craig A., editors, *Proceedings of IJCAI-03 Workshop on Information Integration on the Web (IIWeb-03), August 9-10, 2003, Acapulco, Mexico,* pages 111–116.

Horrocks, I. (1998). The FaCT system. In de Swart, Harrie C. M., editor, *Automated Reasoning with Analytic Tableaux and Related Methods, International Conference, TABLEAUX '98, Oisterwijk, The Netherlands, May 5-8, 1998, Proceedings,* volume 1397 of *Lecture Notes in Computer Science.* Springer.

Horrocks, Ian and Patel-Schneider, Peter F. (2001). The Generation of DAML+OIL. In Goble, Carole A., McGuinness, Deborah L., Möller, Ralf, and Patel-Schneider, Peter F., editors, *Working Notes of the 2001 International Description Logics Workshop (DL-2001), Stanford, CA, USA, August 1-3, 2001,* volume 49 of *CEUR Workshop Proceedings.*

Horrocks, Ian and Patel-Schneider, Peter F. (2004). Reducing OWL Entailment to Description Logic Satisfiability. *Journal of Web Semantics,* 1(4):345–357.

Houston, P. J. (1996). Introduction to DCE and Encina. Whitepaper, Transarc Corp.

Howard, Randy and Kerschberg, Larry (2004). A Framework for Dynamic Semantic Web Services Management. *International Journal of Cooperative Information Systems*, 13(4):441–485.

IBM developerWorks (2004a). New to SOA and Web services. http://www-106.ibm.com/developerworks/webservices/newto/.

IBM developerWorks (2004b). SOA and Web services — Standards. http://www-106.ibm.com/developerworks/views/webservices/standards.jsp.

Junginger, Markus Oliver and Lee, Yugyung (2004). Peer-to-Peer Middleware. In [Mahmoud, 2004], chapter 4, pages 81–107.

Kagal, Lalana, Finin, Timothy W., and Joshi, Anupam (2003). A Policy Based Approach to Security for the Semantic Web. In Fensel, Dieter, Sycara, Katia P., and Mylopoulos, John, editors, *The Semantic Web - ISWC 2003, Second International Semantic Web Conference, Sanibel Island, FL, USA, October 20-23, 2003, Proceedings*, volume 2870 of *Lecture Notes in Computer Science*, pages 402–418. Springer.

Kalbfleisch, C., Krupczak, C., Presuhn, R., and Saperia, J. (1999). RFC 2564: Application Management MIB. http://www.ietf.org/rfc2564.txt.

Kifer, Michael, Lausen, Georg, and Wu, James (1995). Logical Foundations of Object-Oriented and Frame-Based Languages. *Journal of the ACM*, 42(1):741–843.

Lamparter, Steffen, Oberle, Daniel, and Eberhart, Andreas (2005). Approximating Service Utility from Policies and Value Function Patterns. In *6th IEEE International Workshop on Policies for Distributed Systems and Networks (POLICY 2005), 6-8 June 2005, Stockholm, Sweden*, pages 159–168. IEEE Computer Society.

Li, Lei and Horrocks, Ian (2003). A Software Framework for Matchmaking Based on Semantic Web Technology. In *Proceedings of the Twelfth International World Wide Web Conference, WWW2003, Budapest, Hungary, 20-24 May 2003*, pages 331–339. ACM.

Lindfors, Juha and Fleury, Marc (2002). *JMX — Managing J2EE with Java Management Extensions*. Sams. The JBoss Group.

Lord, Phillip W., Bechhofer, Sean, Wilkinson, Mark D., Schiltz, Gary, Gessler, Damian, Hull, Duncan, Goble, Carole A., and Stein, Lincoln (2004). Applying Semantic Web Services to Bioinformatics: Experiences Gained, Lessons Learnt. In McIlraith, Sheila A., Plexousakis, Dimitris, and van Harmelen, Frank, editors, *The Semantic Web - ISWC 2004: Third International Semantic Web Conference,Hiroshima, Japan, November 7-11, 2004. Proceedings*, volume 3298 of *Lecture Notes in Computer Science*, pages 350–364. Springer.

Maedche, Alexander, Motik, Boris, and Stojanovic, Ljiljana (2003). Managing Multiple and Distributed Ontologies in the Semantic Web. *VLDB Journal*, 12(4):286–302.

Mahmoud, Q.H., editor (2004). *Middleware for Communications*. Wiley.

Mandell, Daniel J. and McIlraith, Sheila (2003). Adapting BPEL4WS for the Semantic Web: The Bottom-Up Approach to Web Service Interoperation. In Fensel, Dieter, Sycara, Katia P., and Mylopoulos, John, editors, *The Semantic Web - ISWC 2003, Second International Semantic Web Conference, Sanibel Island, FL, USA, October 20-23, 2003, Proceedings*, volume 2870 of *Lecture Notes in Computer Science*, pages 227–247. Springer.

Manola, Frank and Miller, Eric (2004). RDF Primer. W3C Recommendation. http://www.w3.org/TR/rdf-primer/.

Martin, David, Burstein, Mark, Hobbs, Jerry, Lassila, Ora, McDermott, Drew, McIlraith, Sheila, Narayanan, Srini, Paolucci, Massimo, Parsia, Bijan, Payne, Terry, Sirin, Evren, Srinivasan, Naveen, and Sycara, Katia (2004). OWL-S: Semantic Markup for Web Services. http://www.daml.org/services/owl-s/1.1/.

Masolo, Claudio, Borgo, Stefano, Gangemi, Aldo, Guarino, Nicola, and Oltramari, Alessandro (2003). Ontology Library (final). WonderWeb Deliverable D18. http://wonderweb.semanticweb.org.

Masolo, Claudio, Borgo, Stefano, Gangemi, Aldo, Guarino, Nicola, Oltramari, Alessandro, and Schneider, Luc (2002). The WonderWeb Library of Foundational Ontologies. WonderWeb Deliverable D17. http://wonderweb.semanticweb.org.

Massonet, P. and van Lamsweerde, A. (1997). Analogical Reuse of Requirements Frameworks. In *3rd IEEE International Symposium on Requirements Engineering (RE'97), January 5-8, 1997, Annapolis, MD, USA*, pages 26–39. IEEE Computer Society.

McGuinness, Deborah L. and van Harmelen, Frank (2004). Web Ontology Language (OWL) Overview. http://www.w3.org/TR/owl-features/. W3C Recommendation.

McIlraith, Sheila A., Son, Tran Cao, and Zeng, Honglei (2001). Semantic Web Services. *IEEE Intelligent Systems*, 16(2):46–53.

Mellor, Stephen J., Scott, Kendall, Uhl, Axel, and Weise, Dirk (2004). *MDA Distilled*. Addison-Wesley Professional.

Mika, Peter, Oberle, Daniel, Gangemi, Aldo, and Sabou, Marta (2004a). Foundations for Service Ontologies: Aligning OWL-S to DOLCE. In *The Thirteenth International World Wide Web Conference Proceedings*, pages 563–572. ACM.

Mika, Peter, Sabou, Marta, Gangemi, Aldo, and Oberle, Daniel (2004b). Foundations for OWL-S: Aligning OWL-S to DOLCE. In Payne, Terry, editor, *Papers from 2004 AAAI Spring Symposium - Semantic Web Services*, pages 52–60. AAAI Press. SS-04-06.

Miller, George A., Beckwith, Richard, Fellbaum, Christiane, Gross, Derek, and Miller, Katherine A. (1990). Introduction to WordNet: An On-line Lexical Database. *International Journal of Lexicography*, 3(4):235–244.

Motik, Boris, Oberle, Daniel, Staab, Steffen, Studer, Rudi, and Volz, Raphael (2002). KAON SERVER Architecture. WonderWeb Deliverable D5. http://wonderweb.semanticweb.org.

Motta, Enrico, Domingue, John, Cabraland, Liliana, and Gaspari, Mauro (2003). IRS–II: A Framework and Infrastructure for Semantic Web Services. In *The SemanticWeb - ISWC 2003*, volume 2870 of *LNCS*, pages 306 – 318. Springer.

Narayanan, Srini and McIlraith, Sheila (2003). Analysis and Simulation of Web Services. *Computer Networks*, 42(5):675–693.

Niles, I. and Pease, A. (2001). Origins of the IEEE Standard Upper Ontology. In *Working Notes of the IJCAI-2001 Workshop on the IEEE Standard Upper Ontology, Seattle, Washington, August 6, 2001*.

Noia, T. Di, Sciascio, E. Di, Donini, F. M., and Mongiello, M. (2003). Abductive Matchmaking Using Description Logics. In *Proceedings of the 18th International Joint Conference on Artificial Intelligence (IJCAI 2003)*, pages 337–342, Los Altos. Morgan Kaufmann.

Noy, N. F. and Klein, M. (2002). Ontology Evolution: Not the Same as Schema Evolution. Technical Report SMI-2002-0926, Stanford University.

Noy, Natalya Fridman and Musen, Mark A. (2000). PROMPT: Algorithm and Tool for Automated Ontology Merging and Alignment. In *Proceedings of the Seventeenth National Conference on Artificial Intelligence and Twelfth Conference on on Innovative Applications of Artificial Intelligence, July 30 - August 3, 2000, Austin, Texas, USA*, AAAI-2000 Technical Papers, pages 450–455. AAAI Press / The MIT Press.

Oberle, Daniel (2004). Semantic Management of Middleware. In *Proceedings of the 1st International Doctoral Symposium on Middleware, Toronto, Ontario, Canada*, ACM International Conference Proceeding Series, pages 299 – 303. ACM Press.

Oberle, Daniel, Berendt, Bettina, Hotho, Andreas, and Gonzalez, Jorge (2003a). Conceptual User Tracking. In Ruiz, Ernestina Menasalvas, Segovia, Javier, and Szczepaniak, Piotr S., editors, *Advances in Web Intelligence, First International Atlantic Web Intelligence Conference, AWIC 2003, Madrid, Spain, May 5-6, 2003, Proceedings*, volume 2663 of *Lecture Notes in Artificial Intelligence*, pages 142–154. Springer.

Oberle, Daniel, Eberhart, Andreas, Staab, Steffen, and Volz, Raphael (2004a). Developing and Managing Software Components in an Ontology-based Application Server. In Jacobsen, Hans-Arno, editor, *Middleware 2004, ACM/IFIP/USENIX 5th International Middleware Conference, Toronto, Ontario, Canada*, volume 3231 of *LNCS*, pages 459–478. Springer.

Oberle, Daniel, Hitzler, Pascal, Staab, Steffen, Eberhart, Andreas, Cimiano, Philipp, and Studer, Rudi (2004b). The SmartWeb Foundational Ontology. SmartWeb Project Report.

Oberle, Daniel, Lamparter, Steffen, Eberhart, Andreas, and Staab, Steffen (2005a). Semantic Management of Web Services. Technical report, University of Karlsruhe.

Oberle, Daniel, Lamparter, Steffen, Eberhart, Andreas, Staab, Steffen, Grimm, Stephan, Hitzler, Pascal, Agarwal, Sudhir, and Studer, Rudi (2005b). Semantic Management of Web Services using the Core Ontology of Services. Position Paper. W3C Workshop on Frameworks for Semantics in Web Services.

Oberle, Daniel, Sabou, Marta, Richards, D., and Volz, Raphael (2003b). An Ontology for Semantic Middleware: Extending DAML-S Beyond Web Services. In *On The Move to Meaningful Internet Systems 2003: OTM 2003 Workshops*, volume 2889 of *Lecture Notes in Computer Science*, pages 28–29. Springer.

Oberle, Daniel, Sabou, Marta, and Richards, Debbie (2003c). An Ontology for Semantic Middleware: Extending DAML-S Beyond Web Services. Technical Report 426, University of Karlsruhe, Institute AIFB, 76128 Karlsruhe, Germany.

Oberle, Daniel and Spyns, Peter (2004). The Knowledge Portal OntoWeb. In Staab, Steffen and Studer, Rudi, editors, *Handbook on Ontologies*, International Handbooks on Information Systems, chapter IV, pages 499–517. Springer.

Oberle, Daniel, Staab, Steffen, and Eberhart, Andreas (2005c). Towards Semantic Middleware for Web Application Development. *IEEE Distributed Systems Online*. http://dsonline.computer.org.

Oberle, Daniel, Staab, Steffen, Studer, Rudi, and Volz, Raphael (2003d). KAON SERVER Demonstrator. WonderWeb Deliverable D7. http://wonderweb.semanticweb.org.

Oberle, Daniel, Staab, Steffen, Studer, Rudi, and Volz, Raphael (2005d). Supporting Application Development in the Semantic Web. *ACM Transactions on Internet Technology (TOIT)*, 5(2):359–389.

Oberle, Daniel, Staab, Steffen, and Volz, Raphael (2004c). An Application Server for the Semantic Web. In *The Thirteenth International World Wide Web Conference Alternate Track Papers & Posters*, pages 220–221. ACM.

Oberle, Daniel, Staab, Steffen, and Volz, Raphael (2005e). Three Dimensions of Knowledge Representation in WonderWeb. *Künstliche Intelligenz*, 1:31–35.

Oberle, Daniel, Volz, Raphael, Motik, Boris, and Staab, Steffen (2003e). KAON SERVER Prototype. WonderWeb Deliverable D6. http://wonderweb.semanticweb.org.

Oberle, Daniel, Volz, Raphael, Motik, Boris, and Staab, Steffen (2004d). An Extensible Ontology Software Environment. In Staab, Steffen and Studer, Rudi, editors, *Handbook on Ontologies*, International Handbooks on Information Systems, chapter III, pages 311–333. Springer.

Object Modelling Group (2002). IDL / Language Mapping Specification - Java to IDL. 1.2.

Paolucci, Massimo, Kawamura, Takahiro, Payne, Terry R., and Sycara, Katia P. (2002a). Importing the Semantic Web in UDDI. In Bussler, Christoph, Hull, Richard, McIlraith, Sheila A., Orlowska, Maria E., Pernici, Barbara, and Yang, Jian, editors, *Web Services, E-Business, and the Semantic Web, CAiSE 2002 International Workshop, WES 2002, Toronto, Canada, May 27-28, 2002, Revised Papers*, volume 2512 of *Lecture Notes in Computer Science*, pages 225–236. Springer.

Paolucci, Massimo, Kawamura, Takahiro, Payne, Terry R., and Sycara, Katia P. (2002b). Semantic Matching of Web Services Capabilities. In Horrocks, Ian and Hendler, James A., editors, *The Semantic Web - ISWC 2002, First International Semantic Web Conference, Sardinia,*

Italy, June 9-12, 2002, Proceedings, volume 2342 of *Lecture Notes in Computer Science*, pages 333–347. Springer.

Patil, A., Oundhakar, S., Sheth, A., and Verma, K. (2004). METEOR-S Web Service Annotation Framework. In *The 13th International World Wide Web Conference Proceedings*, pages 553–563. ACM Press.

Pease, A., Niles, I., and Li, J. (2002). Origins of the IEEE Standard Upper Ontology. In *Working Notes of the AAAI-2002 Workshop on Ontologies and the Semantic Web, Edmonton, Canada, July 28-August 1, 2002*.

Pease, Adam (1998). Core Plan Representation. Object Model Focus Group.

Pepper, Steve and Schwab, Sylvia (2003). Curing the Web's Identity Crisis. Technical report, Ontopia (http://www.ontopia.net).

Peters, Randel J. and Oezsu, M. Tamer (1997). An Axiomatic Model of Dynamic Schema Evolution in Objectbase Systems. *ACM Transactions on Database Systems*, 22(1):75–114.

Roman, Dumitru, Lausen, Holger, Keller, Uwe, de Bruijn, Jos, Bussler, Christoph, Domingue, John, Fensel, Dieter, Kifer, Michael, Kopecky, Jacek, Lara, Ruben, Oren, Eyal, Polleres, Axel, and Stollberg, Michael (2005). Web Service Modeling Ontology (WSMO). WSMO Final Draft D2v1.1, SDK WSMO working group.

Russell, Stuart J. and Norvig, Peter (1995). *Artificial Intelligence: a Modern Approach*. Prentice Hall, Pacific Grove, CA, USA.

Sabou, Marta, Oberle, Daniel, and Richards, Debbie (2004). Enhancing Application Servers with Semantics. In Krishnaswamy, Shonali, Loke, Seng W., and Yang, Jian, editors, *1st Australian Workshop on Engineering Service-Oriented Systems (AWESOS 2004) Wednesday, 14 April 2004, Melbourne, Australia. In conjunction with the Australian Software Engineering Conference (ASWEC)*, pages 7–15. Monash University, Australia.

Schmitt, P. H. (2001). Nichtklassische Logiken. Skriptum.

Schneider, Luc (2003). How to Build a Foundational Ontology: The Object-Centered High-level Reference Ontology OCHRE. In Günter, Andreas, Kruse, Rudolf, and Neumann, Bernd, editors, *KI 2003: Advances in Artificial Intelligence, 26th Annual German Conference on AI, KI 2003, Hamburg, Germany, September 15-18, 2003, Proceedings*, volume 2821 of *Lecture Notes in Computer Science*, pages 120–134. Springer.

Schöning, Uwe (2000). *Logik für Informatiker*. Spektrum.

Sheth, Amit and Ramakrishnan, Cartic (2003). Semantic (Web) Technology In Action: Ontology Driven Information Systems for Search, Integration and Analysis. *IEEE Data Engineering Bulletin, Special issue on Making the Semantic Web Real*, 26(4):40–48.

Sivashanmugam, K., Miller, J., Sheth, A., and Verma, K. (2004). Framework for Semantic Web Process Composition. *International Journal of Electronic Commerce (IJEC)*. Special Issue.

Smith, Barry (1996). Mereotopology: A Theory of Parts and Boundaries. *Data & Knowledge Engineering*, 20(3):287–303.

Smith, Barry (2004). Beyond Concepts: Ontology as Reality Representation. In [Varzi and Vieu, 2004], pages 73–85.

Sowa, John. F. (2000). *Knowledge Representation: Logical, Philosophical, and Computational Foundations*. Brooks Cole Publising Co., Pacific Grove, CA, USA.

Spyns, Peter, Oberle, Daniel, Volz, Raphael, Zheng, Jijuan, Jarrar, Mustafa, Sure, York, Studer, Rudi, and Meersman, Robert (2002). OntoWeb - A Semantic Web Community Portal. In Karagiannis, Dimitris and Reimer, Ulrich, editors, *Practical Aspects of Knowledge Management, 4th International Conference, PAKM 2002, Vienna, Austria, December 2-3, 2002, Proceedings*, volume 2569 of *Lecture Notes in Computer Science*, pages 189–200. Springer.

Stell, John G. and West, Matthew (2004). A Four-Dimensionalist Mereotopology. In [Varzi and Vieu, 2004], pages 261–273.

Stojanovic, L., Maedche, A., Motik, B., and Stojanovic, N. (2002a). User-driven Ontology Evolution Management. In Meersman, Robert and Tari, Zahir, editors, *On the Move to Meaningful Internet Systems, 2002 - DOA/CoopIS/ODBASE 2002 Confederated International Conferences DOA, CoopIS and ODBASE 2002 Irvine, California, USA, October 30 - November 1, 2002, Proceedings*, volume 2519 of *Lecture Notes in Computer Science*. Springer.

Stojanovic, Ljiljana (2004). *Methods and Tools for Ontology Evolution*. PhD thesis, Universität Karlsruhe, Institut für Angewandte Informatik und Formale Beschreibungsverfahren, Germany.

Stojanovic, Nenad, Volz, Raphael, and Stojanovic, Ljiljana (2002b). A Reverse Engineering Approach for Migrating Data-intensive Web Sites to the Semantic Web. In Musen, Mark A., Neumann, Bernd, and Studer, Rudi, editors, *Intelligent Information Processing, IFIP 17th World Computer Congress - TC12 Stream on Intelligent Information Processing, August 25-30, 2002, Montréal, Québec, Canada*, volume 221 of *IFIP Conference Proceedings*. Kluwer.

Stuckenschmidt, Heiner and Klein, Michel C. A. (2004). Structure-Based Partitioning of Large Concept Hierarchies. In *The Semantic Web - ISWC 2004: Third International Semantic Web Conference,Hiroshima, Japan, November 7-11, 2004. Proceedings*, volume 3298 of *Lecture Notes in Computer Science*, pages 289–303. Springer.

Sturm, Rick and Bumpus, Winston (1998). *Foundations of Application Management*. Wiley.

Sure, Y., Erdmann, M., Angele, J., Staab, S., Studer, R., and Wenke, D. (2002). OntoEdit: Collaborative ontology development for the Semantic Web. In Horrocks, Ian and Hendler, James A., editors, *The Semantic Web - ISWC 2002, First International Semantic Web Conference, Sardinia, Italy, June 9-12, 2002, Proceedings*, volume 2342 of *Lecture Notes in Computer Science*. Springer.

Tai, Stefan (2004). Transaction Middleware. In [Mahmoud, 2004], chapter 3, pages 53–80.

Tai, Stefan, Khalaf, Rania, and Mikalsen, Thomas A. (2004a). Composition of Coordinated Web Services. In Jacobsen, Hans-Arno, editor, *Middleware 2004, ACM/IFIP/USENIX International Middleware Conference, Toronto, Canada, October 18-20, 2004, Proceedings*, volume 3231 of *Lecture Notes in Computer Science*, pages 294–310. Springer.

Tai, Stefan, Mikalsen, Thomas A., Wohlstadter, Eric, Desai, Nirmit, and Rouvellou, Isabelle (2004b). Transaction Policies for Service-oriented Computing. *Data & Knowledge Engineering*, 51(1):59–79.

Tetlow, Phil, Pan, Jeff, Oberle, Daniel, Wallace, Evan, Uschold, Mike, and Kendall, Elisa (2005). Ontology Driven Architectures and Potential Uses of the Semantic Web in Software Engineering. W3C Working Draft.

Tonti, Gianluca, Bradshaw, Jeffrey M., Jeffers, Renia, Montanari, Rebecca, Suri, Niranjan, and Uszok, Andrzej (2003). Semantic Web Languages for Policy Representation and Reasoning: A Comparison of KAoS, Rei, and Ponder. In Fensel, Dieter, Sycara, Katia P., and Mylopoulos, John, editors, *The Semantic Web - ISWC 2003, Second International Semantic Web Conference, Sanibel Island, FL, USA, October 20-23, 2003, Proceedings*, volume 2870 of *Lecture Notes in Computer Science*, pages 419–437. Springer.

Tosic, V., Ma, W., Pagurek, B., and Esfandiari, B. (2004). Web Service Offerings Infrastructure (WSOI) — A Management Infrastructure for XML Web Services. In [Cho and Ejiri, 2004], pages 817–830.

Trezzo, Jim and Mihic, Matt (2004). Web Services Metadata for the Java Platform. JSR 181, Java Community Process. Early Review Draft Specification.

UDDI Coalition (2000). UDDI Technical White Paper. http://uddi.org.

Ullman, Jeffrey D. (1988). *Principles of Database and Knowledge-base systems*, volume 14 of *Principles of Comuter Science Series*. Computer Science Press.

Uszok, Andrzej, Bradshaw, Jeffrey M., Jeffers, Renia, Tate, Austin, and Dalton, Jeff (2004). Applying KAoS Services to Ensure Policy Compliance for Semantic Web Services Workflow Composition and Enactment. In McIlraith, Sheila A., Plexousakis, Dimitris, and van Harmelen, Frank, editors, *The Semantic Web - ISWC 2004: Third International Semantic Web Conference,Hiroshima, Japan, November 7-11, 2004. Proceedings*, volume 3298 of *Lecture Notes in Computer Science*, pages 425–440. Springer.

van der Aalst, Wil and van Hee, Kees (2002). *Workflow Management*. MIT Press, 1st edition.

van Heijst, Gertjan (1995). *The Role of Ontologies in Knowledge Engineering*. PhD thesis, Universiteit van Amsterdam.

Varzi, Achille C. and Vieu, Laure, editors (2004). *Formal Ontology in Information Systems — Proceedings of the Third International Conference (FOIS 2004)*. IOS Press.

Verma, K., Sivashanmugam, K., Sheth, A., Patil, A., Oundhakar, S., and Miller, J. (2005). METEOR–S WSDI: A Scalable P2P Infrastructure of Registries for Semantic Publication and Discovery of Web Services. *Journal of Information Technology and Management*, 6(1):17–39.

Volz, Raphael, Oberle, Daniel, and Maedche, Alexander (2002). Towards a Modularized Semantic Web. In *Proceedings of the ECAI-02 Workshop on Ontologies and Semantic Interoperability Lyon, July 22, 2002*, volume 64 of *CEUR Workshop Proceedings*.

Volz, Raphael, Oberle, Daniel, Staab, Steffen, and Motik, Boris (2003a). KAON SERVER - A Semantic Web Management System. In *Alternate Track Proceedings of the Twelfth International World Wide Web Conference, WWW2003, Budapest, Hungary, 20-24 May 2003*. ACM.

Volz, Raphael, Oberle, Daniel, Staab, Steffen, and Studer, Rudi (2003b). OntoBroker and OntoEdit Adaptation. WonderWeb Deliverable D9. http://wonderweb.semanticweb.org.

Volz, Raphael, Oberle, Daniel, Staab, Steffen, and Studer, Rudi (2003c). OntoLiFT Prototype. WonderWeb Deliverable D11. http://wonderweb.semanticweb.org.

Volz, Raphael, Oberle, Daniel, Staab, Steffen, and Studer, Rudi (2003d). Triple Client. WonderWeb Deliverable D8. http://wonderweb.semanticweb.org.

Volz, Raphael, Oberle, Daniel, and Studer, Rudi (2003e). Implementing Views for Light-Weight Web Ontologies. In *Proceedings of the Seventh International Database Engineering and Applications Symposium (IDEAS'03), July 16 - 18, 2003, Hong Kong, SAR*, pages 160–170. IEEE Computer Society.

Voskob, Max (2004). UDDI Spec TC V4 Requirement - Taxonomy Support for Semantics. OASIS. http://www.oasis-open.org.

Walls, Craig and Richards, Norman (2003). *XDoclet in Action*. Manning Publications Co.

Welty, Christopher (1995). *An Integrated Representation for Software Development and Discovery*. PhD thesis, Rensselaer Polytechnic Institute Computer Science Department.

Wolff, Frank, Oberle, Daniel, Lamparter, Steffen, and Staab, Steffen (2005). Economical Reflections on Different Options for the Management of Web Services. Technical report, University of Duisburg-Essen, ICB Information Systems and Enterprise Modelling, Germany.

Zaremski, Amy Moormann and Wing, Jeannette M. (1997). Specification Matching of Software Components. *ACM Transactions on Software Engineering and Methodology*, 6(4):333–369.

Index